Religion and the Critical Mind

Religion and the Critical Mind

A Journey for Seekers, Doubters, and the Curious

Anton K. Jacobs

LEXINGTON BOOKS
A division of
ROWMAN & LITTLEFIELD PUBLISHERS, INC.
Lanham • Boulder • New York • Toronto • Plymouth, UK

The Scripture quotations contained herein are from the New Revised Standard Version
Bible, copyright 1989, by the Division of Christian Education of the National Council of
the Churches of Christ in the United States of America. Used by permission. All rights
reserved.

Published by Lexington Books
A division of Rowman & Littlefield Publishers, Inc.
A wholly owned subsidiary of The Rowman & Littlefield Publishing Group, Inc.
4501 Forbes Boulevard, Suite 200, Lanham, Maryland 20706
http://www.lexingtonbooks.com

Estover Road, Plymouth PL6 7PY, United Kingdom

British Library Cataloguing in Publication Information Available

Library of Congress Cataloging-in-Publication Data

Jacobs, Anton K.
  Religion and the critical mind : a journey for seekers, doubters, and the curious / Anton
K. Jacobs.
    p. cm.
  Includes bibliographical references and index.
  ISBN 978-0-7391-4774-0 (cloth : alk. paper)
  1. Religion—Philosophy. 2. Apologetics. I. Title.
  BL51.J235 2010
  210—dc22
                                      2010026645

⊖™ The paper used in this publication meets the minimum requirements of American
National Standard for Information Sciences—Permanence of Paper for Printed Library
Materials, ANSI/NISO Z39.48-1992.

Printed in the United States of America

Contents

Preface and Acknowledgments

This book is an overview of the history of the criticism of religion. It is written for those who want to participate in religion but feel they cannot because of its shortcomings, those whose participation in religion is spoiled by its shortcomings, and those who would simply like an overview of this rich heritage of criticism. It attempts to take the criticisms seriously and suggest, to some extent, what religion might look like if it did the same. So this book is for seekers, doubters, and the curious.

I have tried to compose this work so it can be read and understood by the general reader. I offer my apology to those scholars who may feel that I have glossed over too many important details and qualifications that would characterize more careful scholarly work. And I offer my apology to the general reader insofar as I have failed to render the abstractions of philosophy and theology more clear.

I have had many wonderful teachers and friends along the way who have inspired my mind and encouraged my passion. I would mention especially Harry Bash, Anthony Blasi, Walter Brueggemann, Ed Chasteen, Paul Cheney, Fabio DaSilva, Thomas Keil, M. Douglas Meeks, John W. Riggs, and the late Allen O. Miller. I would mention my parents because they never discouraged my intellectual pursuits, and there were books in our home.

Among those who read early drafts of part or all of the manuscript and offered feedback were Vern Barnet, Melissa Bowers, Ed Chasteen, Clyde and Florence DeWitt, Chuck Dymer, Will Jacobs, Jewel Jumper, Ruth Mosley, John Wiegers, Helen Wilson, Christopher and Andrea Wilt, and especially Jean Jacobs. I want to thank Phyllis Moore, Director of Liberal Studies at the Kansas City Art Institute, who gave me the opportunity to try out these ideas on students. In addition, for all their fine help, I thank my editor, Melissa Wilks, and production editors, Michael Wiles and Ginny Schneider, of Lexington Books. I know I have left out some people who deserve mention, and for that I'm sorry.

For permission to quote extensively from Voltaire's *Philosophical Dictionary*, edited and translated by Theodore Besterman (London: Penguin Books, 1972), thanks goes to the Voltaire Foundation, University of Oxford.

For permission to quote extensively from Bertrand Russell's *Why I Am Not A Christian: And Other Essays On Religion And Related Subjects*, edited by Paul Edwards (London: Unwin Paperbacks, 1975), thanks goes to The Bertrand Russell Peace Foundation Ltd. and the Publishers Taylor & Francis.

The Scripture quotations contained herein are from the New Revised Standard Version Bible, copyright 1989, by the Division of Christian Education of the National Council of the Churches of Christ in the U.S.A. Used by permission. All rights reserved.

Of course, I am solely responsible for the interpretations and claims in this work.

The support and encouragement of my wife is without parallel. I dedicate this book to her

Jean Roth Jacobs

whose life is the exemplar of joyful and passionate care for others.

Anton K. Jacobs
Kansas City
2010

Introduction

The Lamp and the Knife

Western history has given the world two very paradoxical (many would say, mutually incompatible) traditions. One is a philosophical tradition of critical evaluation, encouraging us to find truth through a creative process of looking and thinking. The other is a religious tradition of belief in substantive divine revelation, encouraging us to accept the truth as revealed to us by particular religious authorities. In this sense, we hold dual citizenship—in the Athens of Plato and the Jerusalem of the Bible.[1] Dual citizenship in contrasting realms can be alienating and usually comes with tensions difficult to bear.

A Difficult Journey

In the classical myth of Cupid and Psyche,[2] we have a story that captures the challenge of dealing with gods.

Venus, the god of beauty and fertility, was enraged because people were coming from far and wide to admire the great beauty of a human, Psyche, and to give her homage Venus felt should be hers. So Venus sent her son Cupid (the god of love) to make Psyche fall in love with some kind of being, low and unworthy of love.

Dutifully trying to carry out his mother's wishes while Psyche slept, she awoke, and it so startled Cupid, invisible at that moment, that he pricked himself with his own arrow and fell in love with her. When Psyche is abandoned by her family because of an oracle's prediction that she would marry a monster, Cupid took her as his wife and established her in a grand palace.

Psyche lived in the palace, however, without viewing her husband. Cupid would leave before daylight and return after dark, so Psyche could not actually see him. By avoiding being seen and identified, he was protecting Psyche from the wrath of Venus. Although Psyche knew him only in the dark, he spoke with great love and aroused her passion.

1

One day in her joy, she invited her sisters to visit and see the splendor of her palace. They came. In their jealousy they encouraged her to hide a lamp and knife, and when her husband slept, to light the lamp in order to see him. If he really was the hideous monster as foretold by the oracle, she should cut off his head with the knife. Her curiosity provoked, she acted on the plan.

> So she prepared her lamp and a sharp knife, and hid them out of sight of her husband. When he had fallen into his first sleep, she silently rose and uncovering her lamp beheld not a hideous monster, but the most beautiful and charming of the gods, with his golden ringlets wandering over his snowy neck and crimson cheek, with two dewy wings on his shoulders, whiter than snow, and with shining feathers like the tender blossoms of spring.[3]

He awoke, and he told her how foolish it was to have exposed him since he had disobeyed his mother, who had wished a worse fate for Psyche. He fled, saying, "Love cannot dwell with suspicion."[4]

Then her palace disappeared, and she was put through difficult and dangerous trials by Venus. In the end, Cupid went to Jupiter to plead their cause, and with the good graces and intervention of Jupiter, Psyche was brought to heaven, given immortality, and reunited with her love.

This ancient tale is a good springboard into the venture of the critical evaluation of faith and religion. When we light the lamp to search for enlightenment, we find ourselves, too, faced with great beauty but also surprise and difficulty. We often uncover things we simply do not want to see, some of which may need to be excised.

The whole process is fraught with pain and insecurity and difficulty. We might even find our own religion or sect no longer a place where we can remain in blissful ignorance. Joseph Campbell, recognizing that the spiritual journey for moderns is necessarily an heroic and individual journey, wrote:

> The modern hero, the modern individual who dares to heed the call and seek the mansion of that presence with whom it is our whole destiny to be atoned, cannot, indeed must not, wait for his community to cast off its slough of pride, fear, rationalized avarice, and sanctified misunderstanding. "Live," Nietzsche says, "as though the day were here." It is not society that is to guide and save the creative hero, but precisely the reverse. And so every one of us shares the supreme ordeal—carries the cross of the redeemer—not in the bright moments of his tribe's great victories, but in the silences of his personal despair.[5]

We can—if we hang in there—nurture our own sense of the sacred, the beautiful, and the sublime in faith and religion. If the Western doctrines of revelation and the Eastern doctrines of discovery mean anything, surely they mean this. But the journey is always a perilous trek through the wilderness; nevertheless it offers us hope of a marvelous destination—a place of new appreciation, a de-alienation, a promised land, if you will, whereby we can be at one with ourselves, at peace with the sacred journey, and empowered to worship God and share in God's work of passionate care. With a lamp and a knife, we proceed.

Challenges to Faith

In the nineteenth century many thinkers expected religion and religious faith to die. Individual thinkers had their own particular hopes and fears regarding the demise of religion. Some, like the social critic Karl Marx, thought it could not come soon enough. Others, like the sociologist Emile Durkheim, worried that societies would disintegrate without some kind of religion substitute. What these thinkers shared, though, was a critical view of religion shaped by what came to be known as the *modern worldview.*

The modern worldview has deep roots in human history. Scholars have identified origins of modern thought in ancient Greek philosophy, in the rise of the great religions themselves, and in Hebraic thought as witnessed in the Judeo-Christian scriptures. They have traced its development, suggesting its major breakthrough occurred as part of the Renaissance, especially in the skeptical philosophies of people like René Descartes and in the rise of modern science. But the modern worldview achieved self-conscious articulation and focus during the Enlightenment.[6]

Enlightenment thinkers had great hopes in the power of human reason to construct a new world of enlightenment and liberation. Reason would build this world on the twin pillars of observation and theory—what we know as science. Guided by reason and scientific research, the barriers to knowledge and understanding would be removed.

> The idea was to use the accumulation of knowledge generated by many individuals working freely and creatively for the pursuit of human emancipation and the enrichment of daily life. The scientific domination of nature promised freedom from scarcity, want, and the arbitrariness of natural calamity.[7]

Consequently, the influence of religion would recede as humanity got more rational, innovative, and scientific and less emotional, traditional, and superstitious.

We realize now there was considerable naiveté and miscalculation in their understanding of human reason and of religion—and probably of the world. So far, reason has not delivered as fully as they had expected, nor has religion withered and died away. Human beings continue to manifest a quest for meaning that transcends their everyday lives and even empirical reality itself. There is good reason to believe they always will.

But the modern critiques of religion offered up profound and insightful analyses. Thus these arguments have troubled or comforted many people. Many religious leaders and believers have dismissed the arguments out of hand in a kind of *ad hominem* disparagement of the thinkers' motives or lack of faith. This has been the way especially among the more fundamentalistic in the world's religions. After all, why listen to infidels? The orthodox who are not so fundamentalist will weave elaborate critiques of the critiques—from their religious frame of reference. Other religious leaders have tried to listen to these arguments and incorporate them into their religious worldviews, in a quest for a faith that is authentically modern. This has characterized the liberal wings of religion. Some people, I presume, have embraced the critiques as convenient rationalizations for not taking on the responsibilities and ethical burdens of religious faith, leaving them free, then, to exercise the modern option of secular self-interested individualism. And certainly others have embraced the critiques of religion from a position of authentic skepticism toward the metaphysics of religious claims, and affirmed instead a more thoroughgoing secular humanism, itself a descendant of Enlightenment thought. The anti-religious polemics of thinkers as diverse as Sam Harris, Richard Dawkins, and Christopher Hitchens are the most recent and popular examples of passionately engaged men who care about humanity and who believe religion is outdated and harmful.[8]

But many thinking people, religious and non-religious, who either sense or yearn for some sacred reality beyond the everyday, remain disquieted and uncertain about faith and commitment in the modern, pluralistic world. Simply the availability of so many competing options for one's lifestyle and belief is bewildering, but a major factor has surely been the criticisms of religion. Even if they haven't read the arguments of the modern critics of religion, thoughtful people are aware of them, at least vaguely, because they resonate in the intellectual currents of the culture we all breathe. Believers find themselves wondering about the implications for their faith, in so far as these arguments are true. Frequently their own participation in religious practices is spoiled by the uneasy sense that maybe all this is just a lot of hocus-pocus rooted in one's fears and insecurities and carried by dead tradition. Others find themselves unable to participate in religion or to affirm a faith even though they feel some sense of spiritual reality or yearning.

In recent decades the intellectual picture has become even more complicated. The modern worldview itself has come under sustained criticism from a perspective commonly labeled *postmodern*. What postmodern cultural critics have revealed is that modernism itself undermined any certain foundation for truth and knowledge. Drawing on philosophical argument and anthropological and sociological research, they have made a formidable case that all claims to truth contain contradictions, are built on assumptions easily challenged, and reflect their time and place in history and culture, rendering all human knowledge relative. When I served as a pastor, sometimes in a sermon I would tell my people that no matter how much we have studied, no matter how many hours we have spent working out a belief system about God, liberal or conservative, no matter how convincing we may think our theology is, one bright, undergraduate student, after one semester of philosophy and logic, can shred our arguments with just a few minutes of criticism

This study is for thoughtful people who want to live authentic, integrated, and responsible lives of faith in this postmodern world but who still struggle with serious doubts about their faith and their commitments. My hope is that it will provide them with some of the basic information to understand much of their own uneasiness in these complicated times. For this reason, I review in broad outline the history of the modern critiques of religion as well as the postmodern challenge in order to understand where these arguments come from and in order to take them seriously.

We are people of the twenty-first century. This is our time, and we have inherited excellent criticisms of religious faith and insightful analyses of the human quest for knowledge. I believe it is inauthentic, but also dangerous, to ignore them by trying to return to some pre-modern, authoritarian version of life in which we submit to an unquestioned, unchallenged claim to truth and knowledge. I understand why this would be tempting. In a time of such complexity with all the competing worldviews, not to mention just the stress of getting by everyday in a rapidly changing techno-world, it can look very appealing to retreat into a place of absolute security defined by some authority, be it an infallible Bible, an authoritarian church, or a sectarian ideology of some sort. However, I agree with Gerd Theissen who writes that humanity "has come of age in religion." Responsibility can no longer be shifted "on to the voice of the past." We may be anxious about the task, but we "can no longer avoid it."[9]

My hope is that this study will also provide support for making courageous and socially responsible commitments in a life enriched by religious faith. What I cannot do is remove the doubts and uncertainties or provide an absolutely sure foundation for some faith perspective. What I can do is clarify the issues, highlight the major life options that people choose today, and make a case for participating in particular faith traditions while affirming a faith that transcends sectarianism and embraces human solidarity. I believe this is the kind of liberating and life-affirming stance available to us, in part, because of the critiques of religion. Insofar as this is correct, the Enlightenment fulfilled part of its purpose. What postmodern critics, as well as some horrible history (World Wars I and II, the Holocaust, terrorism), have made clear is that the modern worldview could not substitute for the basic human courage of an unqualified commitment to Life. So I hope to make clear as well that, as Jean-Paul Sartre said, we are "condemned to be free."[10] We must choose. And I want to encourage those who would choose faith and community—against the destructive options of authoritarianism, sectarianism, and self-interested egoism.

A Western Bias

Before entering this journey through time and criticism, I need to make one caveat. I try in this treatment of faith and religion in a postmodern world to be as universal as possible. I want this work to be serviceable to thoughtful people in quest of faith and community regardless of their religious tradition or lack thereof. However, there will be a heavy reliance on Western and Christian texts and thought, for a couple of reasons.

The first is that my own background is Christian. This is what I grew up in, what I've been trained in, and what I know. It has been a varied background, wandering through Lutheran, Baptist, and United Church of Christ traditions, with occasional flirtatious forays into other denominations and religions, but still it has been Christian, and specifically Protestant. While I study and sporadically even participate in other faith traditions, I cannot speak about them with authority. It is extremely difficult as an adult to acquire, for a new cultural tradition, the "feel" one has for one's own familiar culture. This is why people experience culture shock when they spend enough time in a foreign land or a subculture to bump up against differing customs and patterns of thought. With regard to religious participation, this is also why an Episcopalian, for example, accustomed to the solemn dignity of High-Church mass, might have trouble feeling worshipful in the raucous exuberance of a charismatic worship service; although obviously both are Christian, and people worship sincerely in both styles of ritual. While I can study Muslim and Hindu religion, I cannot, without years of immersion, have the same intimate grounding in them that I do in Christianity. Simone Weil was basically correct when she wrote that "the study of different religions does not lead to a real knowledge of them unless we transport ourselves for a time by faith to the very center of whichever one we are studying."[11]

The reason for a Western bias involves more than that I have lived my entire life in the West. It is that the developments of modernist and postmodernist thought, including the major critiques of religion, are part of the Western canon. It is in the West that philosophical and religious streams, sometimes mutually reinforcing, often clashing, have developed *from* classical Greek and Hebrew origins (including other influences) *through* the religious domination of the Middle Ages and the modern "awakenings" of the Renaissance and Enlightenment (including natural science) *to* the current postmodern context characterized by cultural pluralism and relativism. All the authors of the modern critiques of religion reviewed in chapters five through ten of this work shared a small part of the globe encompassing Europe and Great Britain. They are all also, unfortunately, white males.[12] I will refer to them as Enlightenment humanists.

It is possible, as well, that another reason for a Western bias here is that Eastern religious traditions have simply had much less trouble co-existing with modern and postmodern intellectual developments, especially as manifested in natural science. While peoples in the Orient have often resisted the cultural, political, and religious encroachments of the West, so far as I know, there is nothing in Oriental history (until the rise of Maoism) comparable to the West's culture wars between science and religion.[13] These wars continue even today in the United States, as seen in attempts by American school boards to downplay theories of evolution and modern cosmology in public schools. Numerous writers have identified affinities between Eastern thought and modern scientific developments.[14] Fritjof Capra, in *The Tao of Physics*, argues that "the two foundations of twentieth-century physics—quantum theory and relativity theory—both force us to see the world very much in the way a Hindu, Buddhist or Taoist sees it."[15] Until the rise and success of the Chinese Communist Party—whose ideological roots are Western—the problem with religion *as such* seems to have been a Western problem.

Criticism and Critique

Regarding terminology, throughout this work I use *criticism* and *critique* interchangeably. Many, if not most, scholars today use *critique* or *critical theory* because *criticism* (outside the arts) has taken on primarily negative connotations, and because *critical theory* has become a well established branch in philosophy and the social sciences.[16] (Another indication of the all-absorbing nature of a postmodern world: that critical theory could be an intellectual tradition!) Furthermore, *critique* still connotes an interest in challenging current social and cultural formations for the ways in which they inhibit the full development of human beings, whereas *criticism* is largely a neutral term, suggesting a negative evaluation from any given perspective. But many other scholars continue to use *social criticism*.[17] And I suspect *critique* will lose its own power to challenge established institutions as defenders of the status quo themselves appropriate the concept for their own criticisms of the critics.

More important than terminology is meaning. Also throughout this work, I use *criticism* and *critique* broadly for any criticism of religion for whatever reason. This will be seen in chapter 1 on early critiques of religion from within religion itself as well as those in chapters three and four on critiques during the Renaissance and the Reformation. But I am most interested in those discourses that challenge religion as untrue and in some way not good for human beings. We will see early instances of this kind of critique of religion from outside religion in chapter 2. But this characterizes especially the modern critiques from the social critical tradition in the interest of human emancipation stemming largely from Enlightenment impulses. This is a tradition that has hoped for a humanity increasingly liberated from unnecessary and de-humanizing constraints on its development.

I share that Enlightenment concern for human liberation and believe any authentic religious faith will also share that concern. So in chapter 4 we will look more thoroughly at the history and nature of social criticism and the developments in Western thought that laid the foundations for modern critique.

Chapters 5 through 10 will examine the critiques of religion by Voltaire, Karl Marx, Friedrich Nietzsche, Emile Durkheim, Sigmund Freud, and Bertrand Russell. Whatever their faults—and each man had plenty of them—they shared a deep concern for a freer, more humanized humanity. I can understand why many people, concerned primarily or only about their own winnings in our culture of competitive greed, would not be interested in these Enlightenment humanists. I can understand why nationalists, racists, and sectarians would avoid them. I do not understand how any Christian, Jew, Muslim, Buddhist, Hindu—

all of whom share a basic concern for the welfare of humanity—can ignore this rich tradition of critical thought.

Each of the chapters on the major thinkers concludes with "some reflection." My reflections are not meant to be definitive or exhaustive. I would not argue they are always even the most important or most profound reflections that could be made on these thinkers' critiques. They are simply attempts in this journey to appreciate the insight of the critics and draw some implications for people of faith. They could even be skipped by readers who wish to make the journey through the critics without my commentary.

Chapter 11 will take up the development of postmodern thought and its implications for participation in faith and religion. Since postmodern thought debunks the foundations for claims to truth in the modern worldview, some conservative religious thinkers have exploited postmodernism as a tool in their struggle against modern critics and modernizing tendencies in religion.[18] Postmodernism does not seem to me to lend itself to a return to more formerly orthodox or authoritarian ways of being. It does, though, point up the power of human beings as active creators of meaning in their own right. For the individual, this has profound implications for one's responsibility in choice and commitment regarding lifestyle and religion or lack thereof.

In the final chapter I review what seem to me to be the basic options facing reflective moderns when deciding how to live their lives. I also offer a modest case for participation in religion with an open-and-critical faith. There are countless popular books out there that make the case for religious faith, usually for a particular religious faith. There are countless theological works in all major religions doing the same. I do not pretend to offer the answer that everybody else has missed. I just offer the insights that have helped me take seriously the modern critiques of religion, thinking they might be of help to others as well.

Overall I think of this work as a place for spiritual seekers and curious believers to make a brief visit on their journeys. It is written in laypersons' terms (as far as I am capable of doing so). My hope is that it will allow readers to take seriously some of the problems of faith and religion; that it will affirm the value of their quest; and finally that it will be a place from which they can return to their own journey a little better informed, a little more encouraged, and with a little lighter heart.

Notes

1. See Stephen R. L. Clark, *From Athens to Jerusalem: The Love of Wisdom and the Love of God* (Oxford: Clarendon Press, 1984) and Lev Shestov, *Athens and Jerusalem*, trans. Bernard Martin (N.Y.: Simon and Schuster, 1966 [1937]).

2. As told by Thomas Bulfinch, *Bulfinch's Mythology: The Age of Fable, The Age of Chivalry, Legends of Charlemagne* (N.Y.: Avenel Books, 1979), 80-91; original in Apuleius, *The Golden Ass*, trans. William Adlington; rev. S. Gaselee (Ware, Hertfordshire, England: Wordsworth, 1996).

3. Bulfinch, *Bulfinch's Mythology*, 84-85.

4. Bulfinch, *Bulfinch's Mythology*, 85.

5. Joseph Campbell, *The Hero With A Thousand Faces* (Princeton, N.J.: Princeton University Press, 1949), 391.

6. David Harvey, *The Condition of Postmodernity: An Enquiry into the Origins of Cultural Change* (Oxford, Eng.: Basil Blackwell, 1989), 12-13.

7. Harvey, *Postmodernity*, 12.

8. Sam Harris, *The End of Faith: Religion, Terror, and the Future of Reason* (N.Y. & London: W. W. Norton, & Co., 2005); Richard Dawkins, *The God Delusion* (Boston & New York: Houghton Mifflin, 2006); Christopher Hitchens, *God is not Great: How Religion Poisons Everything* (N.Y. & Boston: Twelve, 2007).

9. Gerd Theissen, *A Critical Faith: A Case for Religion* (Phila.: Fortress Press, 1979), 19.

10. Jean-Paul Sartre, *The Philosophy of Jean-Paul Sartre*, ed. Robert Denoon Cumming (N.Y.: Random House, Vintage Books, 1965), 277.

11. Simone Weil, *Waiting for God*, trans. Emma Craufurd (N.Y.: Harper & Row, 1951), 183-184.

12. But see Renate Bridenthal, and Claudia Koonz, eds., *Becoming Visible: Women in European History* (Boston: Houghton Mifflin Co., 1977); also Yosef A. A. ben-Jochannan, *African Origins of The Major "Western Religions"* (Baltimore: Black Classic Press, 1970) and Yosef ben-Jochannan, "The African Contribution to Technology and Science," in *New Dimensions in African History*, ed. John Henrik Clarke (Trenton, N.J. and Asmara, Eritrea: Africa World Press, 1991), 55-62.

13. For a similar claim, see Heinrich Zimmer, "The Meeting of East and West," in *Readings In Eastern Religious Thought*, vol. 1, *Hinduism*, ed. Allie M. Frazier (Phila.: The Westminster Press, 1969), 30.

14. See Joseph Campbell, *Myths To Live By*, (N.Y.: Bantam Books, 1972); William Irwin Thompson, *Coming Into Being: Artifacts and Texts in the Evolution of Consciousness* (N.Y.: St. Martin's Press, 1996); Alan Watts, *The Two Hands of God: The Myths of Polarity* (Toronto: Collier Books, 1963).

15. Fritjof Capra, *The Tao of Physics: An Exploration of the Parallels Between Modern Physics and Eastern Mysticism*, 2nd ed. (Boston: New Science Library, 1985), 18.

16. See David Held, *Introduction to Critical Theory: Horkheimer to Habermas* (Berkeley & Los Angeles: University of California Press, 1980).

17. See Michael Walzer, *The Company of Critics: Social Criticism and Political Commitment in the Twentieth Century* (N.Y.: Basic Books, 1988).

18. See Alan Wolfe, "The Opening of the Evangelical Mind," *Atlantic*, October 2000, 55-76.

Chapter 1

My Prophet Can Beat Up Your Prophet!
Early Critiques of Religion I

There is a boast that young boys will sometimes make in moments of excessive macho posturing. "My daddy can beat up your daddy!" I'm not sure what the point of this brag is except to assert superiority vicariously, thus not having to establish it with one's own fists, but in the record of ancient conflicts between religions something very similar takes place.

Conflicting Gods

In the Hebrew Bible there is an exciting and elaborate story about just such a conflict. This is the celebrated confrontation on Mt. Carmel between Elijah, prophetic representative of Yahweh, and the prophets of Baal. Such an event would have taken place in the ninth century BCE. Elijah was a prophet in the kingdom of Northern Israel.[1] *Yahweh* was the Hebrews' name for their God, usually translated in English Bibles as "the Lord," although *Yahweh* does not mean "the Lord." Its etymology is debated and its meaning uncertain.[2] *Baal* was the name of a major Canaanite deity, a god of fertility and storm, whose name did mean "Lord."[3] The king of Israel at this time was Ahab, and his wife was the historically infamous Jezebel, a Phoenician and worshiper of Baal. According to one scholar, King Ahab was practicing a policy of "religious compromise and coexistence" between the Canaanite and the Hebraic elements of the population.[4] The Bible, of course, puts it more starkly, saying that Ahab "did evil in the sight of the Lord more than all who were before him." Not only did he surpass the wickedness of the worst of previous kings, he took Jezebel as his wife, "and went and served Baal, and worshiped him."[5] Naturally this outraged the Yahwists, and Elijah was moved to challenge the infidelity.

As the story goes, Elijah declared, in the name of the Lord, a drought over the country, and then went into hiding. After a long time, Elijah is called by the Lord to go back to Ahab because the drought is going to end. So Elijah returns to town to confront Ahab. After they mutually accuse each other of being troublemakers in Israel, Elijah orders Ahab to bring all of Israel out to Mt. Carmel along with the hundreds of prophets of Baal.

And so they gather. Elijah challenges the people asking them, "How long will you go limping with two different opinions?" Whichever God is true, that's the one they should follow. He first notes that he is the only prophet of the Lord left, whereas Baal has four hundred and fifty prophets. Clearly not a fair fight. Elijah calls for two bulls. He has the Baal prophets cut up one bull and put it on a pyre. And he tells them to call on Baal to bring fire down and consume the offering. All morning long the Baal prophets march around the pyre calling on the name of Baal, but nothing happens. Elijah taunts them: "Cry aloud! Surely he is a god; either he is meditating, or he has wandered away, or he is on a journey, or perhaps he is asleep and must be awakened." The Baal prophets continue to cry out for Baal. They cut themselves, the story suggesting this was their practice. Nothing happened.

Then it was Elijah's turn. He builds an altar of stones, digs a trench around it, places wood on the altar, cuts up the bull and places it on the wood. Then he has Israelites pour so much water on top of the altar and offering that it thoroughly soaks the altar and fills up the trenches. Then Elijah calls on Yahweh God, the God of Abraham, Isaac, and Jacob, to bring fire down and consume the offering, so the Israelites will know who is truly God. "Then the fire of the Lord fell and consumed the burnt offering, the wood, the stones, and the dust, and even licked up the water that was in the trench."

The people are convinced and prostrate themselves in proclamation of their allegiance to Lord Yahweh. But Elijah is not done. He has the Israelites drag the prophets of Baal off to a dry river bed where Elijah proceeds to kill all of them.[6]

Quite a story! Too bad for the prophets of Baal. What we see in such ancient stories is that attacks on religion are not new. They were not usually attacks on religion as such; nevertheless, competing religious leaders were very much in the business of attacking each other's religion. And, as we can see from this ancient biblical story, these arguments took the form of "My daddy can beat up your daddy." In other words, these were arguments about power. The test of truth of a religion was its power to get things done, especially by bestowing benefits on its adherents and placing curses on their enemies.

Of course, I'm being a bit unfair here to the Elijah tradition. The my-daddy-can-beat-up-your-daddy argument is a better analogy for times and places of polytheism (i.e., where multiple gods were assumed to be real) or henotheism (i.e., where the reality of one god does not exclude the existence of others). The argument, then, was "My god can beat up your god." But the biblical texts containing the Elijah stories were operating from a monotheistic position. His perspective is thus more like, "*Only* my daddy is real." Elijah's mockery of Baal in the story is ironic, tongue-in-cheek, and drippingly sarcastic. In other words, there is only one God. All other gods are false, and, for that reason, powerless.

Monotheism, the belief in one God, came into its most full development with the Hebrews. But monotheism, as an idea and maybe even a practice, predates Judaism. Historians of religion have debated whether monotheism is an evolutionary high point from pre-historical polytheisms or is itself the most "primitive" conception of the divine.[7] The Egyptian pharaoh, Amenhotep IV (he changed his name later to Akhenaton), promoted monotheism in the fourteenth century BCE, but it did not survive his death.[8] It is likely early Judaism did not deny the existence of other gods, but this is much debated. Biblical texts demonstrate a thoroughgoing monotheism from the sixth century BCE.[9] Christianity carried over this monotheism; although its doctrine of the trinity looks very much like polytheism to Jews and Muslims, the latter of whom, following the Qur'an, are certainly among the most consistently and insistently monotheistic. In any case, many early critiques of religion were primarily of the variety of attack on competing religions.

The Prophetic Critique

Other early critiques of religion developed from within religion itself. They, too, were not critiques of religion as such—though some come very close to it. Rather, they were more concerned with the distortions and betrayal of a tradition of belief or practice. The greatest of these, I believe, are found in the Hebrew Bible with the prophets and in the Christian gospels with the Jesus tradition. Some of them were quite insightful and powerful; also brash and sarcastic enough to rival even Karl Marx's caustic wit. But, then, Marx has been called "an Old Testament prophet turned secular humanist."[10]

The Old Testament theologian, Gerhard von Rad, wrote that "the most astonishing phenomenon in the whole of Israel's history" was that at a time when Yahwism was disintegrating, it was able "to re-emerge, with nothing short of volcanic force, in a completely new form, namely in the message of the prophets."[11] Karen Armstrong in *A History of God* argued that the Hebrew prophets "discovered for themselves the overriding duty of compassion."[12] Indeed, the Hebrew prophets developed a case for passionate concern for human welfare as the measuring rod for faithfulness, and they felt led to attack practices of religion that seemed to mask oppression and cruelty or to substitute for justice and kindness.

The prophet, Isaiah, is "generally regarded as the greatest of the Hebrew prophets."[13] He was "the first of the Major Prophets in both Jewish and Christian tradition."[14] He lived in the eighth century BCE, and seemed to have access to the royal house in Judah.[15] This was at a time when the southern kingdom of

Judah and the northern kingdom of Israel found themselves precariously and threateningly situated right between two world powers, Egypt and Assyria. When he looked around and contemplated the fate of Judah, he was appalled at what he saw.

In this tense geo-political situation Isaiah raised his voice of advice and confrontation. He counseled against an alliance with Egypt, probably because he saw it as futile, but also because he saw it as unfaithfulness to give up their protection from Yahweh God and seek protection from the might of a nation serving other gods. He tended to see the Israelites' plight as one of judgment from God, and he called for a renewal of faithfulness to God. He called on Jerusalem to trust God for their security.

In times of international conflict and concern for national security, it is quite common for nations to downplay domestic divisions rooted in injustice and inequality and marshal all their forces for defense. They figure that issues of justice, rights, and exploitation can be put off in the present crisis. But not Isaiah. He seemed to believe even that their national weakness was also a matter of domestic injustice and oppression, and he said so in clear attacks on their practice of religion.

Isaiah insisted that Yahweh is a Holy God. Consequently God calls for righteousness among the people. Isaiah confronts those "who join house to house, who add field to field, until there" is no one left but them. The Lord does not look kindly on them; their own "houses shall be desolate."[16] It is because the Lord demands justice for all. What are you going to do when judgment comes, asks Isaiah, you who enact oppressive and unjust laws, who ignore the needy, steal from the poor, and prey on widows and orphans?[17]

In some of the best known and most oft-quoted verses, the leaders of Judah are called the rulers of Sodom, and the people are called the people of Gomorrah. These are the two infamous cities destroyed, according to tradition, because of their unfaithfulness and their evil ways. Isaiah uses this rather severe name-calling as a lead-in to point out that their ritual allegiance to Yahweh does not make them godly. He follows with a tirade against their religious ritual.

> What to me is the multitude of your sacrifices?
>   Says the Lord;
> I have had enough of burnt offerings of rams
>   and the fat of fed beasts;
> I do not delight in the blood of bulls,
>   or of lambs, or of goats.
> When you come to appear before me,
>   who asked this from your hand?
>   Trample my courts no more;
> bringing offerings is futile;
>   incense is an abomination to me.
> New moon and sabbath and calling of convocation—
>   I cannot endure solemn assemblies with iniquity.

> Your new moons and your appointed festivals
>   my soul hates;
> they have become a burden to me,
>   I am weary of hearing them.
> When you stretch out your hands,
>   I will hide by my eyes from you;
> even though you make many prayers,
>   I will not listen;
>   your hands are full of blood.
> Wash yourselves; make yourselves clean;
>   remove the evil of your doings
>   from before my eyes.[18]

Their religious worship services, their holidays, and their prayers come under condemnation. Typically, religious devotion is a matter of ritual, worship, and prayer, but Isaiah says these things are not what really count. A holy God wants holy works, and religious practices are not holy works.

The prophet is saying that gathering together for worship, singing hymns, and articulating prayers—however elaborate and heartfelt—are not righteousness. So what, then, would honor a holy God? What would fulfill the righteousness of God? Isaiah gives his answer: "cease to do evil, learn to do good; seek justice, rescue the oppressed, defend the orphan, plead for the widow."[19]

Isaiah, like other prophets, wants to be clear that true righteousness is found in human relations, but not just in being nice to or enjoying the company of family and friends. Rather, true righteousness is found in justice and righteousness for all people, but particularly the poor, the oppressed, the powerless, the deprived. I think we could say, if we were to follow Isaiah in this, that righteousness gets its test not so much in a celebration on the Sabbath as in a voting booth on election day. Holiness gets exercised not so much in the prayers written in diaries as in the letters to congresspersons and senators and corporate chieftains who hold the reigns of power over the welfare of people. Faithful and authentic religion is not found primarily in the social clubs and fellowships of communities of faith but in care and work on behalf of those an affluent world continues to exploit and ignore because they do not have the power to resist. These are reasonable extrapolations from Isaiah's critique of religion.

While Isaiah was busy challenging the powers-that-be and their religion in the southern kingdom of Judah, Amos was doing the same in the northern kingdom of Israel.[20]

Amos was a herdsman, caring for sheep and goats, and a dresser of sycamore trees. He lived and worked in the mountain-top village of Tekoa, which was in Judaea, just south of Bethlehem. He was what we might call a rural farmer. Apparently he was not a poor farmer, but he was also not wealthy.

Amos seemed to know a great deal about world events. Probably he learned these things in trips to the cities to trade. Also, before the advent of mass publications, news was eagerly sought and carried by word of mouth. He was apparently quite bright.

This rural farmer decided he had to speak out. He was outraged, and he knew somebody had to say something. So he traveled to the northern kingdom, which was experiencing a period of affluence and expansion. Although he denied being a prophet, he began to do what the prophets do so well—tell it like it is. And in this process of challenging the ruling powers, like Isaiah, he gave us a critique of religion that set compassion and justice against religious ritual. Here is one of the most celebrated of prophetic messages:

> Even though you offer me your burnt offerings and grain offerings,
>   I will not accept them;
> and the offerings of well-being of your fatted animals
>   I will not look upon.
> Take away from me the noise of your songs;
>   I will not listen to the melody of your harps.
> But let justice roll down like waters,
>   and righteousness like an ever-flowing stream.[21]

Isaiah and Amos are the epitome of the prophetic tradition criticizing religion. Their forceful words do not condemn religion as such, but rather view it as empty ritual when it is accompanied by a lack of concern for the welfare of human beings. Unfortunately, as we know too well, those religious traditions rooted in the Book (Judaism, Christianity, Islam) have not always taken the prophetic critique of religion seriously, but there it is, recorded right in the Book a long time ago, a long time before the modern critiques of religion that would come from outside the traditions.

What made these early and damning critiques of religion possible was, according to Karen Armstrong, a shift in the conception of God, a shift carried by the prophets. Whereas the Yahweh God of Moses had been partisan and triumphalist, the Yahweh God of Isaiah and Amos is universal and compassionate.[22] It is telling, I believe, that some of the first critiques of religion are rooted in a concern for human solidarity as manifested in justice and care, and specifically in passionate care for the weakest members of society.

The prophetic challenge to empty religion also found expression in the Christian gospels. Apparently Jesus was remembered as one who challenged the privileges and priorities of religion, much like the prophets before him.

Jesus (c. 4 BCE - c. 29 CE) appeared in Palestine in a time of cultural complexity and political ambiguity. The Jews were a conquered people, ruled as part of the Roman Empire. Their religion was well established, but it had various competing and incompatible schools of thought, the best known of which are the Sadducees and the Pharisees. Their land was a place of trade routes, so they were exposed to various peoples and cultures and lifestyles. These factors meant, among other things, hated enemies without and within, disputes and divi-

sion, and cultural pluralism. If there were a time and place of need for the comforting consolations of religion, surely that was one for the Jews. Jesus, though,
disappoints those for whom religion would be a safe haven of ritual comfort in
such a world, because this charismatic teacher and healer was apparently also a
prophetic critic of religion.[23]

In the Gospel of Mark we find a narrative of controversy between Jesus and
religious leaders. According to the story, Pharisees and scribes notice that Jesus
and his disciples are eating without first washing their hands. There were rituals
of cleansing needed, not only of the hands, but of anything bought at the market
as well as the pots and pans. It was important, according to Pharisaic rules, "to
eat food in a state of ritual purity." The story implies that by confronting Jesus
with his ritual defilement, the scribes and Pharisees wanted "to embarrass [him]
in front of the crowds and thus undermine his authority as a teacher."[24] They ask
him, "Why do your disciples not live according to the traditions of the elders,
but eat with defiled hands?"[25]

Jesus replies "by citing authorities that everyone in the debate would recognize as superior to ancestral traditions: the Law and the prophets."[26] "Isaiah
prophesied rightly about you hypocrites," says Jesus, "as it is written,"

> This people honors me with their lips,
>   but their hearts are far from me;
> in vain do they worship me,
>   teaching human precepts as doctrines.[27]

Jesus follows this quotation from Isaiah with the statement: "You abandon the
commandment of God and hold to human tradition."[28] Jesus points out to them
that in various ways they've figured out how to avoid the hard demands of the
Torah and replaced them with the easy demands of tradition.

Then Jesus calls the crowd together again and gives them this enigmatic
statement: "there is nothing outside a person that by going in can defile, but the
things that come out are what defile."[29] It would appear that Jesus overestimated
his listeners, because later, when Jesus is alone with the disciples, even they ask
him about that statement, "What did you mean by that?"

"Don't you get it?" asks Jesus. What goes into a person can't defile, even
ritually impure foods. What goes into a person passes through the digestive tract
and ends up in the sewer. It doesn't touch the heart, and what defiles people is
what comes out of the heart. Don't you recognize the things that come out of the
wicked heart? Fornication, theft, murder, adultery, greed, wickedness, deceit,
corruption, envy, slander, pride, foolishness. These are the things that defile a
person, not breaking with customs and traditions.[30]

We can see that Jesus is expressing here the spiritual insight that religious
observance, such as purity laws, are not important; what is important is authentic
purity of heart. The truly religious are those whose hearts are devoted to God
and to passionate care for others. Everything else is a matter of human custom

and tradition with, at best, only indirect implications for faithful and responsible living. In other words, religiosity is not the litmus test for faithful living. And so we have another critique of religion from within.

Many other similar instances from the Christian gospels could be cited. A frequently quoted verse occurs in connection with a conflict about sabbath laws, where Jesus says, "The sabbath was made for humankind, and not humankind for the sabbath."[31] It is true, of course, that the gospel writers were in the process of drawing strong distinctions between Judaism and Christianity, especially the Gospels of Matthew and John. So they tended to unfairly caricature the rigidity of Jewish religious law and ritual. Jesus' mean-spirited denunciations of the Scribes and Pharisees in the Gospel of Matthew[32] reflect the troubled relations between Jews and Gentiles a generation after Jesus' death, and so are viewed by many scholars as inauthentic.[33] Nevertheless, the spirit of these scriptural narratives is consistent with the Hebraic prophetic critiques of religion. They show that the prophetic voice of Judaism was carried over into the Christian tradition, and thus provided for later generations of Christians a foundation for the critique of religion from within.

All of these men in these Judeo-Christian texts—Elijah, Isaiah, Amos, Jesus—were themselves religious. Their criticisms of religion, then, were not of religion as such, but of a particular kind of religion. Their criticisms were from within religion. Their interests were true religion and reformation.

The critiques of religion we will examine most closely come during and after the Enlightenment, as part of the modern worldview. They were articulated by people primarily outside religious faith and practice, and thus not as would-be reformations of religion. These are critiques of religion as such. But some important early critiques of religion as such predate modern times.

Notes

1. See Jerome T. Walsh, "Elijah," in *The Anchor Bible Dictionary*, vol. 2, pp. 463-466, ed. David Noel Freedman *et al.* (N.Y.: Doubleday, 1992).

2. YHWH in the original Hebrew, sometimes thought to have been derived from a form of the Hebrew verb "to be." Henry O. Thompson, "Yahweh," in *The Anchor Bible Dictionary*, vol. 6, ed. David Noel Freedman *et al.* (N.Y.: Doubleday, 1992), 1011.

3. John Day, "Baal." in *The Anchor Bible Dictionary*, vol. 1, ed. David Noel Freedman *et al.* (N.Y.: Doubleday, 1992), 545.

4. Winfried Thiel, "Ahab," in *The Anchor Bible Dictionary*, vol. 1, ed. David Noel Freedman *et al.* (N.Y.: Doubleday, 1992), 102.

5. 1 Kings 16:30-31. All biblical quotations, unless otherwise noted, are from the New Revised Standard Version (NRSV).

6. This narrative is found in 1 Kings 18:20-40.

7. See W. Schmidt, *The Origin and Growth of Religion: Facts and Theories*, trans. H. J. Rose (N.Y.: Cooper Square Publisher's, 1972 [1931]) for the case for primitive

monotheism; also E. O. James, *Comparative Religion* (N.Y.: Barnes & Noble, 1961), 198-200; but see, as well, Hans Küng, *Freud and the Problem of God*, enlarged edition, trans. Edward Quinn (New Haven and London: Yale University Press, 1979, 1990), 66-75.

8. James, *Comparative*, 192-199; John B. Noss, *Man's Religions*, 4th ed. (London: Macmillan, 1969), 47.

9. See discussions in Bernhard W. Anderson, *Understanding the Old Testament*, 2nd ed. (Englewood Cliffs, NJ: Prentice-Hall, 1966) and Helmer Ringgren, *Israelite Religion*, trans. David E. Green (Phila.: Fortress Press, 1966).

10. Ashley Montagu and Floyd Matson, *The Dehumanization of Man* (N.Y.: McGraw-Hill, 1983), xviii.

11. Gerhard Von Rad, *Old Testament Theology*, vol. I, *The Theology of Israel's Historical Traditions*, trans. D. M. G. Stalker (N.Y. and Evanston: Harper & Row, 1962), 64.

12. Karen Armstrong, *A History of God: The 4000-Year Quest of Judaism, Christianity and Islam* (N.Y.: Alfred A. Knopf, 1994), 44.

13. Madeleine S. Miller and J. Lane Miller, *Harper's Bible Dictionary* (N.Y.: Harper & Row, 1961), 284.

14. John F. Sawyer, "Isaiah, The Book of," in *The Oxford Companion to the Bible*, ed. Bruce M. Metzger and Michael D. Coogan (N.Y. & Oxford: Oxford University Press, 1993), 325.

15. Christopher S. Seitz, "Isaiah, Book Of (First Isaiah)," in *The Anchor Bible Dictionary*, vol. 3., ed. David Noel Freedman *et al.* (N.Y.: Doubleday, 1992), 477-478.

16. Isaiah 5:8.

17. Isaiah 10:1-3.

18. Isaiah 1:11-16.

19. Isaiah 1:16b-17.

20. The following information about Amos is drawn largely from Anderson, *Understanding*, 232-233, and Walter Brueggemann, *The Prophetic Imagination* (Phila.: Fortress Press, 1978).

21. Amos 5:22-24.

22. Armstrong, *A History*, 43-45.

23. Almost all books on Jesus highlight his challenging religious practices and attitudes; see, for examples, Marcus J. Borg, *Meeting Jesus Again for the First Time: The Historical Jesus & the Heart of Contemporary Faith* (San Francisco: HarperSanFrancisco, 1994), chaps. 3 and 4; John Dominic Crossan, *Jesus: A Revolutionary Biography* (N.Y.: HarperSanFrancisco, 1994), chap. 3; Harry Emerson Fosdick, *The Man from Nazareth: As His Contemporaries Saw Him* (N.Y.: Harper & Row, 1949), chap. 3.

24. Pheme Perkins, "The Gospel of Mark: Introduction, Commentary, and Reflections," in *The New Interpreter's Bible*, vol. VIII, ed. Leander E. Keck et al., pp. 507-733 (Nashville: Abingdon Press, 1995), 606.

25. Mark 7:5.

26. Perkins, "The Gospel of Mark," 606.

27. Mark 7:6-7.

28. Mark 7:8.

29. Mark 7:15.

30. See Mark 7:17-23.

31. Mark 2:27.

32. See Matt. 23.

33. Armstrong, *A History*, 81; see also Robert W. Funk, Roy W. Hoover and The Jesus Seminar, *The Five Gospels: The Search for the Authentic Words of Jesus* (N.Y.: Macmillan, 1993), 238-244; for a critical, albeit somewhat conservative, overview of the ongoing quest for the authentic Jesus, see Ben Witherington, III, *The Jesus Quest: The Third Search for the Jew of Nazareth*, 2nd ed. (Downers Grove, IL: InterVarsity Press, 1997); cf. Eugene M. Boring, "The 'Third Quest' and the Apostolic Faith," *Interpretation* 50/4 (October 1996): 341-354.

Chapter 2

All Sheer Folly
Early Critiques of Religion II

I suppose everyone who has studied the history of colonial America has come across the Calvinist preacher, Jonathan Edwards, and the famous quotation from his sermon, "Sinners in the Hands of an Angry God," in which he characterizes God as one who "holds you over the pit of hell, much as one holds a spider, or some loathsome insect, over the fire, abhors you, and is dreadfully provoked."[1] The use of fear as a motivating factor has been common in the history of religion. Even the earliest critics of religion from outside religion expressed their dismay at religion's tendency to scare people.

The Critique from Without

One of the earliest secular critiques (that is, from outside religion) was that of the Greek philosopher, Epicurus (c. 341-c. 270 BCE) and, later, his follower, the Roman poet, Lucretius (c. 98-c. 55 BCE). What is significant about their criticism and rejection of religion is that, like the moderns, they came to their conclusions as the result of a perspective of natural philosophy.

Natural philosophy underlies the "scientific" perspective. Science says that knowledge of life and the universe are to come from within the realm of nature. This requires naturalistic interpretations and explanations. Whatever is to be known or explained must be natural phenomena—both causes and effects. Scientists cannot claim, for example, that their theory about something is true because God revealed it in a moment of mystical illumination. Although mystical experiences, as William James pointed out, "are usually authoritative over those who have them," mystics cannot demand "that we ought to accept the deliverance of their peculiar experiences, if we are ourselves outsiders and feel no private call thereto."[2] In the scientific frame of reference, "truth" (which, in science, is always understood to be inside quotation marks) results only from the disciplined—albeit creative and sometimes highly intuitive—interplay between reason and observation without resorting to *deus ex machina* explanations. In other words, scientific knowledge can come only from what is in some sense observable and measurable. This is what it means to be empirical. Scientific thought must be justifiable to any scientist, whether Christian, Jew, Muslim, Hindu, humanist, or whatever. Divine activity and revelation are, then, by definition, beyond the very mundane practices of science.

This natural scientific perspective would give the religiously orthodox fits as it became increasingly dominant in Western thought. We can see the seeds of this culture clash in the thought of Epicurus and Lucretius.

Epicurus was a Greek philosopher to whom we trace the concept of Epicureanism; although what we mean by that today is considerably different from what Epicurus and his followers taught. Epicurus was born on the island of Samos of Athenian parents. His father was a teacher. Epicurus began his philosophical studies at an early age. He went to Athens for a while when Aristotle was still living. After traveling to, perhaps also teaching in, various cities, he returned to Athens, bought a house and established a school in 307 or 306 BCE. At the time, Plato's Academy and Aristotle's Lyceum, led by their successors, were still flourishing.[3]

The geopolitical context in which Epicurus lived and taught was so complicated, it gives historians migraines. Alexander the Great died in 323 BCE, and Will Durant speculates that historians tend to end their histories of ancient Greece with that death because "after him the extent and complexity of the Greek world baffle any unified view or continuous narrative."[4]

There were three major competing monarchies (Macedonia, Seleucia, Egypt) and a hundred Greek city-states of varying degrees of independence. "Alexander's rootless empire was too loosely bound together by language, communication, customs, and faith to survive him"; it was divided into five parts by his successors, who were Macedonian chiefs. Wars and revolutions between and within the city-states and between and within the kingdoms meant that leaders and their policies came and went, while the people who could not get out of the way suffered. Athens lost its liberty, regained it, and lost it again. "Barbarian" invaders from the northwest were an ongoing problem, alternately fought and bought off.[5] It was a complicated time.

Cultural developments, too, were decidedly toward pluralism and competition. Indeed, Alexander the Great's conquests spread Greek culture in a process historians call *hellenization*, but they also opened up Greece to all kinds of external and internal cults and sects. Furthermore, science and philosophy had been on the ascendancy among the educated and literate probably since Thales (c. 624-c. 546), who is usually given credit as the founder of Greek philosophy and the scientific perspective.[6] All this meant the weakening of traditional and popular religion, growth in new superstitions and unusual cults, and cultural competition not unlike our culture wars today. "Athens in the third century," according to Durant, "was so disturbed by exotic faiths, nearly all of them promising heaven and threatening hell, that Epicurus, like Lucretius in first-century Rome, felt called upon to denounce religion as hostile to peace of mind and joy of life."[7]

In this context Epicurus established his school, teaching people to use their heads, keep their eyes open, avoid pain, seek pleasure, believe no religion literally, and stay out of politics. A lot of people live like this today without realizing they are Epicureans.

Epicurus taught that all of material reality is made up of atoms. In this he was probably following the earlier teachings of Leucippus (c. 400s BCE) and Democritus (c. 460-370 BCE), although he claimed originality.[8] All the things we see, feel, hear are combinations of atoms of various sizes. Epicurus' view of atoms is not the same as that of modern physics. Among other things, his atoms were solid and indivisible. But we can see how this line of reasoning was on the path to modern scientific views. Everything else, according to Epicurus, is void; i.e., empty space. He reasoned that if there is no empty space, the atoms, which are always in motion (another interesting insight long before modern physics), would not be able to move around and develop into new formations. That's it—atoms and void.

This all seemed obvious to Epicurus because he believed in carefully observing and reasoning about the world around us, and atoms and void are what he observed and reasoned. Something else he noticed while studying reality is that human beings and other animals have a built-in tendency to avoid pain and seek pleasure. He drew the conclusion and developed the argument, then, that the goal of life was the wise and prudent practice of maximizing pleasure and minimizing pain. I say "maximizing pleasure" because he wrote "that pleasure is the beginning and the end of the blessed life."[9] I add "minimizing pain" because when I read Epicurus, it sounds to me like he is more interested in overall comfort than in pleasure.

This is how his *Epicureanism* is different from current understandings of the word. His and his followers' lifestyles, while characterized by plenty of pleasure-full activities, could be quite austere, even ascetic, by our standards. He had the insight that too much thoughtless pleasure can lead to lots more pain than would be necessary if one disciplined one's appetites. In one of his three extant letters, Epicurus wrote:

> For the very reason that pleasure is the chief and the natural good, we do not choose every pleasure, but there are times when we pass by pleasures if they are outweighed by the hardships that follow; and many pains we think better than pleasures when a greater pleasure will come to us once we have undergone the long-continued pains. Every pleasure is a good since it has a nature akin to

ours; nevertheless, not every pleasure is to be chosen. Just so, every pain is an evil, yet not every pain is of a nature to be avoided on all occasions[10]

For Epicurus, the ability to live life with maximum pleasure and minimal pain required prudence, which is "the chief good," even "more precious than philosophy."[11] But prudence, Epicurus argued in his "Principal Doctrines," required knowledge, particularly knowledge that aids us in discerning "the limits of pains and desires." For this, we need the natural sciences.

It is not possible for one to rid himself of his fears about the most important things if he does not understand the nature of the universe but dreads some of the things he has learned in the myths. Therefore, it is not possible to gain unmixed happiness without natural science.[12]

The problem with religion, for Epicurus, was that it was neither rational nor pleasure-full. He attacked religion apparently primarily because it caused people pain. It would have been reasonable to suspect that he objected to religion because it entertained notions about gods and demons beyond human reason and observation. This he did not do. Epicurus was not simple-minded; he recognized we do not "see" atoms either. Rather, we infer their existence. And, oddly enough, he seemed to acknowledge the existence of gods. He just argued that they don't muck around in human affairs, as popular belief suggests. These notions that gods are arbitrarily intervening in everyday life is just a source of anxiety and worry which are painful.[13]

Furthermore, the gods don't have anything to do with punishing or rewarding us after death. When we die, we die. Our souls are part and parcel with our bodies, and when our bodies die, so do we. There is no consciousness, no sensation after death. This is, in a sense, a good thing, Epicurus suggested, because it means no pain. Because it is the cessation of all pain, there is no reason to fear death.[14]

Epicurus would have heartily approved of the attitude toward death that Lord Amberley, the father of Bertrand Russell, displayed in 1876 CE when he wrote to his mother a few days before his death that he looks forward to death "calmly and unmovedly."[15]

When we study the heavens, Epicurus points out in another letter, we need to stick to natural philosophy. The primary disturbance in the minds of people comes from thinking the "celestial bodies are blessed and eternal yet have impulses, actions, and purposes quite inconsistent with divinity." So people "anticipate and foresee eternal suffering as depicted in the myths, or even fear the very lack of consciousness that comes with death as if this could be of concern to them." "Peace of mind," Epicurus argues, is found in being "freed from all this."[16]

It is interesting to note, though, that Epicurus said it would be better, if one were choosing among false realities, to submit to the myths of religion than to the determinism of the physicists of his time. He came down firmly on the side of human freedom, arguing there are consequences from our attitudes and actions—in this life—and we are able to make choices. Determinism meant inescapable slavery; the myths, though, at least offer "a hope for grace through honors paid to the gods."[17] He seemed to root this moral freedom in his scientific view that the atoms themselves were not entirely predictable in their movements, sometimes veering off into new directions—a provocative anticipation, I think, of the uncertainty principle in twentieth-century physics.

Titus Lucretius Carus was an Epicurus dittohead. A Latin poet—the one long poem we have from him, *On the Nature of Things* (*De Rerum Natura*) seems to have followed closely a lost work by Epicurus, and he indicates he is simply presenting Epicurus' teachings.[18] "While walking in his footsteps I follow out his reasonings and teach by my verses," says Lucretius.[19] Russel Geer argues, then, "it is reasonably safe to accept the *De Rerum Natura* as the fullest and most accurate statement of Epicurus' original teachings now extant."[20]

Lucretius resorts to hyperbole when praising Epicurus. Early in *On the Nature of Things* Lucretius says it was Epicurus who dared to raise his head and face down the terrors of religion which had laid humanity "foully prostrate upon earth." Stories "of gods nor thunderbolts nor heaven with threatening roar could quell" his liberating work.[21] Lucretius even calls Epicurus a god—speaking metaphorically, of course—whose feats were greater than those of Hercules.[22]

We know very little if anything about Lucretius. He was almost certainly a Roman noble. His book is addressed to the son of a noble family. The church father, St. Jerome, said Lucretius went crazy after taking a love-potion and committed suicide at an early age, but both Will Durant and George Santayana make the sensible suggestion that we need to be suspicious of a church father's account of someone so thoroughly anti-religious.[23]

Lucretius was a contemporary of Julius Caesar, but Lucretius was observing, thinking, and writing while Caesar was making the conquests that would lead eventually to his dictatorship over Rome. During the time Lucretius was thinking and writing, Rome was in great difficulty, losing its democratic features, manifesting fratricidal warfare and civil war. It had only in the previous hundred years become a world power, and the demands of a far-flung empire put great strains on its political and economic institutions—strains that were killing its democratic institutions and would lead to centuries of successive dictators of varying levels of tyranny and benevolence.[24] Lucretius lived in a time of turbulence and revolution in Rome. "The aristocracy to which he probably belonged was in obvious decay; the world in which he lived was falling apart into a chaos that left no life or fortune secure. His poem is a longing for physical and mental peace."[25]

His poem is an unfinished elaboration of Epicurus' natural philosophy, punctuated regularly by criticisms of religion. Rome contained a pluralistic mix of imported and home-grown gods and spirits. Her gods "were stern, powerful, and aloof." Her spirits "haunted fields, forests, crossroads, and even the home it-self."[26] You were safe, for the most part, at least from the gods, if you did not cross them. But they were seen as behind every unusual physical and natural occurrence in nature. Lucretius viewed the whole religious enterprise as the greatest source of human misery. For Lucretius, the religious leaders—by stir-ring up people about imaginary punishments and rewards in the sweet-and-sour by-and-by—are doing nothing more than generating unnecessary fear and mis-ery for people.

Religion gives "birth to sinful and unholy deeds." Seers disturb people with "terror-speaking tales." It is because "mortals do not understand things, so out of ignorance they explain as from divine power." But the world is just too full of defects to have been created by a god. To suggest that the gods have created "the glorious nature of the world," and that people should then praise them, and that it will all "be eternal and immortal," and that it is a wicked thing to challenge or change what the gods have made—this "is all sheer folly." The fear that any transgression or untoward statement will have to face a "heavy time of reckon-ing" makes "people and nations quake, and proud monarchs shrink into them-selves."[27]

Lucretius raises rhetorical, critical questions that everyone would recognize as common problems for religion that sees God as a supernatural, conscious will who runs the world and intervenes in everyday affairs. These are in the spirit of the challenges by the biblical Job from an earlier time and of those raised in our time by Rabbi Kushner in his best seller, *When Bad Things Happen to Good People*.[28] Lucretius asks, "if Jupiter and other gods" are responsible for storms and lightning, why then do they not strike particularly pernicious sinners and thus make an example of them for others? And why then do they strike the inno-cent of "no foul offence" with "the whirlwind and fire of heaven"? And how can you explain it when lightning is just striking solitary spots for no obvious rea-son? Are the gods exercising or practicing? And why do they not toss down bolts of lightning when there are no clouds? It makes no sense, as well, that sometimes their storms will destroy their own temples and images of them cre-ated in their honor.[29]

It is hard to say whether Lucretius sincerely cares for the human beings he would free from the terrors of religion, but he wants them to know he feels their pain.

> O hapless race of men, when that they charged the gods with such acts and coupled with them bitter wrath! What groaning did they then beget for them-selves, what wounds for us, what tears for our children's children![30]

For all practical purposes, after Lucretius we do not have any significant criticisms of religion as such, certainly not by leading thinkers, until the eigh-teenth century. Then we begin to get very serious criticisms—for many people, devastating criticisms. Historical changes prepared the way for those criticisms, and I will attempt to trace those changes in relatively broad strokes in the next two chapters.

Frames of Reference

It is important to notice from our review of early critiques of religion that they are embedded in a larger picture of society, usually also even of the whole cosmos. Over the years various concepts have been developed to designate this broader, holistic view: *Weltanschauung* (German for *worldview*), *frame of reference, discourse, paradigm.* Sometimes even broader terms have been used for this purpose, such as when we read of "the *Theology* of Karl Barth" or "the social *theory* of Max Weber" or "the *philosophy* of David Hume." The point is that the criticism of religion is one plank in a platform of concerns reflecting an overall perspective of the whole. That overall perspective is itself not always internally consistent nor is it always fully articulated, but it is out of that framework (with its broader philosophical viewpoints) that the critique of religion arises. So Isaiah has a view of a society faithful to the worship of Yahweh from which he criticizes religious practices as empty formalisms in a society not so ordered. Lucretius, with his concern to promote a natural philosophy of knowledge and an ethical philosophy of Epicureanism, rejects religion for its inconsistency with empirical evidence and as a cause of unnecessary pain and misery.

Many religious people justify rejection of the criticisms of religion by rejecting the overall perspective of the critic. This is unfortunate (and an unconvincing cop-out) because it avoids the question whether the criticism is true or has important truth in it. Clearly one need not share Epicurus' and Lucretius' natural philosophy or their view that the goal of life is pleasure to see that religion can and sometimes does scare the bejesus out of people quite unnecessarily. From time to time we hear testimonies by adults reflecting on a childhood characterized by sleepless nights of terror after hearing the sermon of some fire-and-brimstone preacher.

The truth in one plank of a platform of thought simply does not always rest entirely on the legitimacy of the whole platform. Ironically, for example, Marx, who largely shared the natural philosophy of Epicurus and Lucretius and even wrote his doctoral dissertation on Epicurus,[31] criticized religion because it comforted people—a conclusion opposite that of the Epicureans! I would suggest it is simply disingenuous to reject the criticisms because we do not share the overall framework of the critic. The criticisms need to be taken on their own terms, at least initially, before we re-evaluate them. The rule here is simple and reasonable: give them a fair hearing. In so far as they are untrue, forget'em. Insofar as their truthfulness cannot be determined, admit it. In so far as they are true, however, we need to know it, and our faith-claims and religious practices need to be informed, perhaps even disciplined, by their insights.

It is also important to recognize that the overall perspectives themselves re-flect in important ways the time, the culture, and the concerns of the people who "carry" them.[32] For that reason, I have included a few observations about the social context of the critics discussed above and will continue to do so with each critic. (I offer an expanded discussion of the relationship between ideas and his-tory toward the end of chapter 4.)

Let us move on now to the Renaissance and the Reformation—the next peri-ods of Western history to manifest major critiques of religion. These critiques were, like those of the prophets and Jesus, critiques from within religion. The intellectual movements of the Renaissance and Reformation also prepare the way for the rise of science, for self-conscious social criticism, and for the water-shed event of the Enlightenment.

Notes

1. Jonathan Edwards, "Sinners in The Hands of an Angry God," in *The Works of Jonathan Edwards*, vol. II, 1974 ed. (Edinburgh, Scotland: The Banner of Truth Trust, 1834), 10.

2. William James, *The Varieties of Religious Experience: A Study in Human Nature* (N.Y.: The Modern Library, 1902), 414, 415.

3. Carlo Diano, "Epicurus," in *The New Encyclopaedia Britannica*, 15th ed., vol. 4 (Chicago: Encyclopaedia Britannica, 1994); Antony Flew, ed., *A Dictionary of Philoso-phy*, 2nd ed. (N.Y.: St. Martin's Press, 1979), 108-109.

4. Will Durant, *The Story of Civilization: The Life of Greece* (N.Y.: Simon and Schuster, 1966 [1939]), 557.

5. Durant, *Life of Greece*, 557-559

6. Russel M. Geer, introduction to *Letters, Principal Doctrines, and Vatican Say-ings*, by Epicurus (N.Y.: Macmillan, 1964), x.

7. Durant, *Life of Greece*, 565.

8. Geer, introduction, ix.

9. Epicurus, *Letters, Principal Doctrines, and Vatican Sayings*, trans. Russel M. Geer (N.Y.: Macmillan, 1964), 56.

10. Epicurus, *Letters*, 56.

11. Epicurus, *Letters*, 57.

12. Epicurus, *Letters*, 61.

13. Epicurus, *Letters*, 51-52.

14. Epicurus, *Letters*, 54-55.

15. Quoted in Bertrand Russell, *The Autobiography of Bertrand Russell—1872-1914* (Boston and Toronto: Little, Brown and Co., 1967), 12.

16. Epicurus, *Letters*, 30-33.

17. Epicurus, *Letters*, 58.

18. Geer, introduction, x.xxiv-xxv.

19. Lucretius, *On The Nature of Things*, trans. H. A. J. Munro, vol. 12, *Lucretius, Epictetus, Marcus Aurelius*, Great Books of the Western World, ed. Robert Maynard

Hutchins *et al.* (Chicago: Encyclopaedia Britannica; William Benton Publisher, 1952), 61.

20. Geer, introduction, x.xxv.

21. Lucretius, *On The Nature*, 1, 2.

22. Lucretius, *On The Nature*, 61.

23. Will Durant, *The Story of Civilization: Caesar and Christ—A History of Roman Civilization and of Christianity from their beginnings to A.D. 325* (N.Y.: Simon and Schuster, 1944), 154; George Santayana, *Three Philosophical Poets: Lucretius—Dante—Goethe* (Garden City, N.Y.: Doubleday Anchor, 1954), 11.

24. John P. McKay, Bennett D. Hill, and John Buckler, *A History of Western Society*, vol. I, *From Antiquity to the Enlightenment*, 4th ed. (Boston: Houghton Mifflin, 1991), chap. 5 passim.

25. Durant, *Caesar and Christ*, 146-147.

26. McKay *et al.*, *Western Society*, *I*, 144-145.

27. Lucretius, *On The Nature*, 2, 3, 17, 63, 77.

28. Harold S. Kushner, *When Bad Things Happen to Good People* (N.Y.: Avon, 1981).

29. Lucretius, *On The Nature*, 85.

30. Lucretius, *On The Nature*, 76

31. Title: "Differenz der demokritischen und epikureischen Naturphilosophie." See Werner Blumenberg (dargestellter), *Karl Marx: in Selbstzeugnissen und Bilddokumenten* (Reinbeck bei Hamburg: Rowohlt, 1962), 42.

32. See Peter L. Berger and Thomas Luckmann, *The Social Construction of Reality: A Treatise in the Sociology of Knowledge* (Garden City, N.Y.: Anchor Books, 1966).

Chapter 3

Cloppity-Cloppity-Cloppity
Foundations of Modern Critique I

During the Renaissance and the Reformation three developing streams of thought, in particular, would challenge the domination of the Roman Catholic worldview and fight with one another, contributing to the breakup of consensus and to the intellectual foundations on which modern critiques of religion as such would build. I would characterize these three streams as Renaissance humanism, mainline Protestantism, and radical Protestantism.

Renaissance Humanism and Erasmus

The Renaissance usually refers to that period in Western history from sometime in the 1300s through the 1500s. It is especially associated with developments on the Italian peninsula. Long-distance trade had helped support an enormous growth in wealth, and merchant guilds wrested control of the Italian city-states from the nobility; although they then established their own forms of royal rule.[1]

Princes, popes, and wealthy merchants began to invest their wealth in support of arts and letters. Painting, architecture, and literature found patrons ready to commission work that would enrich their lives and display their wealth and prestige. The Renaissance became the age of new learning as the classical art and literature of Greece and Rome were examined, studied, and redone in new forms. The status of artists improved markedly as they received acclaim for their creativity. The idea of the independent creative genius developed. Such geniuses were no longer simply tools of divine creativity; they were creators in their own right.[2] There was a new sense of the power of human agency and the possibility of human development. There arose a concept of an ideal person, a "universal

31

man" who would be multi-talented—"courtier, politician, explorer, artist, scientist, financier."[3] The artists themselves in the fifteenth century believed they were bringing in a new age, closing the door on the dark ages.[4]

The Renaissance spread north of the Alps. "By 1500 Italy exerted a hypnotic influence, and just as the princes of the Western world wished to acquire the services of Italy's great painters and sculptors, so, too, did the artists of this outer world feel themselves drawn to Italy."[5] But in the north the Renaissance had a stronger religious accent. Especially in the writings of people like Thomas More, John Colet, and Desiderius Erasmus, the new learning showed itself in an emphatic concern with ethics—the possibility for social and religious reform, and the potential for human beings to live good and rational lives.[6]

Desiderius Erasmus (c. 1466-1536) spent several years in Italy.[7] He was enchanted by the new learning. He himself studied widely and thoroughly the classics as well as Christian literature. He could write as late as 1517, "Immortal God, what a world I see dawning! Why can I not grow young again?"[8] He was also troubled by the excesses, the violence, the immorality, the exploitation, the inequality, the focus on wealth, the impiety. He thought that humanism among the Italians was "pure paganism," and boasted: "I brought it about that humanism...began nobly to celebrate Christ."[9]

Erasmus has been called "the most distinguished scholar of Northern Europe,"[10] "the greatest European scholar of the 16th century,"[11] "the greatest of the humanists."[12] He loved learning and writing to such an extent that he lived a life of modest means, turning down offers of professorships, bishoprics, even that of a cardinal, so he could remain free to think and study and write what he thought. This early free-lance writer's lifestyle meant shameless pleading with friends and patrons to support his work. "He preferred to beg in freedom rather than decay in bonds."[13] He was able to acquire such support, and, as his fame increased, so did the support from admiring patrons. He lived quite frugally except, presumably, while staying with wealthy patrons desiring the company and wisdom of the great Erasmus. He valued money principally for the freedom to study and write and for buying books.

In or near Rotterdam, Erasmus was born the out-of-wedlock son of a priest and a physician's daughter. He was sent off to school quite young where he developed his deep love of learning. He became an Augustinian monk, but managed to stay out of the cloister through external assignments. He was able, in various ways, to spend considerable time in Paris at the university, in England where he got to know Thomas More and John Colet among others, in Basel where his primary publisher was located, and in Italy where he drank deeply of the Roman Renaissance. He settled in Louvain, Belgium. But wherever he was, he studied, and he wrote.

Erasmus is best known as the epitome of Renaissance humanism—promoting the classics, the faculty of reason, and critical examination of literary and biblical texts—which would contribute to developments in the Enlightenment. He was also a respectful debater with Martin Luther. Although Erasmus agreed with Luther in many ways, they had some basic differences, especially over the issue of free will and the use of reason. And Erasmus never broke with the church, in part, perhaps, because he had some fondness for Pope Leo X, but probably also because Erasmus believed fundamentally in working out differences through debate and discussion, avoiding as much as possible recrimination, vituperation, and certainly violence. He was an opponent of war, pleading with princes to settle conflicts peacefully. He wrote: "There is no peace, even unjust, which is not preferable to the most just of wars."[14] He saw the developing nationalism as an enemy of peace and counted himself a citizen of the world. He corresponded tirelessly not only in defense of his writings but also in lengthy, diligent, and extravagant attempts to remain reconciled with his critics.[15]

This does not mean Erasmus was not a critic. Our interest in him here is as a critic of religion, and a critic he was—one of considerable skill—who with satire and wit criticized almost everything there was to criticize about the church in his time.

One of his earliest published works, *Praise of Folly*,[16] was written almost as a lark after convivial conversations with friends in England. He wrote it quickly but revised it over the years. It is a satire, a long-winded sermon by the goddess Folly. Folly in this discourse is praising herself as the one god who really has given humanity all the real delights and pleasures of its existence. It is an uneven work, shifting at times into what sounds like rather didactic criticism, but it makes its points clearly, and gained for Erasmus both fame and enemies. Folly comments on the whole spectrum of human foibles in politics, economics, and culture. What got most attention from the critics, though, was the criticism of religious practices.

From the superstition of laypersons to the self-important rituals of the supreme pontiff, Folly celebrates her contributions. Springing from my game, says Folly, "drunken and absurd as it is," are the "haughty philosophers and their present-day successors, who are popularly called monks, kings in their purple, pious priests, and thrice-holy pontiffs." Folly reminds her listeners of "those who enjoy deluding themselves with imaginary pardons for their sins." Notice, too, the "people who rely on certain magic signs and prayers thought up by some pious imposter for his own amusement or for gain." They think that by these religious tricks they will receive "wealth, honours, pleasure, plenty, continual good health, long life, a vigorous old age, and finally a seat next to Christ in heaven." Each district has its own saint for some trivial cause or other. And the poor "common ignorant man" comes closer to attributing more to the Virgin Mother than to her son. Christians everywhere are involved in all kinds of superstitions. And in "these varieties of silliness . . . they are readily permitted and encouraged by priests" quite aware of "the profit to be made thereby." Consider the merchants, and there is a "whole tribe" of them who seek gain even "by the meanest methods," and they have got "plenty of sycophantic friars too who will sing their praises and publicly address them as honourable, doubtless hoping that a morsel of these ill-gotten gains will come their way." Let us not forget "the theologians, a remarkably supercilious and touchy lot," ready always to unleash the bolt of denunciation for heresy against "anyone to whom they take a dislike." Christ's apostles would be baffled by the theological subtleties of discussions surrounding the Eucharist, the mother of Christ, baptism, grace and works.

Folly asks: "Who *could* understand all this unless he has frittered away thirty-six whole years over the physics and metaphysics of Aristotle and Scotus?" (Erasmus, in his charm, is not above poking a little fun at himself!) The theologians spend so much time "with these enjoyable tomfooleries, that they haven't even a spare moment in which to read the Gospel or the letters of Paul even once through." Furthermore, they select and twist biblical texts at will, according to their own particular interests. The monks are almost as happy as the theologians in their self-satisfaction, except that "they believe it's the highest form of piety to be so uneducated that they can't even read." And the preaching! We hear so many long-winded exercises of "theological arrogance," "idiotic hypotheses, and further scholastic rubbish" by speakers who are more concerned with "rhetorical excellence" than substance. The upper echelons of the church manifest some of the greatest foolishness. There are the cardinals who might want to consider "that they are not the lords but the stewards of the . . . spiritual riches." And finally we have the popes, the supreme pontiffs. "Think of all the advantages they would lose if they ever showed a sign of wisdom!" Thanks to Folly, they feel they've fulfilled their responsibility by leading in all kinds of pomp and ceremony. These "impious pontiffs" are "the deadliest enemies of the church." They even go forth to participate in that greatest of monstrosities—war![17]

Obviously Erasmus saw enough wrong with the Church to believe it needed reforming. But he was not quite sure what to do, it seems. At the height of Reformation conflict, he did work behind the scenes, encouraging leading churchmen to institute specific reforms he thought might satisfy the Protestants. He vigorously opposed division. He had seen it coming. On September 9, 1517, he wrote in a letter: "In this part of the world I am afraid a great revolution is impending."[18] In less than two months Martin Luther would issue his ninety-five theses challenging the theology and practice of indulgences. Erasmus tried to remain a moderating, pacifying, and reconciling influence as the Reformation exploded around him. He was an enlightened man with a sensitive heart and a keen mind in an age of violent polarization. He came to be vilified by the hardliners on both sides. Old and ill, he became morose; although he surely found comfort in the letters and visits of admirers.[19] After his death in 1536, some of his books were banned and burned in Spain and Italy. In 1559 all of his works were placed on the Roman index of prohibited books.[20] It would have broken his heart.

Mainline Protestantism and Martin Luther

The religious rebellion of the 1500s shattered the Roman church, ultimately dividing Western Christianity into a variety of churches, denominations, and sects. There were numerous key players in this movement called the Reformation, which could be called the Separation. The best known are John Calvin in Geneva, Ulrich Zwingli in Zürich, and Martin Luther in Saxony. Martin Luther (1483-1546) is commonly seen as the major player, not least of which because his efforts set it all in motion. He was an Augustinian monk with a penchant for spiritual struggle.

Luther was born in the village of Eisleben in Saxony, his father a businessman in copper mining who wanted Luther to become a lawyer.[21] So Martin began studies at the University of Erfurt. After a visit home in 1502, on his way back to the university, he encountered a violent thunderstorm that scared him out of his wits. Lightening drove him to the ground, and he made a vow, then, to become a monk. He prayed to St. Anne, the patron saint of the mining profession: "St. Anne help me! I will become a monk."[22] He fulfilled his vow two weeks later by entering the Augustinian monastery at Erfurt.

Luther was a man tormented by terror at the wrath of God, dread at the judgment of Christ, panic at the power of Satan. For a while, he found some peace in the monastery. "Luther in later life remarked that during the first year in the monastery the Devil is very quiet."[23] Primarily he felt agony and torment, feeling himself in what he characterized as at war with the devil, always burdened by his own unworthiness. Then the day came for Martin to say his first Mass. Everything seemed fine; he "took his place before the altar and began to recite the introductory portion of the mass until he came to the words, 'We offer unto thee the living, the true, the eternal God.'" Later Luther wrote:

> At these words I was utterly stupefied and terror-stricken. I thought to myself, "With what tongue shall I address such Majesty, seeing that all men ought to tremble in the presence of even an earthly prince? Who am I, that I should lift up mine eyes or raise my hands to the divine Majesty? The angels surround him. At his nod the earth trembles. And shall I, a miserable little pigmy, say, 'I want this, I ask for that'? For I am dust and ashes and full of sin and I am speaking to the living, the eternal, and the true God."[24]

Luther later had another conversion experience, more important, at least for the rest of the world, than the one that led him into the monastery. This second conversion led him into the activities that would shatter Western Christian unity. Luther was an exemplary monk but found no peace in his devotion. While studying Paul's letter to the Romans, he experienced a new enlightenment and a new birth. Here are his words:

Night and day I pondered until I saw the connection between the justice of God
and the statement that "the just shall live by his faith." Then I grasped that the
justice of God is that righteousness by which through grace and sheer mercy
God justifies us through faith. Thereupon I felt myself to be reborn and to have
gone through open doors into paradise.[25]

Luther experienced grace, found a new peace, gained the courage and confidence to become the leading reformer of the Church and ultimately to change
the history of the world. But while the old agony and torment were gone, he still
faced many difficulties, doubts, and struggles. The experience of anxiety and
temptation followed him throughout his life. "I did not learn my theology all at
once," wrote Luther, "but I had to search deeper for it, where my temptations
took me. . . . Not understanding, reading, or speculation, but living, nay rather
dying and being damned make a theologian."[26]

Luther began to have very serious doubts about many of the practices and
beliefs of the church. In addition, he thought the church was corrupt, and in
many ways he was right. Others of his generation had similar doubts and criticisms. Indeed, J. H. Plumb points out that even before Luther's time "criticism
of clerical worldliness, of monkish foolishness, of papal avarice, of Roman
decadence" from north of the Alps had been often "sharp and prolonged."[27] We
have already seen it in Erasmus's *Praise of Folly*, first published in 1509. But as
early as 1378 the English theologian, John Wycliffe, "began a systematic attack
on the beliefs and practices of the church."[28] In *The Trialogus* he referred to the
papacy as the antichrist and railed against the church's "infinite blasphemies."[29]

What really ticked Luther off, leading him to take a public stand that would
start a domino effect of religious diversity in Western history, was the practice
of selling indulgences—offering people forgiveness or release of their dead rela-
tives from purgatory for financial contributions to the church. It was a particularly unfortunate, exploitative, and cynical practice. Luther went public with his
criticisms. The Pope, Luther said, "would do better to sell St. Peter's and give
the money to the poor folk who are being fleeced by the hawkers of indulgences."[30] The defenders of the practice stiffened. The dispute rapidly became
one about the power and role of the papacy. Luther began to publish much more
serious criticisms of the church and became embroiled in a life-threatening
struggle with church leaders.

We have already seen that Luther was severe with himself in his own spiritual struggles. He was clearly a man of deep, powerful, and uninhibited emo-
tions. So, with his life at stake as well, he was especially ferocious as a dispu-
tant.

In response to a criticism from a leading Dominican, Luther wrote: "Like an
insidious devil you pervert the scriptures." In an inquiry to a Cardinal, Luther
said of the Pope, "His Holiness abuses Scriptures. I deny that he is above Scripture." Luther argued the papacy was merely a human institution, and identified

the papacy as the antichrist. When he rejected ordination as a sacrament, he said the clergy regard the laity as dogs. Under order of excommunication, in a fit of rage, and receiving offers of help from knights who supported him (but which he rejected), he asked why we don't rise up and "assault these monsters of perdition, these cardinals, these popes, and the whole swarm of the Roman Sodom, who corrupt youth and the Church of God?" In his *Address to the German Nobility* Luther argued against the power of the church over the state, and against the idea that only the pope could interpret scripture or call a council. He called for reducing the number of orders, spoke against irrevocable vows and the burning of heretics, and argued that clergy should be allowed to marry. He claimed the bull of excommunication was guilty of "horrible blasphemies." The bull "is the sum of all impiety, blasphemy, ignorance, impudence, hypocrisy, lying—in a word, it is Satan and his Antichrist." "And as they excommunicated me for the sacrilege of heresy," he wrote, "so I excommunicate them in the name of the sacred truth of God. Christ will judge whose excommunication will stand." In a letter to his superior, friend, and confessor he wrote that Christ and the pope "are diametrically contrary." Upon being invited to the Diet of Worms and unsure whether he would get a fair hearing or just be required to recant, he wrote a letter that said: "This shall be my recantation at Worms: 'Previously I said the pope is the vicar of Christ. I recant. Now I say the pope is the adversary of Christ and the apostle of the Devil.'"[31] Only by the narrowest definition of criticism could we avoid viewing Luther as a critic of religion; albeit, not religion as such.

Later he would turn his critical ferocity against the German peasants during their rebellion, against the Anabaptists, against usurers, people who did not love music, the Zwinglians, and, unfortunately, against Jews, among others. He was simply a vehemently critical man. This is not to say Luther had no charm. He was loved and respected by many, followed by more. He was a laugher, a drinker, a lover of music, and a spell-binding table companion. He showed respect in debate with opponents who showed him respect. But he was a man of polarity which manifested itself in every venue of opposition.

The Reformation meant not only division between Protestantism and Catholicism. It also meant division among Protestants. Luther in all his color and charm tended also toward a character most moderns would see as unbending. The psychoanalyst Erich Fromm analyzed Luther as authoritarian.[32] It is possible that this was fairly typical of men of power in Luther's day; however, Erasmus's humanism was remarkably tolerant and conciliatory, and Roland Bainton's biography of Luther identifies, in the maelstrom surrounding Luther's clashes with the Catholic Church, numerous personalities of considerable civility and thoughtfulness. One particularly heartbreaking event (for Protestants) occurred at the height of Luther's power.

There was a moment when the major Protestant groups came close to unifying. Among the Reformation leaders there had been ongoing debates about a variety of doctrinal and ecclesiastical matters. In 1529 the German and Protestant Prince Philip of Hesse invited the major leaders to a meeting at Marburg to see if they could not achieve some kind of unity. Philip believed that the church would be better served if Protestants could achieve a common confession and confederation. Among the leaders who attended were the Swiss reformer Ulrich Zwingli from Zürich and Luther and Philipp Melancthon from Saxony. [33]

Luther and Melancthon drew up fifteen articles of doctrine they felt every-body should agree to. Zwingli, the other Swiss reformers, and some of the Germans, were able to agree with fourteen of them. [34] The one article to which they could not come to agreement was about the Eucharist.

The Roman Catholic Church had developed the doctrine that the bread and wine are actually transformed into the body and blood of Christ. Luther moved away from this position, rejecting the idea that the bread and wine were actually changed into Christ's body and blood. However, he still "felt himself bound . . . to teach the real presence of Christ's body and blood not in place of, but in, with, and under the bread and wine." [35] Zwingli and the other reformers, on the other hand, argued that the Lord's Supper is a memorial at which Christ is spiritually present but not materially; in other words, Christ's real, material body and blood are not in the elements of the Lord's Supper. (Two hundred years later Voltaire wrote sardonically: "So, while those who were called Papists ate God but not bread, the Lutherans ate both bread and God. Soon after there came the Calvinists who ate bread and did not eat God.") [36]

The Protestants at Marburg could not come to final agreement; the reformed and Lutheran churches were unable to unite, and the rest is history. At the end of the meeting at Marburg, Zwingli, offered his hand in Christian fellowship. Luther refused to shake hands, saying, "Your spirit is not our spirit." [37] Melancthon later wrote: "We told the Zwinglians that we wondered how their consciences would allow them to call us brethren when they held that our doctrine was erroneous." [38]

I retell this story to underscore the observation that while the critical mind is essential for human liberation, it can easily become an exasperatingly and unnecessarily divisive and intolerant mind. Karen Armstrong has pointed out that

> it has been suggested that [Luther's] belligerent character did great harm to the Reformation. At the beginning of his career as a Reformer many of his ideas were held by orthodox Catholics, and they could have given the Church a new vitality, but Luther's aggressive tactics caused them to be regarded with unnecessary suspicion. [39]

Insofar as that is true, Erasmus was certainly one of the victims. Even though I want to affirm the importance of criticism, I also want to encourage humility and especially its social counterpart: tolerance.

While Erasmus indulged in wide-ranging criticism, including criticism of religion, even calling for reform, he never risked a serious breach with the church, deferring to its time-honored wisdom. And his manner of criticism was gentlemanly humane, as befits a Renaissance scholar. Robert Blackley Drummond wrote that Erasmus's breadth was his weakness, just as narrowness was Luther's strength. Erasmus, whatever doubts he entertained, "knew well how to convey them without committing himself to any positive statement." It certainly was not heretical to raise critical questions about the Bible and church fathers, especially since he said he would retract his claims if the church pronounced them erroneous.[40] Luther's criticisms were of a very different and even inflammatory nature, and they gave no quarter. Nevertheless, neither Erasmus nor Luther ever really turned their critical analyses to the structures of society in any significant way.

The feudal economic and political organization of society received Luther's explicit blessing by his affirmation of princes and magistrates as representatives of God, his support of obedience to the state, and his condemnation of the Peasants' rebellion. Bainton wrote that Luther "would tolerate no wanton disturbance of the ancient ways." His first and overriding concern was religion, and "the forms of the external life are indifferent and may be left to be determined by circumstance."[41] Harry Emerson Fosdick pointed out that Luther did struggle with some ambivalence regarding his stand toward the state, even admitting that discipleship could sometimes require a rebuke of the princes or denial of allegiance, but "in the end he placed the church dangerously under the dominion of the state."[42] (So three hundred years later Marx could write: "Christians live in states with differing constitutions, some in a republic, others in an absolute monarchy, and still others in a constitutional monarchy. Christianity does not decide on the *quality* of constitutions since it knows no distinction among them.")[43]

The radical wing of the Reformation was a different matter.

Radical Protestantism and the Anabaptists

The Amish are a Christian religious community that has traditionally abstained from "many of the standard components of modern civilization: automobiles, radio and television, high school and college, movies, air conditioning, jewelry and cosmetics, life insurance, cameras, musical instruments," and much more.[44] The Pennsylvania Amish were featured in the popular 1985 movie *Witness*.[45] I lived for some time in a small, rural town in northern Indiana near a large community of Amish. Some of the Amish would visit my town for the services of the local physician. Occasionally on a summer evening, with the windows open, I would hear the creaking sounds of an Amish horse-drawn wagon going down the street with the distinctive cloppity-cloppity-cloppity of the horses' hoofs. That sound—cloppity-cloppity-cloppity—was a reminder that the way we moderns live, with all our modern technological devices, is not necessary.

The Amish have their historical roots in the radical wing of the Reformation as "descendants of the sixteenth-century Swiss Anabaptists."[46] It is a complicated picture because of the multiplicity of sects and theologies, but the radical wing of the Reformation (also called the *left wing*) refers to those Protestant groups who were rejected by and in turn rejected both the Catholic and the Protestant establishment churches. These were some forty or more radical sects,[47] generically labeled by their opponents *Anabaptists* (from Greek meaning baptized again or rebaptized) because they rejected infant baptism as meaningless and submitted to an adult baptism, typically by immersion. In the Schleitheim Confession of Faith, prepared at a conference of Anabaptist Swiss Brethren in 1527, they wrote:

> Baptism shall be given to all those who have learned repentance and amendment of life, and who believe truly that their sins are taken away by Christ . . . and . . . who . . . request it. . . . This excludes all infant baptism, the highest and chief abomination of the pope.[48]

This is probably the one practice they all had in common. (Some of the mainline Protestant authorities took ironical glee in executing Anabaptists by drowning.[49])

The radical Protestants found their justifications in a literal adherence to biblical texts, and their early leaders came from among the clergy and intelligentsia. Much of their following, though, was from elements experiencing intense social and economic discomfort, recruited especially from "among the lower classes, when the miserable failure of the peasant revolt had caused deep distrust of the Lutheran cause."[50]

Their reading of Christian responsibility with regard to the organization of church and community was indeed radical. To them, the church Luther established looked very much like the institutions he vacated, albeit encoded with a different theology. They carried a challenge to the social organization of their time, usually more implicitly than explicitly. They desired to re-create, as closely as possible, the "true church" here on earth.[51] The church, they believed, had fallen from the golden age of the apostolic fathers. The orthodox churches (Catholic and Protestant) had become militaristic, coercive, hierarchical, and tied up with the state. The true church, as seen in the New Testament, was to be voluntaristic (made up entirely of freely choosing, baptized adults), communistic (sharing all material wealth), pacifistic (not even serving in military or police forces), and separate from the state or civil government. They tended to see themselves as the only true believers and set themselves apart from the rest of society.[52] Again, from the Schleitheim Confession of Faith:

> A separation shall be made from the evil and from the wickedness which the devil planted in the world; in this manner, simply that we shall not have fellowship with them and not run with them in the multitude of their abominations.

This is the way it is: Since all who do not walk in the obedience of faith, and have not united themselves with god so that they wish to do His will, are a great abomination before God, it is not possible for anything to grow or issue from them except abominable things.[53]

The mainline Protestant reformers viewed these Anabaptist doctrines and practices as spiritualizing and revolutionary. Franklin Littell, in *The Origins of Sectarian Protestantism*, argues that the Anabaptists themselves were not spiritualizing or revolutionary, especially in the way other more marginal elements of the left wing were. He suggests the mainline Protestant leaders misperceived the Anabaptists by focusing on the most radical groups, and not recognizing how similar and humane the Anabaptists were to the mainline Protestants.[54] However, we can see why the established churches, as well as the state, would view with considerable alarm the radical notions of pacifism, voluntarism, communism, and disestablishment. While the Anabaptists were still in favor of good order, it was certainly not the order of the reformed churches or even the state at that time. We can understand why the defenders of the establishment would think they were facing serious criticism—more implicit than explicit. Being viewed as living in abomination would sound like criticism to most people.

Some of the more extreme elements of the left wing of the Reformation advocated violent revolution, suggesting the kingdom of God would be established by the sword. This included Thomas Münzer, an early leader of the peasants' rebellion. He had apocalyptic visions for a new world order, inspired by the book of Revelation. Bernt Rothmann in 1534 established a new community in Münster and taught that defense of the faith would mean arming themselves "not only with the humble weapons of the apostles for suffering, but also with the glorious armour of David for vengeance . . . in order . . . to eradicate all ungodliness."[55] One of Rothmann's followers, Jan Benkelsz, whom Vivian Green identifies as "both a megalomaniac and a mystic" sought to legalize polygamy. He was proclaimed the messianic king of the world.[56] Most Anabaptists faced severe persecution, even death, by Protestant and Catholic authorities alike, but these explicitly revolutionary elements were dealt with especially quickly and brutally.

It is reasonable to suspect that had any of the revolutionary elements of the left wing of the Reformation been successful, it would not now be viewed as so thoroughly pacifistic. Nevertheless, it is true that a majority of the leaders and groups of the radical Reformation were strictly pacifist. The Schleitheim Confession stated:

there will also unquestionably fall from us the unchristian, devilish weapons of force—such as sword, armor and the like, and all their use [either] for friends or against one's enemies—by virtue of the word of Christ, Resist not [him that is] evil.[57]

In their pacifism, I would agree, they got their New Testament literalism right.

Among the radical reformers were the Hutterites of Moravia (after Jacob Hutter, executed in 1536) who ended up migrating to South Dakota in the United States and Canada; the Mennonites (after Menno Simons) who also ended up migrating to the Americas and are known today as the Amish and the Mennonites.[58]

The radical Protestants' criticism of religion was still a criticism from within religion. It was socially radical largely because of their holistic view of church and community, rooted in biblical literalism, and because of their location in a time and place where separation of church and state was not yet a reality. (The establishments in the United States, Canada, or Mexico today do not feel threatened by Amish communities in their midst. Actually we find them charmingly quaint.)

The critique of the Anabaptists was not a modern critique. It did not celebrate the powers of human reason, freedom, and creativity, nor critically challenge religious authority as such. It was not concerned with the liberation of humanity from unnecessary social fetters. It was substituting a kinder, gentler authoritarian system for others, less humane and more arbitrary; although Marx's collaborator Friedrich Engels viewed Thomas Münzer as a forerunner of revolutionary communism.[59] All in all, as Vivian Green writes: "The universe remained a supernatural entity governed by the providential dispensation of God."[60]

Such a universe would last for about two hundred more years. In the meantime the accumulating forces of rational criticism, the development of science, and other social changes would eventuate in the "enlightened" mind ready to view life and the world as secular realms of natural forces. In this modern frame of reference, religion would become vulnerable to the cultural critics who saw religion as unnecessary, often harmful, and something to be superseded.

Notes

1. The background of the Renaissance in this section draws primarily from John P. McKay, Bennett D. Hill, John Buckler, *A History of Western Society*, vol. I, *From Antiquity to the Enlightenment*, 4th ed (Boston: Houghton Mifflin, 1991) and J. H. Plumb, *The Italian Renaissance: A Concise Survey of Its History and Culture* (N.Y. and Evanston: Harper & Row; Harper Torchbooks, 1961).

2. McKay et al., *Western Society*, I, 398-399.

3. Roland H. Bainton, *Here I Stand: A Life of Martin Luther* (Nashville: Abingdon Press, 1978), 95.

4. Plumb, *Italian Renaissance*, 32.

5. Plumb, *Italian Renaissance*, 145.

6. McKay et al., *Western Society*, I, 405-409.

7. The biographical information about Erasmus is primarily from Will Durant, *The Story of Civilization: The Reformation—A History of European Civilization from Wyclif to Calvin: 1300-1564* (N.Y.: Simon and Schuster, 1957), chaps. 14 and 19.

8. Quoted in Plumb, *Italian Renaissance*, 143.

9. Quoted in McKay et al., *Western Society, I*, 407.

10. Plumb, *Italian Renaissance*, 143.

11. James D. Tracy, "Erasmus," *The New Encyclopaedia Britannica*, 15th ed., vol. 18 (Chicago: Encyclopaedia Britannica, 1994), 489.

12. Durant, *The Reformation*, 271.

13. Durant, *The Reformation*, 274.

14. Durant, *The Reformation*, 287.

15. See Desiderius Erasmus, "Letter to Maarten Van Dorp 1515," in *Praise of Folly* and *Letter to Maarten Van Dorp*, trans. Betty Radice (London: Penguin, 1993), 135-172.

16. Desiderius Erasmus, *Praise of Folly*, in *Praise of Folly* and *Letter to Maarten Van Dorp*, translated by Betty Radice, introduction and notes by A. H. T. Levi (London: Penguin, 1993).

17. Erasmus, *Praise of Folly*, 21, 63-64, 64, 65, 66, 76, 86, 89-91, 91, 93, 94, 96, 101-102, 108, 108-109, 109, 110, 110-111.

18. Quoted in Durant, *The Reformation*, 292.

19. See Durant, *The Reformation*, 436.

20. A. H. T. Levi, introduction to *Praise of Folly* and *Letter to Maarten Van Dorp 1515*, by Erasmus (London: Penguin, 1993), xxxiv.

21. My primary source for Luther's biography is Bainton, *Here I Stand*.

22. Quoted in Bainton, *Here I Stand*, 25.

23. Bainton, *Here I Stand*, 27.

24. Quoted in Bainton, *Here I Stand*, 30.

25. Quoted in Bainton, *Here I Stand*, 49.

26. Quoted by Timothy George in James A. Weaver, in Douglas C. Weaver, ed., *A Cloud of Witnesses: Sermon Illustrations and Devotionals from the Christian Heritage* (Macon, GA: Smyth & Helwys, 1993), 69.

27. Plumb, *Italian Renaissance*, 93.

28. John Stacey, "Wycliffe, John," *The New Encyclopaedia Britannica*, 15th ed., vol. 12 (Chicago: Encyclopaedia Britannica, 1994), 786.

29. John Wycliffe, "from *The Trialogus*," in *Great Voices of the Reformation: An Anthology*, ed. Harry Emerson Fosdick (N.Y.: The Modern Library, 1952), 25-26.

30. Quoted in Bainton, *Here I Stand*, 61.

31. Quotations in Bainton, *Here I Stand*, 68, 73, 84, 88, 106, 115, 119, 120, 126, 125, 139.

32. Erich Fromm, *Escape from Freedom* (N.Y.: Avon, 1941), chap. 3.

33. Bainton, *Here I Stand*, 249.

34. Eric W. Gritsch, *Martin—God's Court Jester: Luther in Retrospect* (Phila.: Fortress Press, 1983), 67.

35. Geoffrey W. Bromiley, "Zwingli, Huldrych," *The New Encyclopaedia Britannica*, 15th ed., vol. 12, 946-947 (Chicago: Encyclopaedia Britannica, 1994), 946.

36. Quoted in A. J. Ayer, *Voltaire* (N.Y.: Random House, 1986), 102.

37. Durant, *The Reformation*, 412.

38. Quoted in Durant, *The Reformation*, 412.

39. Karen Armstrong, *A History of God: The 4000-Year Quest of Judaism, Christianity and Islam* (N.Y.: Alfred A. Knopf, 1994), 279.

40. Robert Blackley Drummond, "Erasmus: A Biographical Note," in *The Christian Reader: Inspirational and Devotional Classics*, ed. Stanley Irving Stuber (N.Y.: Association Press, 1952 [Drummond's note, 1873]), 197.

41. Bainton, *Here I Stand*, 190.

42. Harry Emerson Fosdick, ed., *Great Voices of the Reformation: An Anthology* (N.Y.: The Modern Library, 1984), 73-74.

43. Karl Marx, *Writings of the Young Marx on Philosophy and Society*, trans. and ed. Loyd D. Easton and Kurt H. Guddat (Garden City, N.Y.: Anchor Books, 1967), 128.

44. William M. Kephart and William W. Zellner, *Extraordinary Groups: An Examination of Unconventional Life-Styles*, 5th ed. (N.Y.: St. Martin's Press, 1994), 7.

45. Peter Weir, dir., *Witness*, Paramount Pictures, 1985.

46. Kephart and Zellner, *Extraordinary Groups*, 5.

47. According to Sherrin Marshall Wyntjes, "Women in the Reformation Era," in *Becoming Visible: Women in European History*, ed. Renate Bridenthal and Claudia Koonz, (Boston: Houghton Mifflin Co., 1977), 172.

48. "*The Schleitheim Confession of Faith*," in *Great Voices of the Reformation: An Anthology*, ed. Harry Emerson Fosdick (N.Y.: The Modern Library, 1952), 288.

49. Williston Walker, *A History of the Christian Church*, 3rd ed., rev. Robert T. Handy, Cyril C. Richardson, and Wilhelm Pauck (N.Y.: Charles Scribner's Sons, 1970), 327.

50. Walker, *A History*, 328; see also Vivian Green, *A New History of Christianity* (N.Y.: Continuum, 1996), 153.

51. Franklin Hamlin Littell, *The Origins of Sectarian Protestantism: A Study of the Anabaptist View of the Church*, (N.Y.: Macmillan, 1964), 44.

52. Green, *A New History*, 153.

53. "*Schleitheim Confession*," 289.

54. Littell, *Origins*, 24.

55. Quoted in Green, *A New History*, 154.

56. Green, *A New History*, 154.

57. "*Schleitheim Confession*," 289.

58. Green, *A New History*, 155.

59. Frederick Engels, "The Peasant War in Germany," in *Marx & Engels On Religion*, ed. Reinhold Niebuhr (N.Y.: Schocken Books, 1964 [1850]), 109-118.

60. Green, *A New History*, 155.

Chapter 4

His Eyes Will Be Dazzled
Foundations of Modern Critique II

When you think about it, the idea that human beings can criticize religion is pretty remarkable. The pretension and arrogance of it all scandalizes those who are unable to distinguish between their religion and the transcendent sacred reality to which that religion points. It is to act in the spirit of Prometheus. Prometheus was the Titan in Greek mythology who defied the gods by stealing fire from heaven and giving it to humanity which gave humanity the power to conquer and subdue the world.[1] Karl Marx celebrated the myth of Prometheus as the representative myth for the great historical program of critical philosophy.[2] In the preface to his doctoral thesis, Marx wrote that "Prometheus is the foremost saint and martyr in the philosopher's calendar."[3]

For Marx and others, the development of critical philosophy, as critique of society, would help humanity understand its own alienation and oppression, and spur it to change the world into a place of freedom and security for all. Indeed, critique, as it has come down to us through the history of Western philosophy, is a Promethean project. And the arrogance of it not withstanding, it is an essential practice for human liberation and maybe even for spiritual transcendence.

Origins of Critique

The idea of a modern critique of society is usually traced to classical Greek philosophy, especially the work of Plato (c. 428-347 BCE).[4] Plato's basic idea regarding society was that there are ideal forms for organizing the institutions of human life toward which we should strive. But in order to understand those ideal forms, we have to evaluate and criticize the way things are currently done, because our eyes are clouded by our experience. In other words, through the use of critical reason we can learn to recognize the cultural mystifications that restrict human potential, and begin, then, to shape visible reality toward the invisible ideal.[5]

Plato's cave in his work, *The Republic*, is a celebrated myth about the problem of "seeing" clearly.

> And now . . . let me show in a figure how far our nature is enlightened or unenlightened:—Behold! human beings living in an underground den, which has a mouth open towards the light and reaching all along the den; here they have been from their childhood, and have their legs and necks chained so that they cannot move, and can only see before them, being prevented by the chains from turning round their heads. Above and behind them a fire is blazing at a distance, and between the fire and the prisoners there is a raised way; and you will see, if you look, a low wall built along the way.[6]

Other men are walking "along the wall carrying all sorts of vessels, and statues and figures of animals made of wood and stone and various materials, which appear over the wall." Some of them are talking with one another; others are silent. All the prisoners can see are the shadows of themselves and the objects carried, cast by the fire on the opposite wall. For them, then, this is all there is to reality.[7]

This is like us. But what happens when one of them gets free of his chains, is able to see over the wall, and look at the light? He experiences pain and discomfort, but he sees his former life—the shadows and the others—for what they are. And if he is compelled to climb out of the den and see the sun and the world and all that is in it? "When he approaches the light his eyes will be dazzled," and again he is discomfited, but again he gains truer sight. He begins to reason about the way things really are, and he finds that he pities his former fellows. Even if there are special rewards for recognizing the passing shadows in that former state, he would never return.[8]

Plato wants this journey upwards out of the den to be interpreted as "the ascent of the soul into the intellectual world." It is a hard and difficult path, the path to enlightenment, and it requires great effort, but it is essential in order to understand what is true and good and beautiful. Whoever "would act rationally either in public or private life must have his eye fixed."[9]

It could be a life-long project to identify all the social critics who have used the myth of Plato's cave to characterize the process of enlightenment. Plato himself, of course, was walking in the footsteps of his teacher Socrates (c. 470-399 BCE) who was put to death by the authorities on charges of corrupting the young and whose life and teachings Plato creatively chronicled.[10] What Socrates, and Plato after him, did, however, was put into motion a way of approaching the structures and institutions of society. This was the way of criticism, and it implied, naturally enough, that social organization was malleable. It could be changed. Furthermore, it should be changed, so people could live the good life. The first step toward social change was mental change. Human consciousness would need to be raised to a new level, where the given, everyday reality could be perceived clearly for the deficient reality it is. Then new possibilities could be imagined. This called for social criticism.

The odd thing, historically, though, is that a strong tradition of social critique did not develop and, except for minor voices here and there, lay dormant largely until the Enlightenment. Paul Strathern, commenting on the history of philosophy, makes the strong argument that "for nearly two thousand years" after the "golden era" of Socrates, Plato, and Aristotle, "nothing happened." He adds a qualification, though, acknowledging the powerful work of Plotinus (205-270 CE), St. Augustine (354-430 CE), Averroës (1126-1198 CE), and Thomas Aquinas (1225-1274 CE): "At least, nothing original happened," he writes.[11]

Strathern may be overstating the case, but there has been the traditional view that the Middle Ages were not productive in creative philosophy, including social theory. (The early Medieval period was often formerly identified as the "Dark Ages.") Sociologist Harry Barnes writes: "There were few advances in social philosophy from the sixth to the ninth century."[12]

There are dissenting voices, of course, and it might depend, in part, on how closely you look. Frederick Copleston, who took a very close look, suggested the Medieval period has had a bad rap because powerful philosophers in the early modern period were so heavily critical of scholasticism (some of it warranted) and the Medieval domination of philosophy by theology that they did not bother to investigate for themselves. He wrote that "they condemned it unseen and unheard, without knowledge either of the rich variety of mediaeval thought or of its profundity."[13] It is also possible that Copleston—as a Jesuit—was more inclined to appreciate the efforts and spirit of scholasticism.

To be sure, though, toward the end of the Medieval period some strongly critical voices began to be heard. Harry Barnes calls to our attention that Pierre Dubois (1255-1321) proposed such reforms as to lead some modern scholars to hail him "as the chief social radical of the Middle Ages" and that Marsilius of Padua (1270-1342) "attacked the Catholic church with something of the spirit and modernity of the Deists and Voltaire."[14] Among other things, Dubois argued that the church in France should be independent of Rome, the papacy should have no temporal authority, there should be an international court, and women should have equal political rights.[15] Marsilius maintained that the state should be supreme over the church and clergy. He attacked the institution of the papacy and seemed to presume, in anticipation of the Reformation, that the Bible is the only rule for faith. Furthermore, Marsilius argued, government should be by the consent of the governed; all law should be decided by legislators with the practical interests of the people and community in mind; the prince should be subordinate to and the enforcer of law; and the prince should be elected rather than hereditary.[16]

These are striking efforts when we remember these men were writing in a time when radical social criticism was potentially a capital offense. Marsilius and a collaborator were denounced in a 1327 papal bull as "sons of perdition and fruits of malediction."[17] Obviously Dubois and Marsilius reflect the struggle between church and state so very characteristic of the Middle Ages, but they also manifest the developing sentiment of nationalism and concurrent ideas of popular sovereignty. Their tool was social criticism, and while they criticized the church, these were still criticisms from within and not criticisms of religion as such.

Michael Walzer argues that social criticism, "as a self-conscious activity, a chosen role, is a recent phenomenon." Walzer speculates that the Hebrew prophets, the Greek sophists, "the Roman satirists, the preaching friars of the Middle Ages, the humanists of the Renaissance"—all must have in some sense been self-consciously aware of their role as social critics. "It is true, however, that throughout the Middle Ages and into early modern times, criticism was concerned almost exclusively with the individual moral character and intellectual commitment: wicked actions and false doctrines."[18]

Walzer is correct, so far as I know, that the *self-conscious selection* of social criticism as one's project, if not vocation, in life awaited modern times. But we have already seen that some critics were concerned about more than wicked actions and false doctrines. Furthermore, in a society as culturally integrated as the West in the late Middle Ages, concern about "wicked actions and false doctrines" led inexorably to issues of church, state, and economy. When that relatively integrated culture opened up during the Renaissance to new forms of art and literature (ironically through a renewed study of the old—classical Greece and Rome), and when it came apart during the Reformation, a new era of religious criticism opened up. As we saw, it began as reforming and competitive criticism of religion from within. In the historical context of the sixteenth century, it quickly developed into fragmented forces of struggle for the minds and hearts of humanity and resulted in two centuries of religious unrest and warfare. Will Durant observed, correctly, "In a society where government, law, and morality are bound up with a religious creed, any attack upon that creed is viewed as menacing the foundations of social order itself."[19]

The modern worldview, then, developed concomitantly with social criticism and criticism of religion. It was furthered, largely inadvertently, by the Renaissance and Reformation.

Contributions of the Renaissance and the Reformation

The Reformation made its contribution to the modern worldview, largely indirectly, as did the Renaissance before it. Richard Tarnas points out that the Protestant Reformation "questioned, criticized, and often expelled altogether" many of "the accretions brought into Christianity by the Roman Church." Among other things, these included "the complex organizational structures, the priestly hierarchy and its spiritual authority . . . and finally the Mother Church herself." Indeed, it was argued, that only biblical authority was authoritative.[20]

What we might notice is that if only the Bible is authoritative, there is a distinctive shift to individual, subjective authority because, in fact, this means interpretive authority is relegated to the reader—every reader—of the Bible. It becomes almost impossible, then, to legitimate the authority of a church over its members. And these church members, in turn, have to assume responsibility for reading, thinking, and interpreting. This opens the door to "heresy," setting the stage for the enormous Western culture war between religion and philosophy, and religion and science. Incidentally, the stage is also set for those modern religious leaders who manipulate their followers into believing they have freely chosen to believe what the leaders have convinced them they must believe.

The Catholic Church was not crushed by the Reformation. A Catholic Counter-Reformation was initiated in which the worst abuses of the church were reformed, but in which orthodoxy was also reaffirmed vis-à-vis Protestantism. Both sides of Christianity, then, were anchored in competing orthodoxies that amounted to a "religious backlash against the Renaissance's pagan Hellenism, naturalism, and secularism."[21] From that point on, to take a natural scientific perspective seriously implied a place of operation outside Christianity. Criticism of Christianity as such or scientific discoveries inconsistent with the orthodox religious cosmology placed one in an implicitly heretical position and therefore outside the realm of legitimate discourse. Minds were liberated by the Reformation, but they were supposed to choose the correct belief—an impossible condition to maintain without an authoritarian coercion that became increasingly difficult to justify theologically or philosophically. The Renaissance awakened a humanistic spirit of open inquiry and reflection that would not go back to sleep. When the Enlightenment arrived, its greatest contributions would be in the realms of political, economic, and social thought, but it would of necessity be defined in large part in opposition to faith and religion.

On other levels, the Reformation contributed to secularization and opened paths to the Enlightenment. The Protestant emphasis on personal autonomy, while ambiguous in the reformers, especially Luther and Calvin,[22] "served as a continuation of the Renaissance impulse."[23] By undermining "the theological authority of the Catholic Church," Tarnas writes, "the Reformation opened the way in the West for religious pluralism, then religious skepticism, and finally a complete breakdown in the until then relatively homogeneous Christian world view."[24] While the Reformation resulted in a setback for the Renaissance spirit, it also undermined the uniformity and absolutism that could keep that spirit in check.

Also in complex ways the Reformation contributed to political and economic shifts. "The Reformation's new sense of personal religious self-responsibility and the priesthood of all believers also abetted the growth of political liberalism and individual rights."[25] The peculiar blend of Calvinist and Lutheran thought resulted in an affirmation of and emphasis on work in the world, thereby providing legitimation for rational economic activity.[26] Max Weber argued that Protestantism brought the asceticism of monasticism out of the monastery, injecting it into everyday life. And so the "waste of time" became "the first and in principle the deadliest of sins,"[27]—a useful ethic for the burgeoning bourgeoisie and their need for a disciplined work force.

Protestantism fragmented the sacred canopy of Medieval Christendom.[28] Instead of competing with the state for control, churches had to compete with each other in courting the favor of particular nation-states. Men like Luther, Calvin, and Zwingli "could hold their ground and make progress against the tremendous power of Rome, only as they carried along with them the consent and backing of their governments."[29] They also needed the state to repress the subversive left-wing elements of the Reformation. The same was true for the Catholic Church as it sought to limit Protestant gains and keeps its own adherents enfolded. This development coincided with and probably promoted the growing spirit of nationalism.[30]

The unraveling of the whole cloth of the Medieval worldview with its intricate coherent merger of Aristotelian and biblical cosmology opened the way for the scientific revolution. The reformers had strengthened the distinction between creator and the creation, human beings included in the latter. "By disenchanting the world of immanent divinity . . . the Reformation better allowed for its radical revision by modern science."[31] Only the scriptures and certain pronouncements by the church were outside the bounds of critical discourse. This would change as the biblical and theological cosmology cracked under the impact of the "Copernican revolution."

The Rise of Modern Science

Thomas Kuhn called the rise of modern science "the Copernican revolution."[32] We reviewed Epicurus' and Lucretius' view of the universe in chapter 2—a universe of unlimited space and atomic matter—basically the view of the Greek thinkers Leucippus and Democritus in the fifth century BCE. We should not forget that the dominant Western cosmology was quite different. From the fourth century BCE until the Copernican revolution in the 1600 and 1700s, the dominant view of the universe was the two-sphere model. It had the earth as "a tiny sphere suspended stationary at the geometric center of a much larger rotating sphere which carried the stars." Moving between the earth and the sphere of stars was the sun, and beyond that, there was nothing at all.[33] This view had been worked out in detail by Aristotle and handed on, with modifications, to the medieval world. The Roman astronomer and mathematician, Ptolemy (c. 100-170), had built his cosmology, with modifications, on this view.

This cosmology accorded well with most astronomical observations, navigational and survey purposes, and the biblical view. Ian Barbour writes: "Aristotelian cosmology and Christian theology were merged to form the *medieval picture of the universe*."[34] Then Nicolaus Copernicus (1473-1543), in his struggle to account for the anomalous movements of the planets, altered that model to include an earth that rotated on its axis and orbited around the sun. In his *On the Revolutions of the Heavenly Spheres*, published in 1543, Copernicus wrote:

> if we transfer the motion of the Sun to the Earth, taking the Sun to be at rest, then morning and evening risings and settings of Stars will be unaffected, while the stationary points, retrogressions, and progressions of the Planets are due not to their own motions, but to that of the Earth, which their appearances reflect. Finally we shall place the Sun himself at the center of the Universe. All this is suggested by the systematic procession of events and the harmony of the whole Universe, if only we face the facts, as they say, "with both eyes open."[35]

Everybody was not entirely interested in facing the facts with both eyes open, at least not these facts or from a natural scientific framework. The Copernican innovations set off a revolution in scientific matters that alarmed religious leaders and others. It called into question the religiously dominated, holistic view of the cosmos from an essentially secular (i.e., natural philosophical) frame of reference. Even before *On the Revolutions* was published, Martin Luther had some things to say about Copernicus, this "upstart astrologer who strove to show that the earth revolves, not the heavens or the firmament, the sun and the moon." Luther said, "This fool wishes to reverse the entire science of astronomy; but sacred Scripture tells us that Joshua commanded the sun to stand still, and not the earth."[36] John Calvin asked, "Who will venture to place the authority of Copernicus above that of the Holy Spirit?"[37] Copernicus, like Erasmus, fell victim to the hardening of positions in the wake of the Reformation. In 1616 *On the Revolutions* was placed on the Index of banned writings of the Catholic Church, where it remained until 1835.[38]

Nevertheless, the Copernican thesis slowly gained converts. Successful scientific work continued, dismantling the Aristotelian cosmos, which Copernicus had never entirely abandoned. Johannes Kepler (1571-1630) established the elliptical orbits of planets, suggested the conception of the solar system as a machine, and extended William Gilbert's (1544-1603) view of the earth as a magnet to the other celestial bodies. Galileo Galilei (1564-1642) built telescopes and began multiple observations that further buttressed Copernicanism. What's more, the telescope popularized astronomy in a way the ethereal cosmological and mathematical work of Galileo and his predecessors could not. Thomas Digges (c. 1546-1595) and Giordano Bruno (1548?-1600) developed and popularized the idea that the universe was infinite. And Bruno resurrected the idea that the universe is made up of atoms.[39] This presented scientists with the challenge of reconciling the conceptions of the heavens and the earth since the Aristotelian view suggested "that celestial and terrestrial objects and processes are utterly different in kind.[40] We recognize here the earlier insights of thinkers like Democritus, Leucippus, Epicurus, and Lucretius, who had been dismissed in an Aristotelian universe but whose works had been recovered by Renaissance humanists.

René Descartes (1596-1650) is remembered today more as a philosopher and a mathematician. Indeed, his development of a rationalist philosophy has led many thinkers to credit him with launching modern philosophy and, in contrast to Kuhn's emphasis on Copernicus, modern science. Denning Miller wrote that "modern science and civilization could well be dated from 1619, to mark the year in which a young French soldier [René Descartes] lay dreaming by the Danube."[41] Richard Tarnas wrote: "Descartes enthroned human reason as the supreme authority in matters of knowledge, capable of distinguishing certain metaphysical truth and of achieving certain scientific understanding of the material world."[42] Paul Strathern said: "By the end of the sixteenth century, philosophy had stopped. It was Descartes who started it up again.[43]

But Tarnas also wrote: "More than any other single factor, it was the Copernican insight that provoked and symbolized the drastic, fundamental break from the ancient and medieval universe to that of the modern era."[44] And others have argued that Descartes's creative attempts to develop a holistic, integrated cosmology, with key insights about motion and optics, though much of it mistaken, gave fruitful leads to others who surpassed him in fulfilling the Copernican promise.[45] Clearly both Copernicus and Descartes are given credit for much of the rise of modern science. Another key player was Isaac Newton.

Scientists were still faced with a discontinuity between the physics of the heavens and that of the earth. The necessary component for breaking down the conceptual terrestrial-celestial dichotomy and providing a powerful cosmological theory of the whole was gravity, the idea and development of which were hit upon by Robert Hooke (1635-1703) and Isaac Newton (1642-1727) about the same time. Newton's mathematical techniques were remarkable achievements that allowed the computation of "both the shape and the speed of celestial and terrestrial trajectories" with great precision. It would be another half century of research and argument before the revolution was complete. But after Newton "most scientists and educated laymen conceived the universe to be an infinite neutral space inhabited by an infinite number of corpuscles [atoms] whose motions were governed by a few passive laws like inertia and by a few active principles like gravity."[46] The Copernican revolution was complete.

Educated people no longer lived in an Aristotelian world ruled by God but in a Newtonian universe that looked a lot like an infinite mechanism governed by its own natural laws. The implications for the Western religious worldview were immense. "In the clockwork universe God frequently appeared to be only the clockmaker, the Being who had shaped the atomic parts, established the laws of their motion, set them to work, and then left them to run themselves."[47] The biblical view of the cosmos was discredited. Miracles became incredible. Deism (the view that God exists but does not intervene in the operation of nature) became, then, a view favored by important thinkers, especially in the seventeenth and eighteenth centuries. "By the end of the eighteenth century an increasing number of [people] saw no need to posit the existence of God" at all.[48] The Western world was ready for modern social critics who would view their project, in part, as the liberation of humanity from the constraints, superstitions, and alienation of religion.

Ideas and History

When reviewing, as we have, the ideas of thinkers and reformers, it is easy to give the distorted impression that history is a matter of changing ideas and the influence of those ideas. It is never so simple. Human history is not merely a history of ideas, and the history of ideas is not merely a history of thinkers. It is important to recognize that changing ideas develop in a cultural context of changing social, economic, and political factors. History is a matter of living, breathing, acting people exercising their wills—in pursuit of power and piety, security and stimulation, reform and reaction, influence and escape, wealth and freedom, war and peace, advantage and love, status and humility, work and recreation—in utterly complex conditions of social forces over which few individuals have any control.

The Renaissance and Reformation periods were characterized on the political-economic level by such things as a growing middle class of merchants and farmers who competed with the landed nobility for protection and advantage. The monarchs struggled for power with the nobility, the church, other monarchs, and on occasion with the peasants. The cultural efflorescence of the Renaissance owes a great deal to the wealth accrued from trade especially between the Italian city-states and the East, and to the rulers of the city-states who supported the arts in their endeavors to display the extravagance of wealth. The corruption of the papacy and the papal states as a result of participation in the prodigality of kingdom building and Renaissance culture gave fuel to critics and reformers. And so it goes.

The rise of modern science, too, was not independent of factors external to science itself. Herbert Butterfield points out that "the advent of the printed book on the one hand, and of the woodcut and the engraving on the other, had greatly transformed the problem of scientific communication from the time of the Renaissance." Furthermore, the solution to the problem of gravity required theoretical developments in mathematics. "Without the achievements of the mathematicians the scientific revolution, as we know it, would have been impossible." Advances in technology and the desire for new technology, usually for reasons other than scientific, were also essential factors for scientific advance.

> It has been argued that the growing number of mechanical objects in the world at large had induced also a sort of specialised interest or a modern attitude of mind—an interest in the sheer question of the way in which things worked, and a disposition to look upon nature with the same preoccupation. . . . And clocks worked by wheels were still a surprisingly new thing in the world when there appeared in the fourteenth century the suggestion that the heavenly bodies might be like a piece of clockwork. The early propaganda on behalf of the scientific movement laid remarkable stress on the utilitarian results that were expected from it; and this was one of the grounds on which the scientists or the scientific societies called for the patronage of kings.

The telescope and microscope could be regarded as by-products "of the glass- and metal-polishing industries in Holland." And it is only after the discovery of the air-pump that we got "the use of the blow-pipe in chemical analysis."[49]

Jonathan Miller argued that the prevalence of the smelter's furnace provided Galen with his theoretical model for the heart, and that William Harvey's ability to see the heart as a pump depended on the widespread use of mechanical pumps.

> By the end of the sixteenth century mechanical pumps were a significant part of the developing technology of Western Europe. Coal and metal mines were being deepened to supply the needs of growing cities. Engineers were bedeviled by the problems of seepage, and forceful pumps were the only way of keeping the shafts empty. Contemporary handbooks of metallurgy included pages of pumping mechanisms.

Miller points out that historians are not entirely agreed on the influence of the fire-pump on Harvey's revolutionary insight into the heart as a pump, "but it seems unlikely that Harvey would have departed so radically from the traditional theory if the technological images of propulsion had not encouraged him to think along such lines."[50]

Wars are of enormous influence on the outcome of ideas. We can hardly imagine what our world would look like today, had key battles and wars gone other than they did. What would Judaism and Christianity be like if the rebellion in Palestine had succeeded in throwing off Roman rule in 70 CE? What would

American Christianity look like had the South been successful in its secession? Imagine how different the Mideast might be, in its Arab-Israeli conflicts without the Holocaust. Will Durant, in his review of the invasions of the Moslems into Christian Europe in the 800s and 900s, notes that the invasion of Italy was defeated in 916 by "the combined forces of the pope, the Greek and German emperors, and the cities of southern and central Italy." He points out that had Rome fallen, "Constantinople would have been wedged in between two concentrations of Moslem power." And he writes: "On such chances of battle hung the theology of billions of men."[51]

The interactive dynamic between what people think and what they experience and do is usually obvious with even a casually close look at their biographies. The caution and gentility of Erasmus's writings could be seen as influenced as much by fear of religious and political repression as by his own pacific personality. Furthermore, his work depended on powerful patrons, among whom were Henry VIII of England, Pope Leo X, Charles V of Spain, François I of France, and Ferdinand of Austria![52] Luther's ideas were necessary for the institutional changes associated with the Reformation, but Luther's ability to live and work depended on powerful German princes to resist the Holy Roman Emperor and the pope. Anabaptist leadership may have come from disaffected intellectuals, but its following came from a disenfranchised and disempowered peasantry.

Near 1737, the Puritan pastor Jonathan Edwards, writing from his small town of Northampton, in the American colony of Massachusetts, said that the people of that rural area were "as sober, orderly, and good sort of people, as in any part of New England," and largely free of corruption, vice, error, "and a variety of sects and opinions." He showed sociological insight in his explanation: "Our being so far *within* the land, at a distance from sea-ports, and in a corner of the country, has doubtless been *one reason* why we have not been so much corrupted with *vice*, as most other parts."[53] The sea-port nearest his town was Boston—where one could find all the alien enterprises and philosophies and divisions against which the Puritan preachers of the hinterlands were preaching. But 1700s Boston, as an outpost of the emerging modern world, was to carry the day, and those small New England towns were to lose their pristine culture and succumb to a new world of variety and multiplicity.

Jonathan Edwards lost his battle to keep even Northampton strict and Calvinist. He even lost his job. In 1750 he was fired by his congregation, in part, for insisting on "moral" requirements for church membership. His biographers are agreed that an additional factor in his firing was his vehement preaching against the excesses of the commercial interests; in other words, the practices of early American capitalists.[54] The sociologist C. Wright Mills put it well when he wrote: "Neither the life of an individual nor the history of a society can be understood without understanding both."[55]

While it is not my intention to provide a sociology of the critics and their ideas or a historical explanation of them, I do think it is important to acknowl-

edge the historical and cultural contexts in which they thought. In Plato's philosophical project, climbing out of the cave suggested the possibility of finding
eternal truth apart from historical context. This is a doubtful possibility. It is
clear that through cultural cross-fertilization we achieve some transcendence of
our own culture in our thinking. Through historical study we transcend to some
extent our own time. And certainly people have creative and imaginative ideas
before their time. But the creativity and the imagination as well as the conceptu-
alization and the formulation of ideas always manifest the influence of their time
and place in history and culture.

It is for this reason that Karl Marx (to the surprise of students new to Marxian studies) spent considerable ink criticizing utopian socialists and communists.
He noted that these movements subvert themselves by trying to think a history
before the history can embody the ideas.[56] A relatively recent example of sociological naiveté is brought to our attention by John Peters. He points out that
"Carl Sagan and others designed a message to be sent to outer space with *Voy-
ager* in the 1970s that was supposed to be stripped of any extraneous cultural
coding." Now, more than twenty-five years later, we realize that that supposedly
culturally and historically transcendent image showed a couple with 1970s hair-
dos, the man doing the speaking, and the woman posed "half demure, half
sexy." And they "are clearly white, though whites are not the majority race of
the planet"! Peters writes: "Even in its attempts to transcend itself, a historical
moment only reveals its blindness to its own face."[57]

Modern Critics of Religion

From the end of the seventeenth century until the middle of the twentieth, major
thinkers in the West constructed more-or-less systematic critiques of religion.
These critiques were largely of religion as such; although they were typically
directed at Western religions, especially Christianity.

Some of these critiques dismantled the classical arguments for the existence
of God developed by earlier brainy people like Aristotle, Saint Anselm, and St.
Thomas Aquinas. The Scottish philosopher, David Hume (1711-1776), and the
German philosopher, Immanuel Kant (1724-1804), in the eighteenth century,
and the Danish—and Christian!—philosopher, Søren Kierkegaard (1813-1855),
in the nineteenth century—all carefully examined the traditional proofs of God
and demonstrated that they did not succeed. To oversimplify the findings of
these complex critiques: what they basically showed was that all the arguments
for God's existence depended on the assumption that God exists. So they were
not proofs at all. Although occasionally believers will try to resurrect the old
arguments for God's existence by giving them new twists,[58] it is commonly accepted today, by both believers and nonbelievers, that the existence of God is
beyond rational or empirical proofs. "For if God does not exist," wrote Kierke-

gaard, "it would of course be impossible to prove it; and if he does exist it would be folly to attempt it."[59]

My concern in this work is not with those metaphysical critiques, which debunk the so-called proofs of God's existence.[60] Rather, it is with what E. D. Klemke calls "cultural critiques" of religion.[61] These are in many ways the more troubling for spiritual seekers because they focus on historical, sociological, psychological, and political problems of faith and religion, so they are challenging even for those who have a deep sense of the reality of the divine.

In the next six chapters I review six modern thinkers' cultural critiques of religion. To be sure, there are others, but these six are especially important for their lasting influence, and they were critics, for all practical purposes, *from outside* whose criticisms are of religion *as such*. Five of them are well known to scholars and the educated public. Those five are: Voltaire, French author and philosopher, typically seen as the preeminent thinker of the Enlightenment; Karl Marx, German social theorist, commonly viewed as the founding father of communism and most branches of socialism; Friedrich Nietzsche, German philosopher, viewed as initiating what has come to be postmodern thought; Sigmund Freud, Austrian physician, primary founder of psychoanalysis and central point of reference in psychiatry and psychology (in opposition as well as agreement); and Bertrand Russell, English philosopher and mathematician, whose influence on mathematics, science, philosophy, and political thought has been wide-ranging.

The sixth critic is not so well known outside the scholarly world. He is Emile Durkheim, French social scientist, one of the important founding parents of modern sociology. A caveat is in order for Durkheim. Of the six, he is the one unequivocal in his belief that religion was important for society as a source of social cohesion and worried about its eventual demise even though he was a nonbeliever himself. Unlike the other five, he did not see liberation from the "fetters" and "illusions" of religion as a great gain for humanity. So he is not properly a "critic" in the same sense as the other five. However, he did a great deal of study and analysis of religion, providing a sociological explanation for it and, in the process, denying any objective, transcendental reality to the Divine. He also took the side of the secularists who fought the Catholic Church over who would control public education in France. All this is certainly *implicitly* critical from any believer's standpoint.

Nietzsche, too, was different from the other five in one very important respect. While he was interested in furthering human liberation—a major concern of modern, Enlightenment thought—he did not seem to think this could be accomplished by an extension of human reason—as did Enlightenment thought. In fact, besides criticizing religion, he attacked science and reason, among other things (such as nationalism and anti-Semitism!), as manifestations of the nonrational will to power and domination. For this reason, he has been characterized by some as an "irrationalist" and a "nihilist."

Of the six, three had a Christian background (Voltaire, Nietzsche, Russell); two had a Jewish background (Durkheim, Freud); and one was mixed in that his parents had converted from Judaism to Christianity around the time of his birth (Marx). They were different from one another in many other ways as well, but they had several things in common. They were all furthering the Enlightenment project of demystifying the world through critical analysis. Each of them produced a critical analysis of religion. And they all had a passion for informing and expanding the minds of human beings, apparently in the belief that a better-thinking humanity would be a better-off humanity.

Notes

1. Bulfinch, *Mythology*, 12-13; also Aeschylus. *Prometheus Bound*, trans. G. M. Cookson, vol. 5, *Aeschylus, Sophocles, Euripides, Aristophanes*, Great Books of the Western World, ed. Robert Maynard Hutchins et al. (Chicago: Encyclopaedia Britannica; William Benton Publisher, 1952 [c. 458 BCE]).

2. Marx, *Writings of the Young Marx*, 52.

3. Karl Marx, *Karl Marx: Selected Writings*, ed. David McLellan (Oxford: Oxford University Press, 1977), 13.

4. Trent Schroyer, *The Critique of Domination: The Origins and Development of Critical Theory* (Boston: Beacon Press, 1973), 15.

5. Schroyer, *Critique*, 15.

6. Plato, *The Republic*, trans. Benjamin Jowett, vol. 7, *The Dialogues of Plato*, Great Books of the Western World, ed. Robert Maynard Hutchins et al. (Chicago: Encyclopaedia Britannica; William Benton Publisher, 1952), 388-389.

7. Plato, *The Republic*, 388.

8. Plato, *The Republic*, 388-389.

9. Plato, *The Republic*, 389.

10. See Plato, *Apology; Crito; Phaedo*, trans. Benjamin Jowett, vol. 7, *The Dialogues of Plato*, Great Books of the Western World, ed. Robert Maynard Hutchins et al. (Chicago: Encyclopaedia Britannica; William Benton Publisher, 1952).

11. Paul Strathern, *Descartes in 90 Minutes* (Chicago: Ivan R. Dee, 1996), 7.

12. Harry Elmer Barnes, "Chapter I: Ancient and Medieval Social Philosophy," in *An Introduction to the History of Sociology*, ed. Harry Elmer Barnes, 3-28, (Chicago & London: University of Chicago Press, 1948), 17.

13. Frederick Copleston, *A History of Philosophy*, vol. 2, *Mediaeval Philosophy*, part 1 (Garden City, N.Y.: Doubleday & Co.; Image Books, 1950), 14-15, 15.

14. Barnes, "Chapter I," 21.

15. Will Durant, *The Story of Civilization: The Age of Faith—A History of Medieval Civilization—Christian, Islamic, and Judaic—from Constantine to Dante: A.D. 325-1300* (N.Y.: Simon and Schuster, 1950), 697.

16. Frederick Copleston, *A History of Philosophy*, vol. 3, *Late Mediaeval and Renaissance Philosophy*, part 1 (Garden City, N.Y.: Doubleday & Co.; Image Books, 1953), chap. 1, passim.

17. Copleston, *History*, v. 3, 182-183.

18. Walzer, *Company*, 4, 5.

19. Durant, *Age of Faith*, 251.

20. Richard Tarnas, *The Passion of the Western Mind: Understanding the Ideas That Have Shaped Our World View* (N.Y.: Ballantine Books, 1991), 236.

21. Tarnas, *Passion*, 238.

22. On Luther's and Calvin's ambivalence, see Fromm, *Escape*, chapter 3.

23. Tarnas, *Passion*, 239.

24. Tarnas, *Passion*, 240.

25. Tarnas, *Passion*, 244; see also Steven Lukes, *Individualism* (N.Y.: Harper & Row, 1973).

26. Max Weber, *The Protestant Ethic and the Spirit of Capitalism*, trans. Talcott Parsons (N.Y.: Charles Scribner's Sons, 1958 [1904-05]); see also Kurt Samuelson, *Religion and Economic Action: A Critique of Max Weber*, trans. E. Geoffrey French, ed. D. C. Coleman (N.Y. and Evanston: Harper & Row, 1961).

27. Weber, *Protestant Ethic*, 157.

28. This phrase is from Peter L. Berger, *The Sacred Canopy: Elements of a Sociological Theory of Religion* (Garden City, N.Y.: Doubleday & Co., 1967).

29. Fosdick, *Great Voices*, 283.

30. See Ernest Gellner, *Nations and Nationalism* (Oxford, England: Basil Blackwell, 1983), 40-41, 78, 142.

31. Tarnas, *Passion*, 241.

32. Thomas S. Kuhn, *The Copernican Revolution: Planetary Astronomy in the Development of Western Thought* (Cambridge, Mass., & London, England: Harvard University Press, 1957).

33. Kuhn, *Copernican Revolution*, 27.

34. Ian G. Barbour, *Religion and Science: Historical and Contemporary Issues* (San Francisco: HarperSanFrancisco; HarperCollins, 1997), 5.

35. Quoted in Kuhn, *Copernican Revolution*, 154.

36. Quoted in Kuhn, *Copernican Revolution*, 191.

37. Quoted in Kuhn, *Copernican Revolution*, 192.

38. Kuhn, *Copernican Revolution*, 192; Ernest Nagel, "The Enlightenment: The Scientific Revolution," in *The Columbia History of the World*, ed. John A. Garraty and Peter Gay (N.Y.: Harper & Row, 1972), 686.

39. Kuhn, *Copernican Revolution*, 212, 219-225, 233-237, 245-246.

40. Nagel, "The Enlightenment," 686.

41. Denning Miller, *Popular Mathematics: The Understanding and Enjoyment of Mathematics* (N.Y.: Coward-McCann, 1942), 215.

42. Tarnas, *Passion*, 279.

43. Strathern, *Descartes*, 7.

44. Tarnas, *Passion*, 248.

45. Nagel, "The Enlightenment," 689; Kuhn, *Copernican Revolution*, 238-242.

46. Kuhn, *Copernican Revolution*, 248-254, 256, 257, 260.

47. Kuhn, *Copernican Revolution*, 263.

48. Kuhn, *Copernican Revolution*, 263.

49. H. Butterfield, *The Origins of Modern Science 1300-1800* (London: Bell & Hyman, 1957), 73, 89, 92-94.

50. Jonathan Miller, *The Body In Question* (N.Y.: Random House, 1978), 186-187, 208, 210.

51. Durant, *Age of Faith*, 290.

52. Levi, introduction, 1.

53. Jonathan Edwards, *A Faithful Narrative of the Surprising Work of God*, in *The Works of Jonathan Edwards*, vol. I, 1974 ed. (Edinburgh, Scotland: The Banner of Truth Trust, 1834 [1737]), 346.

54. Perry Miller, *Jonathan Edwards* (n.p.: William Sloane Associates, 1949), 218-219, 324-325; Patricia J. Tracy, *Jonathan Edwards, Pastor: Religion and Society in Eighteenth-Century Northampton* (N.Y.: Hill and Wang, 1980), 130.

55. C. Wright Mills, *The Sociological Imagination* (N.Y.: Oxford University Press, 1959), 3.

56. Karl Marx and Friedrich Engels, *The Communist Manifesto*, in the Norton Critical Edition with annotations, sources, and background, ed. Frederic L. Bender (N.Y. & London: W. W. Norton, 1988 [1848]), 32-35.

57. John Durham Peters, *Speaking into the Air: A History of the Idea of Communication* (Chicago and London: University of Chicago Press, 1999), 255.

58. See, for example, Patrick Glynn, *God, The Evidence: The Reconciliation of Faith and Reason in a Postsecular World* (Rocklin, Calif.: Forum, 1999); also "The Existence of God: A Debate Between Bertrand Russell and Father F. C. Copleston, SJ," in *Why I Am Not a Christian: And Other Essays on Religion and Related Subjects*, by Russell, ed. Paul Edwards, 133-153 (London: Unwin Paperbacks, 1975 [1948]).

59. Søren Kierkegaard, "Against Proofs of God," in *To Believe or Not To Believe: Readings in the Philosophy of Religion*, ed. E. D. Klemke (Fort Worth, Tex.: Harcourt Brace Jovanovich, 1992), 127.

60. Generally, the "proofs" are those arguments offered by St. Anselm (1033-1109), St. Thomas Aquinas (1225-1274), and René Descartes (1596-1650); the best known and fairly damning critiques of the proofs were by David Hume (1711-1776) and Immanuel Kant (1724-1804). The proofs and the critiques are parts of larger works, but they have been frequently excerpted and anthologized. One such anthology is E. D. Klemke, ed., *To Believe or Not To Believe: Readings in the Philosophy of Religion* (Fort Worth, Tex.: Harcourt Brace Jovanovich, 1992)

61. Klemke, ed., *To Believe or Not To Believe*, 144.

Chapter 5

Metaphysico-Theologo-Cosmonigology
Modern Critics of Religion: Voltaire
(1694-1778)

Those who feel they live in a rocky love-hate relationship with religion will find a kindred spirit in Voltaire. Those who appreciate their freedom to ongoingly explore that love-hate relationship should thank him. Will and Ariel Durant wrote, "When we cease to honor Voltaire we shall be unworthy of freedom."[1] No other individual, before his time, offered publicly so much observation, thought, and feeling in exposing the shortcomings of religion and religious thought. In addition, he exposed the limits of reason to resolve all ultimate questions of belief (even though he believed in the power of reason to resolve human problems). And he worked in a time and place where the risks of saying these things were considerable.

Some Historical Context

The period of the Enlightenment in Western history is seen by some as encompassing the eighteenth century, by others as more strictly limited to the latter half of that century.[2] The German philosopher Immanuel Kant wrote a key essay in 1784, titled, "What is Enlightenment?" In it he says the motto of enlightenment is "Have courage to use your own reason." He suggests it is extremely difficult for an individual to overcome mental subservience to outside authority, but that a society of freedom would make it possible for a public to enlighten itself. He adds that while we do not yet really live in an age of enlightenment, "we have clear indications that the field has now been opened wherein" people can rationally examine matters of religion "free from outside direction."[3]

61

The Enlightenment was a time of challenging traditional authority and promoting reason. "This century begins to see the triumph of reason," wrote Voltaire in a letter of 1760.[4] The Renaissance, the Reformation, and the rise of modern science contributed much to prepare the culture for the Enlightenment. A variety of forces—the breakdown of the feudalistic organization of society, the advance of nationalism, the developments of industrialization and urbanization, and the rise of capitalism and the capitalist classes (the *bourgeoisie*)—cracked open the cultural hegemony of nobility and church. Through that crack poured forth ideas challenging tradition and established authority in all social institutions. Enlightenment thinkers promoted the argument that human beings could, through the wise use of reason joined with passion, create and recreate their societies.

This suggested, of course, the disenchantment of the world, in the sense that the structure of society was not God-ordained; rather it was a natural historical reality open to change and thus to progress as led by people of critical reason. This called for social criticism of all institutions. The Enlightenment thinkers and those who followed them offered up critiques of political, economic, and social structures along with the ideologies that justified those structures. One very important plank in their project, in many ways the first plank, was the criticism of religion.

The Enlightenment began in England,[5] but by the middle of the eighteenth century, Paris had become "the intellectual capital of Europe," rendering France the center of the Enlightenment.[6] The French philosophers (known as the *philosophes*) were persons of letters and proponents of reason, committed to writing and publishing for an educated public.

In hindsight we can see they were preparing the way for the French Revolution. Toward the end of the century the *philosophes* expected and some agitated for a revolution. Their passions for enlightening reason and greater justice "reflected the visible increases in knowledge and technique, in wealth, welfare, and civilization" which they could observe all around them.[7] Yet that very progress highlighted the contrast to the France of the eighteenth century, still headed by a hereditary monarch over a declining nobility and supported by the "traditional organizations and orthodoxy of churches."[8] France, during the reigns of Louis XIV and Louis XV, according to Theodore Besterman,

> was the most powerful and, superficially, the wealthiest country in the world. But this power and this wealth had been mined by megalomaniac kings and a corruptly incompetent nobility and governing class. Such as it was it was based on a population of peasants who lived in misery and ignorance. Even when their poverty was intermittently relieved by temporary rises in the price of farm produce, they were still wretched, for they were broken by numerous and complex taxes and obligations.[9]

Such was the social context in which these early modern thinkers had to fight their culture wars. In many ways the most significant front in their battles was religion.

The *philosophes* came to be known as anti-Christian because they were quite critical of religion but especially of the Catholic Christianity as practiced in France. For this reason, Will and Ariel Durant argue that the debate was not so much between philosophy and religion as between the *philosophes* and French Catholic Christianity.[10] In a sense, that is correct, but the *philosophes* were wide-ranging thinkers who directed their attention at everything they knew anything about and at some things about which they knew very little. They were bold thinkers and writers. Given their time and place in history, they knew quite a bit about the religion practiced in Europe before and since the Reformation; they knew imperfectly other religions as reported by the many travelers to other continents in that age of exploration. Some of the *philosophes*, it is true, were born-again atheists opposed to any religion at all. But what all the *philosophes*, believer and unbeliever alike, bitterly criticized was narrow, intolerant, superstitious, and coercive religion. This is the religion that "prompted the tortures of the Inquisition," that "enforced its doctrines by the sword," that blessed tyranny and oppression, that "ground down the face of the poor," and that "was the natural enemy of all learning and advancement."[11] This kind of religion, of course, was not limited to French Catholic Christianity in the eighteenth century, and Voltaire's satirical short story, "History of Scarmentado's Travels," takes aim at intolerance, hatred, and irrationality not only in Christianity but also in Islam, Judaism, and Hinduism.[12]

The domination of French culture by the Catholic Church's hierarchy was resented by significant minorities of every class in France except the peasantry. The Church had exercised, through the state, a censorious repression of free thinking and competing ideas. Many of the clergy themselves were serious doubters, some even atheists. At his death in 1733 Jean Meslier, a poor parish priest who had served his people faithfully, left a manuscript of harsh criticism of religion and the terrors done in its name. Published by the *philosophes*, it called for rejection of faith and religion, the promotion of reason and scientific education, and the abolition of private property.[13]

So the latter half of the eighteenth century was the time of direct and indirect but certainly blatant attacks on religion. There were many who exercised their quills on this project, especially among the French. Among the more notable were Didier Diderot (1713-1784), Guillaume Raynal (1713-1796), Claude Adrien Helvétius (1715-1771), Jean Le Rond d'Alembert (1717-1783), Baron Paul Henri Dietrich d'Holbach (1723-1789). The most prominent, whose influence proved most long-lasting, was Voltaire.

Some Biography

Voltaire was a poet, a playwright, an essayist, a historian, a novelist, and a phe-nomenally prolific correspondent. He set out early in life to be a man of letters, and he succeeded in a way few ever have. He lived to write. His was an ency-clopedic mind, and he worked ceaselessly until his death shortly before his eighty-fourth birthday. He was funny, serious, satirical, quick to anger and quick to forgive. "Though there were no limits to his toleration of a man's beliefs and morals, he found it difficult to forgive bad manners"—especially when mani-fested in personal attacks.[14] He was charming, sometimes ingratiating, some-times mean. He was kind and generous, "the first great practical philanthropist of his century."[15] He was a successful financier, able to make himself wealthy and therefore not dependent on his writing to live. In his *Mémoires* he wrote: "I saw so many poor and despised men of letters that I decided long ago not to add to their number."[16] He sought fame and found it. He also found dangerous noto-riety. He satirized the powerful in his plays and poems, criticized religion with the erudition and thoroughness of a Jesuit, and promoted tolerance and the rule of reason in a society hanging onto the divine right of kings and the cultural he-gemony of Catholic Christianity. For such indelicacies, he was imprisoned twice, banned from Paris more than once, and sometimes on the run ahead of warrants for his arrest.

Voltaire was born in Paris as François Marie Arouet to a father who was a successful attorney and a mother of minor nobility. Voltaire believed he was illegitimate, but the evidence is inconclusive. His mother died when he was seven. He was educated by Jesuits at a school that trained men "to take their place in the world as leaders," then tutored by a skeptical abbé. At his father's insistence, he studied law for several years but went on to do his own thing in spite of his father's opposition.[17]

The young Voltaire began writing poems and plays. In addition, he seems to have been an irresistibly charming companion, full of himself always, but tender hearted, entertaining, and witty. Will and Ariel Durant write that "he pranced from one host or hostess to another, welcomed even in lordly circles for his sparkling verse and ready wit, imbibing and effusing heresy, and playing the gallant."[18] He became well known at a young age and lived a long time.

His poems and plays were of variable quality and met with variable success. He was never good, though, at recognizing the line beyond which he could not cross without giving serious offence. He was imprisoned in the Bastille for one poem in 1717. (Besterman believes, in this case, he was not really the author and thus falsely accused.)[19] It was about this time that he took the name Arouet de Voltaire.

He was imprisoned again in 1726 because he planned to kill a nobleman who had had him beaten after the two exchanged insults regarding Voltaire's lack of noble pedigree. He obtained release by promising to go to England.

Voltaire loved England. He spent a couple of years there before he was allowed to return to France. He learned English very rapidly and met almost every noteworthy in science, the arts, and public affairs. He found the country refreshingly free for thinkers to express themselves without fear of the state, and he was pleased with the weakness of religion, which had split into many different sects, officially tolerated. He wrote a laudatory book about many aspects of England. Among other things about religion, he says: "If there were only one religion in England, there would be danger of tyranny; if there were two, they would cut each other's throats; but there are thirty, and they live happily together in peace."[20] However, the book was "no dispassionate description of English realities; he was using England as a whip to stir up revolt in France against oppression by state or Church."[21] When it was published surreptitiously in France, he had to flee a warrant for his arrest.

Around 1730 he began an affair with a married woman, Émilie, the Marquise du Châtelet, that lasted until her death in 1749. For all practical purposes, they were inseparable. Her husband, a military officer, was remarkably tolerant of this relationship, even with Voltaire living at their château at Cirey in Champagne. This was probably the most significant companionship Voltaire experienced in his life. Émilie herself was a worthy companion, an intellectual in her own right. Voltaire had great respect for her. In his *Mémoires* Voltaire writes: "Seldom has so fine a mind and so much taste been united with so much ardour for learning; but she also loved the world and all the amusements of her age and sex."[22]

Her death occurred in childbirth, which was the result of an affair with another man. Biographers have suggested this affair was, in part, the consequence of Voltaire's losing much of his passion for Émilie, which was itself, in part, the result of Voltaire's new found passion for his widowed niece. In any case, Voltaire was greatly sorrowful at Émilie's death, at first blaming her lover, and then, in typically Voltairean fashion, forgiving him. When she died, he wrote: "I have not lost a mistress, I have lost half of myself, a soul for whom mine was made."[23]

The last twenty years of his life were spent at an estate he bought and developed at Ferney, several miles outside Switzerland. Ferney was a beautiful location, far enough from Paris and close enough to the Swiss border that he could get out of the country faster than a warrant for arrest could be served.

This was not a retirement; he never retired. He continued to work hard, not only at his craft of writing, but also against injustice and intolerance, as well as on the gardens and buildings of his estate. He entertained lavishly and had a great many visitors since he had become quite famous throughout Europe.

Always painfully conscious of the finitude of time, he tried to protect it as much as possible. He once wrote: "It is frightful the time we spend in talk. We ought not to lose a minute. The greatest expenditure we can make is of time."[24] And, since most guests were self-invited, he had trouble with guests who overstayed. Apparently, to get free of such guests, sometimes he would go to bed

feigning illness, even terminal. The story is told that when one such guest returned the next day, Voltaire said, "Tell him I am dying again. And if he comes
any more, say I am dead and buried."[25]

Voltaire was generous and kind to his employees—gardeners, servants, and
their families. He was also philanthropic in his dealings with the community. It
is interesting to note that this famous critic of religion rebuilt the rundown parish
church at Ferney. He "adorned it with the proud inscription in letters of gold
Deo erexit Voltaire ('Built for God by Voltaire')."[26]

He died during a triumphal return to Paris in 1778.

Voltaire on Religion

Theodore Besterman writes that Voltaire's idea of reason was "the search for the
true and the good."[27] It was also a critical reason, informed by the spirit of science. So it was a matter of examining the evidence of one's senses and thinking
through whatever topic was under consideration. We could say that for him, like
the umpire or the referee, it was a matter of calling it as you see it. Voltaire
writes: "Reason consists of always seeing things as they are."[28] It was a practice
of looking at life with your eyes open, not neglecting any evidence and trusting
the structures of logical thought. He had great hope in the power of reason:
"Reason is gentle, humane, tolerant; she smothers discord, strengthens goodness, and renders obedience to the law so attractive that coercion is no longer
necessary to uphold it."[29] Reason was also inspired by a passion for the welfare
of humanity. Voltaire believed that humanity could get along well with one another if only people would be rational.[30] He writes: "It is obvious to the whole
world that a service is better than an injury, that gentleness is preferable to anger." This insight and its application depends on the use of "our reason to dis-
cern the shades of goodness and badness."[31]

For us moderns, to understand reason in this sense, really to understand the
use of reason in the Enlightenment and until the twentieth century, we need to
remember that it was not yet seen as separate from the concern for a better
world. The reduction of reason to the dispassionate, "value-free" zone of logic
and critical thinking had not occurred, and science had not yet prided itself on
being value-free. Reason and science had not yet divorced, on grounds of in-
compatibility, the concern for human emancipation.

Voltaire was inspired by an acute sense of empathy for human suffering and
especially the need for freedom and justice. "Voltaire's master idea, one can
almost speak of an obsession, was the idea of justice, for to him that which is
just is that which is true and good."[32] For this reason, Voltaire was notably im-
patient with the notion that this is the best of all possible worlds and any theological legitimation of that sentiment. He greatly admired the poetry of Alexander Pope but argued with Pope's suggestion in Pope's "Essay on Man" that
"whatever is, is right."[33] We get the concept *Panglossian* from a character in

Candide, one of Voltaire's works still widely read today. Pangloss was a professor of "metaphysico-theologo-cosmonigology." Throughout the novel, in spite of all kinds of calamities, Pangloss displays a naïve optimism, insisting that everything is at it should be. "'It is demonstrated,' he said, 'that things cannot be otherwise: for, since everything was made for a purpose, everything is necessarily for the best purpose.'"[34] *Candide* was published in 1759.

In 1755, on a Sunday morning, with the churches crowded for All Saints' Day, Lisbon, Portugal, had been hit by an earthquake of two shocks, forty minutes apart, that destroyed nine thousand buildings, and killed, ultimately 30,000 people.[35] Voltaire could not reconcile this calamity with the idea of a just God or that this is the best of all possible worlds. He wrote the "*Poéme sur la désastre de Lisbonne*" (poem on the disaster of Lisbon). It is a despairing poem that laments the evil in the world that plagues humanity. It begins:

> Oh wretched man, earth-fated to be cursed;
> Abyss of plagues, and miseries the worst!
> Horrors on horrors, griefs on griefs must show,
> That man's the victim of unceasing woe,
> And lamentations which inspire my strain,
> Prove that philosophy is false and vain.[36]

He went through two different endings because his friends found its despair so problematic.[37] He concluded with the idea that humankind's only real joy is hope.[38] In the preface to the poem, Voltaire wrote that the author of the "The Lisbon Earthquake" is not writing "against the illustrious Pope" but rather "against the abuse of the new maxim, 'whatever is, is right.'" This author "maintains that ancient sad truth acknowledged by all men, that there is evil upon earth; he acknowledges that the words 'whatever is, is right,' if understood in a positive sense, and without any hopes of a happy future state, only insult us in our present misery."[39]

Voltaire carried his concern for reason and justice in a culture saturated with religion but being challenged by secularizing tendencies. He read and wrote a great deal about religion. He applied an informed, critical, and historical mind to the sacred texts and traditional doctrines of religion, what later came to be called higher criticism or the historical-critical method. He was *demythologizing* biblical texts two hundred years before Rudolf Bultmann gave liberal Christianity that concept.[40] These efforts can be seen as his attack on what he, and others, considered the superstitions, absurdities, stupidity, and intolerance of religion.

Voltaire pilloried the conflicts between competing religious parties with savage satire, but he was enraged at any injustice of repression or persecution for religious reasons. He was set off especially by an edict in 1759 making it a crime punishable by death to attack the Church. Voltaire resolved to make the attack a war, calling on all the *philosophes* and any others who would take up his cry, "*Écrasez L'Infâme!*" (Crush the infamy!) which he used repeatedly and which became associated with him.[41] In 1763 he produced an outline of the history of Christian persecution and brutality in his *Treatise on Tolerance.*[42]

Another one of the works of Voltaire still read today is the *Philosophical Dictionary*. It is a collection of short essays, many of them on religious themes. The Durants called the book essentially "an arsenal of arguments against Christianity as Voltaire knew it."[43] Within this little book are represented most of Voltaire's arguments regarding religion.

Among other things, Voltaire was strongly critical of religion's tendency to argue, debate, pronounce, and persecute on questions of ultimate realities—realities that could not be settled by rational argument **or** empirical evidence. In his essay on the soul, he points out that the earliest Hebrew writings had no clear conception of an immortal soul. Besides all the cogitation over the exact nature and mortality or immortality of the soul is useless. He writes: "O man! This god has given you understanding in order to behave well, and not to penetrate the essence of the things he has created." In an essay on the historical debates on the nature of Jesus, displaying his satire to good effect, Voltaire writes:

> Here is an incomprehensible question that has exercised curiosity, sophistic subtlety, acrimony, intrigue, fury to dominate, rage to persecute, blind and bloody fanaticism, barbarous credulity, and has produced more horrors than the ambition of princes, though this has produced much. Is Jesus [the] word? If he is [the] word did he emanate from god in time or before time? If he emanated from god is he coeternal and consubstantial with him or is he of a similar substance? Is he distinct from him or is he not? Was he made or begotten? Can he beget in his turn? Has he paternity or the quality of production without paternity? Was the holy ghost made or begotten or produced or does he proceed from the father, from the son or from both? Can he beget, can he produce? If his hypostasis is consubstantial with the hypostasis of the father and the son, how is it possible for him not to do the same things as these two persons who are himself?
>
> Christians . . . quibbled, hated each other, excommunicated each other because of some of these dogmas, so inaccessible to the human mind.

In an essay on the debate over whether all is good, Voltaire writes that for those who like to argue over the "inexplicable chaos" of the problem of good and evil, it is merely "an intellectual exercise. . . . [T]hey are convicts who play with their chains." At the end of all chapters on metaphysics, he concludes, we should write that this is simply not clear.[44]

In his essay on Genesis Voltaire applies his hand to biblical criticism. He discusses textual problems of consistency as well as the pre-scientific understanding of the world underlying its stories of creation, the fall, the flood, and Sodom and Gomorrah. Voltaire points out that ancient views saw light as having a source other than the sun; thus, could the sun and moon be created four days after the light. The heavens were also seen as a hard material, turning over our heads, and there were reservoirs of water, a notion not corrected because the ancients did not have the modern discoveries of astronomy. He observes that many ancient peoples, before the Hebrews settled in those lands, held a belief that the world was created in six periods, suggesting the Hebrews were offering up that belief in new dress. Voltaire notes that in one chapter male and female are created; then in the next chapter the female is fashioned from a rib of the male. Voltaire applies satirical reason to the tree of knowledge of good and evil:

> It is difficult to conceive that there has been a tree that taught good and evil, as there are pear trees and apricot trees. Besides, why did not god want man to know good and evil? Would not the contrary have been much more worthy of god, and much more necessary to man? It appears to my poor reason that god should have ordered man to eat a great deal of this fruit; but reason must submit.

Voltaire calls it to the reader's attention that there is no mention of the devil in the appearance of a serpent; the Hebraic use of the plural *Elohim* implies an early belief in more than one god; the garden of delight manifests a common belief that there was a better, golden age in primitive times; and other ancient histories have no mention of a universal flood. Voltaire writes: "We must not be startled by words, but worship the spirit, and hark back to the times in which was written this book."[45]

It should be noted that Voltaire's biblical criticism was not original. Critical study of biblical texts had been promoted during the Renaissance, and critical histories of the Old and New Testaments had been published in the 1600s.[46] Voltaire himself had an extensive theological library. He said he had two hundred books on Christianity and had read all of them, which he characterized as "like going the rounds of a lunatic asylum."[47] Voltaire's works were, however, much more widely read than the scholars of academia and most other independent scholars for that matter. Such critical reviews of Genesis in the 1600 and 1700s notwithstanding, still today professors who expound these views are dismissed by fundamentalist seminaries.

Obviously Voltaire was no orthodox believer. But was he a believer at all? This question has been addressed by numerous scholars. A. J. Ayer and John Gray, among others, have identified him as a deist. Will and Ariel Durant argued that he was a theist. Theodore Besterman makes the case that he was an atheist.[48] (I suppose such a conclusion hinges, as Besterman indicates, on one's definitions of *deism*, *theism*, and *atheism*.) I would, to be innocent of evasion, say that I think the evidence best supports Voltaire as a deist; although I concede strong statements by Voltaire that support theism.

Besterman, in arguing that Voltaire was an atheist, suggests that Voltaire's affirmations of belief were a practical expedient. Besterman writes: "The most common direct or indirect theme of Voltaire's references to god is that of expediency."[49] Besterman read everything extant that Voltaire ever wrote, so I have to respect his judgment; although that is not my impression from my more selective reading. Certainly Voltaire made statements that manifest an expedient approach to religion. For example, from the *Philosophical Dictionary*:

> I should want no dealings with an atheist prince who thought it useful to have
> me pounded in a mortar: I am quite sure that I would be pounded. If I were a
> sovereign I should want no dealings with atheist courtiers whose interest it was
> to have me poisoned: I should have to take antidotes at random every day. It is
> thus absolutely necessary for princes and peoples to have deeply engraved in
> their minds the notion of a supreme being, creator, ruler, remunerator and aven-
> ger.[50]

And Besterman points out that it is from Voltaire that we get the sentiment: "If
god did not exist, he would have to be invented."[51]

But I am inclined to read Voltaire as simply terribly ambivalent about belief
in God. There are numerous passages in his writings in which he affirms a divine creator from the evidence of the creation—what today we call the argument
by design. On the other hand, he addresses at times the extreme difficulty in
maintaining a rational belief in God, but in the same breath he exclaims the irrationality of its opposite.

Voltaire frequently sought to distill from religion a relatively simple faith,
without dogma and superstition. In an essay on the priest in the *Philosophical
Dictionary* he writes:

> When a priest says: 'Worship god, be just, indulgent, compassionate,' then he
> is a very good doctor. When he says: 'Believe me or you will be burned,' he is
> a murderer.[52]

And in the essay on religion:

> After our holy religion, which is undoubtedly the only good one, which would
> be the least bad?
>   Would it not be the simplest? Would it not be that which taught much mo-
> rality and very little dogma? that which tended to make men just without mak-
> ing them absurd? that which did not order one to believe in things that are im-
> possible, contradictory, injurious to divinity, and pernicious to mankind, and
> which dared not menace with eternal punishment anyone possessing common
> sense? Would it not be that which did not uphold its belief with executioners,
> and did not inundate the earth with blood on account of unintelligible soph-
> isms? that in which an ambiguity, a play on words and two or three forged
> charters would not make a sovereign and a god, out of an often incestuous,
> murderous and poisoning priest? that which did not subject kings to this priest?
> which taught only the worship of one god, justice, tolerance and humanity?[53]

I suppose an answer to Voltaire's true belief could be sought in speculation
whether Voltaire would have bothered much at all with religion had he lived in a
time and place more secular, where religion could be conveniently ignored, as is
certainly the case in Europe today. In today's world he could find plenty of instances of tolerant and rational religion—contemporary manifestations of characteristics he admired in the Quakers of his day—found easily in liberal Protes-

tantism. He would also have the option of Bertrand Russell's thoroughgoing secular humanism and atheism. But then Russell, too, wrote a lot on religion. Which way would Voltaire go? Would he still be ambivalent? I don't have even a good guess.

Some Reflection

Voltaire's ambivalence about the existence of God may reflect a more fundamental ambivalence between two sensibilities—that of the poet/religious and that of the scientist/philosopher. We see here, again, the conflict between Athens and Jerusalem. It seems to me there is in personalities a counterpart to the tension between cultural traditions of reason and religion. And most of us, I would guess, are simply more one than the other. There is a sensibility that is particularly attuned to the subtle, the nuanced, the ambiguous, the interplay between shadow and light, the spaces between categories. This is the sensibility of the poet and the mystic. These are the people who have an ear for the music of the spheres. There is another sensibility particularly attuned to categories, distinctions, differences, logic, and system. This is the sensibility of the empirical scientist and the philosopher. These are the people who have an eye for the spheres' elliptical orbits.

Voltaire was indeed a poet and playwright, but it might be noteworthy that we do not read his poetry or perform his plays. We read his essays, which are didactic and satirical, and his novellas and short stories, which are obvious parables (*Candide*, *Zadig*, etc.) whose messages are "in your face," so to speak. In the *Philosophical Dictionary* Voltaire satirizes the theologians' use of the concept of *grace*.[54] He is quite right in poking fun at all the categories of grace developed by theologians trying to systematize and categorize religious experience. But one gets the sense that Voltaire has no feel for this concept whatsoever. Tallentyre writes: Voltaire "had as little feeling for art as for nature."[55] Besterman writes: "Voltaire's character: the unrelaxing effort to see things clearly, as they really are, cannot produce the kind of high poetry represented by *Paradise Lost*."[56] Besterman also writes that "Shakespeare had an incomparable gift . . . for turning words into music, a gift that Voltaire simply did not possess."[57] It makes one wonder: perhaps Voltaire really did not have that aesthetic or mystical sensibility required of the religious and maybe even the great poet.

This is not a fault, of course. And in Voltaire's case it was a great strength and resulted in grand gifts to the world. He applied his clear, rational and empirical mind to exposing the historical absurdities resulting from turning the ineffable experience of the holy into dogma and ecclesiastical and political policies. His battle cheer, *Écrasez L'Infâme*, represented an early, important campaign, in the West at least, in depriving religion of its power for intolerance and brutality. Unfortunately his gifts are still needed. "When we . . . observe," writes A. J. Ayer, "such things as the recrudescence of fundamentalism in the United States, the horrors of religious fanaticism in the Middle East, the appalling danger which the stubbornness of political intolerance presents to the whole world, we must surely conclude that we can still profit by the example of the lucidity, the acumen, the intellectual honesty and the moral courage of Voltaire."[58]

Ironically, though not surprisingly, Voltaire's gifts have also contributed to the quest of the spiritual explorer. Will and Ariel Durant put it this way (and I close the chapter with this quotation):

> We can appreciate Christianity better today than he could then, because he fought with some success to moderate its dogmas and violence. We can feel the power and splendor of the Old Testament, the beauty and elevation of the New, because we are free to think of them as the labor and inspiration of fallible men. We can be grateful for the ethics of Christ, because he no longer threatens us with hell, nor curses the men and cities that will not hear him. We can feel the nobility of St. Francis of Assisi, because we are no longer asked to believe that St. Francis Xavier was heard in several languages while he spoke in one. We can feel the poetry and drama of religious ritual now that the transient triumph of toleration leaves us free to worship or abstain. We can accept a hundred legends as profound symbols or illuminating allegories, because we are no longer required to accept their literal truth. We have learned to sympathize with that which we once loved and had to leave, as we retain a tender memory for the loves of our youth. And to whom, more than to any other one man, do we owe this precious and epochal liberation? To Voltaire.[59]

Notes

1. Will and Ariel Durant, *The Story of Civilization: The Age of Voltaire—A History of Civilization in Western Europe from 1715 to 1756, with Special Emphasis on the Conflict between Religion and Philosophy* (N.Y.: Simon and Schuster, 1965), 786.

2. See, respectively, Hellmut O. Pappe, "Enlightenment," in *Dictionary of the History of Ideas: Studies of Selected Pivotal Ideas*, vol. IV, ed. Philip P. Wiener (N.Y.: Charles Scribner's Sons, 1973), 89; and Ayer, *Voltaire*, 93.

3. Immanuel Kant, "What is Enlightenment?" in *Foundations of the Metaphysics of Morals* and *What is Enlightenment?* trans. Lewis White Beck (Indianapolis: Bobbs-Merrill, 1959 [1784]), 85, 90.

4. Quoted in Durant, *Age of Voltaire*, 744.

5. Pappe, "Enlightenment," 89.

6. Durant, *Age of Voltaire*, 607.

7. E. J. Hobsbawm, *The Age of Revolution, 1789-1848* (N.Y. and Toronto: Mentor; New American Library, 1962), 38.

8. Hobsbawm, *Age of Revolution*, 39.

9. Theodore Besterman, *Voltaire* (N.Y.: Harcourt, Brace & World, 1969), 532.

10. Durant, *Age of Voltaire*, 605.

11. S. G. Tallentyre, *The Life of Voltaire* (N.Y.: Loring & Mussey, n.d.), 381.

12. Voltaire, "History of Scarmentado's Travels," in *Candide, Zadig and Selected Stories*, trans. Donald M. Frame (N.Y.: New American Library, 1961 [1756]).

13. Durant, *Age of Voltaire*, 608-611, 611-617.

14. Besterman, *Voltaire*, 105.

15. Tallentyre, *Life of Voltaire*, 496.

16. Quoted in Besterman, *Voltaire*, 160.

17. See Besterman, *Voltaire*, chapter one, quotation on p. 32.

18. Durant, *Age of Voltaire*, 34.

19. Besterman, *Voltaire*, 62, 68.

20. Voltaire, *Philosophical Letters*, trans. Ernest Dilworth (Indianapolis, Ind.: Bobbs-Merrill, 1961 [1733/34]), 26.

21. Durant, *Age of Voltaire*, 369.

22. Quoted in Besterman, *Voltaire*, 224.

23. Quoted in Durant, *Age of Voltaire*, 391.

24. Quoted in Durant, *Age of Voltaire*, 373.

25. Quoted in Tallentyre, *Life of Voltaire*, 365.

26. Ayer, *Voltaire*, 31.

27. Theodore Besterman, introduction to *Philosophical Dictionary*, by Voltaire, (London: Penguin Books, 1972), 10. Quotation Rights for this work: by permission of the Voltaire Foundation, University of Oxford.

28. Voltaire, *Philosophical Dictionary*, ed. and trans. Theodore Besterman (London: Penguin Books, 1972 [1764]), 188.

29. Voltaire, *Treatise on Tolerance*, trans. Brian Masters, ed. Simon Harvey (Cambridge: Cambridge University Press, 2000 [1763]), 25.

30. Ayer, *Voltaire*, 170-171.

31. Voltaire, *Philosophical Dictionary*, 272.

32. Besterman, introduction, 10.

33. Alexander Pope, *An Essay On Man*, ed. Frank Brady (Indianapolis: Bobbs-Merrill; The Library of Liberal Arts, 1965 [1733-34]), 55.

34. Voltaire, *Candide*, trans. Lowell Blair (N.Y.: Bantam Books, 1959 [1759]), 18.

35. Blake Ehrlich and Luis de Sousa Rebelo, "Lisbon," *The New Encyclopaedia Britannica*, 15th ed., vol. 23, (Chicago: Encyclopaedia Britannica, 1994), 76.

36. Voltaire, "The Lisbon Earthquake," in *The Portable Voltaire*, trans. Tobias Smollett et al., ed. Ben Ray Redman (N.Y.: The Viking Press, 1963 [1755]), 560.

37. See Durant, *Age of Voltaire*, 722-723.

38. Voltaire, "Lisbon Earthquake," 569.

39. Voltaire, "Lisbon Earthquake," 558.

40. See "New Testament and Mythology" in Rudolf Bultmann, et al., *Kerygma and Myth*, ed. Hans Werner Bartsch (N.Y. and Evanston: Harper Torchbooks; Harper & Row, 1961), 1-44.

41. Durant, *Age of Voltaire*, 737.

42. Voltaire, *Treatise on Tolerance*.

43. Durant, *Age of Voltaire*, 742.

44. Voltaire, *Philosophical Dictionary*, 27, 47, 73-74.

45. Voltaire, *Philosophical Dictionary*, 215-228.

46. J. C. O'Neill, "Biblical Criticism: History of Biblical Criticism," in *The Anchor Bible Dictionary*, ed. David Noel Freedman et al., vol. 1, (N.Y.: Doubleday, 1992), 727.

47. Quoted in Durant, *Age of Voltaire*, 745.

48. Ayer, *Voltaire*, 110; John Gray, *Voltaire* (N.Y.: Routledge, 1999), 27; Durant, *Age of Voltaire*, 716; Besterman, *Voltaire*, chapter 17; also Voltaire, *Philosophical Dictionary*, 58n.

49. Besterman, *Voltaire*, 220.

50. Voltaire, *Philosophical Dictionary*, 57.

51. Quoted in Besterman, *Voltaire*, 221.

52. Voltaire, *Philosophical Dictionary*, 346-347.

53. Voltaire, *Philosophical Dictionary*, 356-357.

54. Voltaire, *Philosophical Dictionary*, 229-231.

55. Tallentyre, *Life of Voltaire*, 357.

56. Besterman, *Voltaire*, 99.

57. Besterman, *Voltaire*, 147.

58. Ayer, *Voltaire*, 174.

59. Durant, *Age of Voltaire*, 753-754.

Chapter 6

The Sigh of the Oppressed Creature
Modern Critics of Religion: Karl Marx
(1818-1883)

I attended a big high school that served a wide geographical portion of suburban St. Louis. Its students were a cross section of white suburban America in the early 1960s. That school district included neighborhoods from the upper middle class to what Lillian Rubin called the "hard-living" working poor.[1] It became obvious to me that the economic background of students' families made a significant difference in students' everyday lives.

Some students simply had resources that allowed them more options. They had a parent at home (today called a "soccer mom") who could pick them up after extra-curricular activities (since the school buses quit running hours earlier). When they were old enough to drive, they had access to family cars. They were able to play with the best sporting equipment, buy records to play on fine high-fidelity-stereo systems, and date and travel without having a job. This meant they also had time to participate in various sports, clubs, and other activities. The few who did work somehow seemed to get relatively comfortable jobs with flexible hours. Most of them made very good grades, and they talked about going to college. I remember being surprised whenever I learned one of these affluent students did not make all As and Bs.

Other students had working parents and sometimes broken homes. To have any spending money, they had to work at jobs, typically in low-paying restaurants, gas stations, and retail sales. To have access to a car, they had to buy it and insurance themselves. Those who participated in extra-curricular activities had to find a way home, and often somehow juggle a job that competed for those afternoon and evening hours. I was likewise surprised whenever one of these students did make all As and Bs. (Those who dropped out of high school were almost always from these hard-living working-class families.)

75

It all seemed terribly unjust to me. It looked like the only sure way to have advantages was to choose very carefully the family into which you were born! It seemed that all families could not be affluent, but I did not quite understand why not or why the working-class folk were not angry about it—until I got to college and began to study Marxist thought.

Karl Marx is the great bogeyman for many, if not most Americans. Decades of conflict with "Marxist" states (the former Soviet Union, China, North Korea) and "Marxist" revolutions (in Asia, Africa and Latin America) and more than a hundred years of Western capitalist propaganda against socialism and communism have created a popular image of Marx as some kind of raving and misguided madman. His writings have been credited with duping devious leaders and innocent peoples into eliminating freedom and private property through totalitarian states. I know people who think they have adequately dismissed the teachings of a professor by saying, "He/she's a Marxist." Francis Wheen has noted that in Britain and America the "educated middle classes . . . are often perversely proud of their refusal to engage with Marx."[2] Red-baiting still turns up in the most peculiar places. In an undated but relatively recent booklet defending creationist science, the biologist Stephen J. Gould is cited among the "Sources" and identified as "*Marxist* Professor at Harvard University"![3]

Furthermore, the distortions and abuses by many "Marxist" leaders and movements have reinforced this view painted by opponents of Marxist thought and practice. Ernst Bloch even wrote that "Marxism suffers not so much from its enemies as from its alleged friends."[4]

Marx did indeed rave a lot, and he was a revolutionary, but he was no madman. He was an unusually well-informed and brilliant social theorist who provided us with some of our most profound analyses of modern culture and society. He understood the dynamics and saw some of the problems of modern capitalism quite early in its development. In this he showed the kind of insight that most thinkers are able to fulfill only well after events. He foresaw, among other things, capitalist globalization, the pauperization of the lowest elements in capitalist societies, the widening gap in income between workers and capitalists, the dependence on technology, the "growth of huge, quasi-monopolistic corporations, and periodic recessions."[5]

I do not want to defend Marx against what Ernst Bloch called the "significantly inadequate, one-dimensional, or obviously distorted" knowledge of Marx in the West—at least not anymore than I already have. Plenty of Marxian scholars have done that quite well, if only people would read them—or Marx himself. But the student must take into account Terrell Carver's wise observation that "it takes an effort of will on anyone's part to escape an easy (and lazy) equation among Marx, Engels, and Marxism."[6] My concern is with Marx's view of religion which has been oft-cited and influential way out of proportion to his comments. He was not much interested in religion, viewing it as personally irrelevant, thoroughly discredited by Ludwig Feuerbach in *The Essence of Christianity*,[7] and a dying institution.

Some Historical Context

Karl Marx finished writing *The Communist Manifesto* early in 1848—fifty-nine years after the start of the French Revolution; sixty-six years before the start of World War I. The French Revolution marked the beginning of the end of the old order in Europe. World War I completed the demise of the old order.

The old order was a medieval social and political system dominated by a more-or-less united front of monarchy, church, and aristocracy. E. J. Hobsbawm has written that "the French Revolution ended the European Middle Ages."[8] This is true, but the old order struggled to maintain control against the forces of change throughout the nineteenth century. Out of the chaos of the French Revolution including wars with other European countries, the French military officer from Corsica, Napoleon Bonaparte, came to rule over France and its armies. Even though he declared himself emperor in 1804, French armies under his leadership continued to carry the ideals of the Revolution in its conquests. The German philosopher Georg Hegel was at the University of Jena when the city fell to Napoleon's army in 1806. Already inspired by the progressive promise of the French Revolution, Hegel wrote in a letter:

> The emperor—this world-soul—I saw him ride through the city. . . . [I]t is indeed a wonderful sensation to see such an individual, concentrated on this stage here, riding a horse, spread over the world, dominant over it. . . . From Thursday to Monday such progress is possible only by this extraordinary man, whom it is impossible not to admire.[9]

Nevertheless and unfortunately, before Napoleon's reign was finished, "imperial conquest and exploitation" took precedence over liberation.[10]

After the defeat of Napoleon, the world powers at the Congress of Vienna in 1815 had sought to restore the monarchical status quo, in so far as possible, throughout Europe. But social changes, civil unrest, and revolutionary movements made that restoration nearly impossible to hold.

Interwoven with the political struggles was a burgeoning capitalism accompanied by the expansion of industrialization and urbanization. This meant a growing *bourgeoisie* (capitalist class) who sought increased political power for its own interests. The economic changes also meant the increasing emancipation of the peasants from the aristocracy, revolutionary gains in agriculture, and a growing proletariat. Secularization—the erosion of religious domination over culture and government—was advanced by political challenges to the church as well as philosophical and pragmatic critiques of religion.

There were four identifiable currents of political opposition agitating against the old order. One was liberalism, which sought to establish representative government with suffrage held by the propertied. One was the radically democratic, which sought republican government and a franchise for more than just the propertied. A third was nationalism, growing elements in Western nations who identified with the nation-state and promoted national glory. (It is surprising to most people born any time in the last hundred years to learn that nationalist sentiment, with all its emotional power to mobilize masses and crush dissent, is a fairly recent historical development, having become a powerful ideology just since the French Revolution.) And then there was socialism, which promoted a radical emphasis on community, cooperation, and sharing the fruits of the Industrial Revolution.[11]

Waves of discontent, beginning in 1830, culminated in the 1848 uprisings that saw revolutions in France, Italy, the German states, the Habsburg empire and Switzerland; somewhat less acute unrest in Spain, Denmark, and Rumania; and sporadic actions in Ireland, Greece, and Britain.[12] The revolutions of 1848 failed in their immediate aims (although not completely).[13] But the political and cultural conflicts generating them would continue to dominate the European scene until World War I finally broke the back of the old order of monarchy and nobility.

Some Biography[14]

Marx was one of the most brilliant and perceptive thinkers of the nineteenth century. There are frequent statements of praise for his mind, among both friends and enemies. The young socialist and journalist, Moses Hess, while still on good terms with Marx, wrote in a letter:

> Dr Marx (that is my idol's name) is still a very young man—about twenty-four at the most. He will give medieval religion and philosophy their *coup de grâce*; he combines the deepest philosophical seriousness with the most biting wit. Imagine Rousseau, Voltaire, Holbach, Lessing, Heine and Hegel fused into one person—I say fused not juxtaposed—and you have Dr Marx.[15]

Marx was deeply committed to working for a society of justice and freedom. His whole being was centered around this project. Even as a young man in 1835 he wrote: "The chief guide which must direct us in the choice of a profession is the welfare of mankind and our own perfection."[16]

For Marx, though, there was no way that his commitment would result in a life of quiet contribution to profession and community. He seems to have been a combative personality that would have shown itself no matter what, but once he took the side of the lower classes and set his mind to work at social critical analysis for revolutionary causes, he was on the path to a life of struggle. Two scholars in an encyclopedia article wrote: "Above all, Marx was a fighter, willing to sacrifice anything in the battle for his conception of a better society."[17]

Certainly that is true. A particularly poignant story comes from 1880, two years before his death, while Marx was vacationing. He ran into the American journalist, John Swinton, who engaged him in a wide-ranging discussion. During a pause, Swinton asked simply, "What is?" Swinton, writes: "And it seemed as though his mind were inverted for a moment while he looked upon the roaring sea in front and the restless multitude upon the beach. . . . [I]n deep and solemn tone, he replied: 'Struggle!'"[18]

Marx was born in 1818 at Trier in the Rhineland, which had been occupied by the French in 1797 and remained a part of France until the Congress of Vienna in 1815. It was a university town, a religious center, and a commercial crossroads. It was a cultural context where the ideals of the Enlightenment were valued.[19]

His father owned several wineries and was a modestly successful lawyer—an educated member of the middle class. Although a son and nephew to rabbis, he converted to Lutheranism, probably before Karl's birth, because under Prussian rule Jews were barred from practicing in the professions. He had also "been steeped in free French ideas of politics, religion, life and art, becoming 'a real eighteenth-century "Frenchman" who knew his Voltaire and Rousseau by heart.'"[20]

Marx's mother was Dutch and a daughter of a rabbi, and from a family that tended to produce rabbis. She was a relatively uneducated "woman whose interests began and ended with her family, over whom she fussed and fretted ceaselessly."[21]

Marx entered the University of Bonn in 1835 to study law. He transferred to the University of Berlin in 1836, where his encounters with Hegelian philosophy and that of the radical Young Hegelians led him to switch to philosophy. Like Voltaire, this meant a serious break with his father who did not appreciate Marx's enthusiastic embrace of such an impractical course of study. From then on, their relationship was strained, and Marx did not even attend his father's funeral in 1838. Marx lost any chance of a career in philosophy when Friedrich Wilhelm IV came to power in Prussia in 1840, and the Young Hegelians came under attack. Marx ended up submitting his dissertation to the University of Jena and was awarded his doctorate in 1841.[22]

Marx attempted to make a living as a journalist. He edited, between 1842 and 1848, several radical publications. However, their inflammatory rhetoric and critical perspective consistently led to their suppression. Marx was expelled from one country after another—Prussia, France, and Belgium. He finally settled in London in 1849, where he remained for the rest of his life, largely impoverished, while he researched political economy and wrote the theoretical underpinnings for revolutionary practice.[23] Intermittently he worked with international political and labor organizations—notably the Communist League and the International Working Men's Association.

He married his childhood sweetheart Jenny von Westphalen in 1843. They were deeply devoted to one another, and theirs was a happy marriage if not a happy life.[24] They tried to maintain the bourgeois lifestyle in which both had grown up but almost always lived on the edge of financial disaster. Their possessions of any value were from time to time in the pawn shop or sold outright. They were often hounded by creditors. They wanted for adequate nourishment and health care at times. And they survived largely through miniscule royalties, modest inheritances, and the largesse of friends, especially that of Friedrich

Engels who was helping run his father's textile firm in Manchester.[25] Three of their six children died, in part, from inadequate nutrition and health care. Marx himself was plagued by incessant health problems.[26]

Marx met Friedrich Engels in France, and they discovered they were complementary soul-mates. For the rest of Marx's life, Engels was his collaborator, closest friend, and financial benefactor. Only once, for sure, did they have a serious falling out, when Marx showed particular insensitivity to the death of Engels's common-law wife.[27]

Marx himself was a devoted family man. American students, in particular, put it to Marx's discredit that he did not get and hold a regular job, so his family would not have to suffer. He did attempt such jobs twice but was unsuccessful. These students do not realize that for a German intellectual revolutionary immigrant in mid-nineteenth-century England, this would have almost certainly "meant grinding employment as well as grinding poverty, the cessation of any cultural advantages for the children, and the end of his career as an 'ideas man' for contemporary communism."[28] But his commitment to his life project did mean that his family suffered the consequences of impoverishment. He felt this painfully. He had originally put off the marriage until he had a paying position. He expressed more than once his regret that his family had suffered the way they did, and had he to do it over again, he would not have married.

He was nevertheless a devoted and doting father and grandfather. Visitors were struck by the remarkable contrast between the warm, humorous, playful, indulgent family man and the pugnacious, sarcastic political philosopher. Actually there were similar, albeit less strong, impressions on the part of visitors, especially in his later years, between the warm and personal Marx they met and the aggressively polemical Marx they had anticipated. Presumably Marx had mellowed with age.[29]

His wife Jenny died of cancer on December, 2, 1881. His daughter, "Jennychen," died of cancer at the age of thirty-eight on January 11, 1883. Brokenhearted, Marx himself died March 14, 1883.

Marx on Religion

The following discussion will be rather abstract, but understanding Marx requires some grasp of these abstractions. I am simplifying, hoping the oversimplification is not irresponsibly distorting. Marxian scholars are notoriously combative and unforgiving regarding sins of distortion and interpretation. If the reader remembers that my oversimplified distortions are meant to be helpful rather than faultlessly precise, we should be okay.

Marx takes a dialectical view of history. We can think of *interactive* as a rough synonym for *dialectical*. *Dialectic* comes from the Greek meaning "debate," "discussion," "speech." In Plato's dialogues Socrates debates others in a lively give-and-take that moves toward an increasing clarity of ideas. This dialectical process of argument was seen as a form of reasoning. In those Socratic dialogues, Socrates kept the debate going by identifying the contradictions in the last claim made.

The German philosopher Georg Hegel (1770-1831), in some of the most complicated prose in history, used this dialectical model to interpret history.[30] Hegel thought that both philosophy and history "followed a dialectical path, in which" contradictory realities would clash and give rise to new realities containing new contradictions "that themselves required resolution."[31] Marx appropriated Hegel's model, modifying it considerably in ways we need not go into. Marx's perspective has been called "historical materialism," "dialectical materialism," "historical dialectics" and "dialectical-historical materialism." Whatever the label, it views history as the process of conflict between opposing social classes. This conflict, according to Marx, is the key to social change over time and to the internal dynamics of society at any given time.

In any historical period, says Marx, society is made up of interrelated groups with sometimes converging, sometimes opposing interests. When the fundamental interests of these groups are opposed, the society is seen as containing contradictions that lead to conflict. For the most part, the dominant class has the power to control the thinking of the dominated classes. Thus they accept their domination as well as the violent suppression of rebellion when it occurs. But at crucial historical times the dynamics of change will give rise to a new class whose developing interests are hampered by the old structure. A period of revolutionary conflict sets in until the new class accumulates enough power to change the structure of society to better serve its interests. Some Hegelian-Marxist scholars have identified this process as *thesis—antithesis—synthesis* or *affirmation—negation—negation of the negation.* Marx ridiculed such semantics.[32]

An example: the Middle Ages in Europe were characterized by a basic economic system of nobility and serfdom, with a monarchical government that protected the interests of the nobility. Economic changes gave rise to increasing numbers of capitalists whose enterprising ways did not fit well within the structures of the feudalistic economic system and were thus restricted by the nobility and monarchy.[33] As the capitalists got stronger, they challenged the old system and put in place a new system—capitalism, with constitutional government that protected their interests. This, in simplistic form, is how the historical materialist view sees history changing.

If we were to take a slice of time out of history (sort of like stopping a movie to view one frame) the historical materialist sees the ongoing conflict in a social structure on two interactive levels: the superstructure, i.e., the social institutions (politics, law, education, art, religion, science, and philosophy) and the material, i.e., the economic foundation (the organization of the economic system).[34] There is a dialectical relationship between the superstructure and the material foundation. The superstructure is the realm of ideas, especially the kind of reflective knowledge necessary to operate the social system. The material foundation is the manner in which our lives are organized by the economic system. The economic system is the foundation for society because it is the process whereby society extracts from nature the necessities of life—food, shelter, and so on. And the superstructural institutions are dependent on the economic system. If the economic system did not produce a surplus, there could not be politicians, lawyers, teachers, preachers, and philosophers because everybody would have to be working in the fields—gathering, hunting, cultivating, husbanding, and so on.

Most of the time the dominant class of the economic system controls the superstructure, thus using art, religion, science and philosophy as ideological justification of the system, and using politics and law to enforce it against the subordinate classes. Marx and Engels wrote, in *The German Ideology*: "The ideas of the ruling class are in every epoch the ruling ideas, i.e., the class which is the ruling *material* force of society, is at the same time its ruling *intellectual* force."[35] Today this domination of culture is commonly called *hegemony*. As a new burgeoning class suffers from its position in the economic system, critical ideas and philosophies arise that challenge the system. If that new class gains enough power from its position in the economy to organize themselves into a political force, then revolution is possible.

Today we in the West typically view our current economic system as organized into upper classes, middle classes, and lower or working classes, and we "see" this structure in the ways our work and social life are organized. The upper classes usually own most of the property and technology, including the corporations where the lower classes are hired, bossed around, and fired. The middle classes are more mixed—most working for someone else but many (professionals and small business owners) self-employed. These class divisions also manifest themselves in our neighborhoods, shops, homes, schools, etc. This is what I became aware of in my high school. Marx believed that the development of capitalism was resulting in a society divided by two antagonistic classes—the *bourgeoisie* (i.e., the capitalists who own the means of production) and the proletariat (who have to sell their labor as workers to the *bourgeoisie*).[36]

Marx simply identified the same basic conflict of interest between these two groups that Adam Smith, the "father" of capitalist theory, had seen.[37] It is in the interest of the capitalists, as a class, to pay the workers no more than they have to and to influence government policy to keep the workers as powerless as possible; just the opposite is in the workers' interest. Marx wrote that wages and profit stand opposed in a hostile relationship.[38] This conflict of interest is built into the capitalist system, and over time, except for occasional workers' gains, the capitalists tend to win. Winning here means keeping most of the excess wealth created in the process of production and giving back to the workers only enough to keep them from revolting.

What the capitalists will do in the process of winning, however, says Marx, will prepare the conditions for a socialistic society. Three developments especially will prepare history for its next, and final, stage of development. One, the capitalists will develop the technology and increase the wealth of society to such an extent that there will be no reason for everybody to be working all the time, and there will be, in fact, more than enough wealth for everybody. "The bourgeoisie," wrote Marx, "during its rule of scarce one hundred years, has created more massive and more colossal productive forces than have all preceding generations together."[39] Second, in doing so, capitalism will undermine traditional cultural restraints (such as religion!) on the rational, critical, and humanistic understanding of humanity and society. "The bourgeoisie . . . has put an end to all feudal, patriarchal, idyllic relations" and "drowned the most heavenly ecstasies of religious fervor."[40] Third, capitalism will also politicize the proletariat by dragging it into capital's own internecine struggles and international conflict at the same time that it generates an increasingly larger class of workers concentrated together in factories where they will interact and organize into unions and political parties.[41]

With the stage set, then, the recurrent crises of the capitalist economic cycle (today called "depressions") will threaten the whole system by absurdly destroying productive forces because it has produced too much![42] Political agitation by alliances of class-conscious workers and radical bourgeois "exiles" will lead to an ever-growing understanding of the system and the causes for its injustice, exploitation, and oppression. Eventually, as the workers gain a true understanding of their position in the system and of their collective interests as a class, they will revolt and establish a socialistic state of justice, community, and freedom.[43]

Once class divisions have been eliminated and all human beings are free to pursue their full human development, the need for a state apparatus (government) will become unnecessary. This is because the state was instituted and maintained in history primarily to protect the interests of the dominant classes. When there is no longer a dominant class, there is no longer any need for the state, as presently understood. It will wither away, claims Marx, except for some coordinating administration. Humanity collectively will establish a communistic society of cooperation, equality and freedom where the gain of one will be the gain of all and vice versa.[44]

This ideal condition of fully human emancipation would mean that humanity will no longer suffer from alienation. The concept of *alienation* is a key concept in Marx's thought and essential for understanding his view of religion. Our everyday understanding of alienation is estrangement from others accompanied by psychological discomfort. Marx's view of alienation is different. For Marx, alienation is a condition in which human beings have generated social structures that take on a life of their own and that act back upon their creators, denying them freedom and fulfillment.[45] This alienation is seen in that both capitalists and workers are spending all their time and energy working and struggling in a system of competitive greed that nobody has any control over. They experience the world (nature and culture) as alien powers to which they must conform. They do not experience themselves as the active, creative, and productive agents of their world. They are denied the possibility of fully enjoying life and developing their creative potential—for philosophy, for art, for family, for even choosing what kinds of work they would like to do from one day to the next.

Until the rise of capitalism, with its development of technology and organization generating abundant wealth, humanity could not get free from this compulsory drudgery and class conflict. It was a slave to nature. And until the rise of secular, enlightened philosophy, humanity perceived its social structures as created by divine powers. This is how Marx sees religion as most perniciously alienating—by encouraging the perception of human historically created social structures as divine and eternal. Human beings are enslaved by social structures they created because they do not perceive the structures as their own creation.

Marx believed that the happy marriage between capitalistic organization and technological advance would mean that for the first time in history more than enough of the necessities of life for all could be produced. The enlightened philosophical critique of religion would expose the reality that human beings collectively create the human culture they inhabit. This implies, then, the possibility of taking charge of their institutions and re-organizing them in such a way that everybody could be emancipated from the necessity of life-limiting labor or from exploiting others to do it. The de-alienation of humanity would mean an emancipated humanity. Since Marx believed that the religious veil had already been lifted, it remained for critical theorists, like him, to expose the "natural law" theories of capitalism as ideological justification, which is what he attempted in *Capital*.

In *Capital* Marx wrote: "The religious world is but the reflex of the real world."[46] This was his basic view of religion. Religion is an expression of alienation. He wrote: "*Man makes religion*, religion does not make man. And indeed religion is the self-consciousness and self-regard of man who has either not yet found or has already lost himself."[47] Since, for Marx, there is no objective divine reality, religion is a matter of attributing personal and supernatural reality to the forces of society which people experienced as external to themselves—as alien.

According to Marx, until modern times, religion had always played the role of justifying and legitimating the exploitative class structures of history. In other words, religion was an ideology.[48] But modern philosophical developments had thrown off this veil of illusion, preparing the way for humanistic social critique in the interest of human emancipation. This work had been largely done, so Marx believed, by Ludwig Feuerbach. It remained only for Marx to mention this fait accompli and go on to the crucial work of exposing the unjust and exploitative nature of capitalism and to organize the new industrial classes into a revolutionary force. But in the little he said about religion, almost entirely in his early writings, he made the claims which constitute his critique of religion, and which have been so widely quoted.

We have seen that he viewed religion as alienating and as an ideological accomplice of the status quo. Unlike some of the more simplistic political analyses of religion, it was not Marx's view that unbelieving ruling classes cynically and deceitfully employed religion to appease the lower classes. Denys Turner has pointed out that although Marx thought "it is in the interests of the ruling classes that people should indulge in" religion, "he did not, for a moment, suppose that one could explain the pervasiveness of religion among the oppressed classes of his day in terms of their oppressors' interests and power."[49] Rather, his analysis of religion is rooted in a more basic view of its place in human experience.

His most fundamental claim is that religion is a *true* "expression of real suffering." Marx was writing almost a hundred years after Voltaire, which was some distance from the history and the immediate reality of the kind of severe suffering religion could inflict through repression, persecution, and intolerance. Furthermore, the threat of eternal damnation was not strongly felt or even taken very seriously in the European culture of Marx's time, certainly not in his immediate social circles. So unlike Voltaire and, before him, Epicurus and Lucretius, Marx did not focus on religion as an independent source of suffering itself. Rather, he saw it as a result of suffering. He writes:

> *Religious* suffering is the *expression* of real suffering and at the same time the *protest* against real suffering. Religion is the sigh of the oppressed creature, the heart of a heartless world, as it is the spirit of spiritless conditions. It is the *opium* of the people.
>
> The abolition of religion as people's *illusory* happiness is the demand for their *real* happiness. The demand to abandon illusions about their condition is a *demand to abandon a condition which requires illusions*. The criticism of religion is thus in *embryo* a *criticism of the vale of tears* whose *halo* is religion.[50]

Religion is the expression of the real pain and misery people experience in an unfree world. But as a religious expression, it gives illusory happiness because it does not address the real conditions that are the source of alienation and oppression. It is an opiate in the sense that it provides false hope in another world and renders tolerable conditions that should not be tolerated. The critique of religion was necessary, Marx believed, before humanity could properly see itself clearly.

> The criticism of religion disillusions man so that he thinks, acts, and shapes his reality like a disillusioned man who has come to his senses, so that he revolves around himself and thus around his true sun. Religion is only the illusory sun that revolves around man so long as he does not revolve about himself.[51]

Marx's confident hope, then, was that as humanity recognized religion for what it is—a cry for help and false comfort, the voice of alienation itself—humanity would cease looking to religion for consolation and turn its critical eye to the real social conditions that it had the power to change.

> Thus it is the *task of history*, once the *otherworldly truth* has disappeared, to establish the *truth of this world*. The immediate *task of philosophy* which is in the service of history is to unmask human self-alienation in its *unholy forms* now that it has been unmasked in its *holy form*. Thus the criticism of heaven turns into the criticism of the earth, the *criticism of religion* into the *criticism of law*, and the *criticism of theology* into the *criticism of politics*.[52]

Some Reflection

Marx was an atheist. For him, "the truth of this world" is all the truth there is. This is the *materialism* in "historical materialism." Obviously we have here an assumption about reality that renders any theism or view of a transcendent spiritual reality meaningless. The believer and the seeker cannot go there; although they might visit the site as a matter of their own reflections about ultimate reality. Such reflections are the province of what the philosophers call metaphysics and ontology—two highfalutin words denoting the philosophical quest for the ultimate and essential nature of reality. Marx had no use for such stuff. For him, all that mattered was making the world a comfortable and livable space for everybody. While the believer and the seeker typically will not share Marx's materialist assumption, there is something in that single-minded devotion to the emancipation of humanity that should strike some chords in the faith of religious exponents. The central plank in the ethical systems of the world's major religions is regard and care for one's fellow human beings.[53]

Marx's view of religion sees the origin of religion in human suffering. It is the idea that religious sentiment is generated by the deficiencies and the deprivations of human life. This was not an uncommon view among thinkers in the human sciences in the nineteenth and early twentieth-centuries. We will see it again in Freud and Russell. In this perspective, religion is merely a quest for a "magic helper."[54]

Marx admirably and consistently resisted the temptation to paint any kind of detailed picture of the future emancipated communist society. But in one celebrated, poetic passage he and Engels wrote that in the "communist society, where nobody has one exclusive sphere of activity but each can become accomplished in any branch he wishes, society regulates the general production and thus makes it possible for me to do one thing today and another tomorrow, to hunt in the morning, fish in the afternoon, rear cattle in the evening, criticise after dinner, just as I have a mind, without ever becoming hunter, fisherman, shepherd or critic."[55] Let us imagine, for a moment, such a truly liberated society—one in which the organization of the economy and technology is socialized so that wealth is truly shared, and individuals are free to pursue their various interests, to enjoy family, friends, and life, and to choose the kind of work they do during the minimal hours necessary. If life were no longer a matter of fierce competition, of worry, anxiety, and struggle to make a living, of being bossed and exploited by capitalists—would religion then disappear? Of course, we cannot say with certainty outside the experience of such a world, but the idea seems, on the face of it, absurd. Few serious students of religion today believe that the origin of religion lies in material deprivation or even primarily in human suffering of any kind.

In a newspaper spiritual advice column, the Reverend Billy Graham wrote that "the human heart has a spiritual emptiness . . . that only God can fill."[56] All spiritual thinkers would not say it quite like that, but the basic idea would be affirmed by most religious people—certainly by theists such as Jews, Christians, and Muslims. The spiritual quest is more than a flight from suffering.

However, there is another important truth that Marx can help us remember. The human heart also has some needs that we should not try to fill with God. As Marx made so very clear, we are material beings whose very existence and meaning depend on the fulfillment of such needs as food and water, human intimacy, sexuality, shelter, good health, and creative work. God is no substitute for these things. And these are things it is our job as stewards of life and nature on our planet to acquire for ourselves and our communities. There come periods, of course, when we have to do without one or more of these basic human needs, and we lean on spirituality, then, to get through such times. I think most spiritual seekers recognize this as a stopgap measure. God is no substitute for the very real physical and non-physical things human beings need for a fulfilling life.

It is obvious that there are people for whom religion is a solace for the pain and struggle of life. Every leader of a religious community knows people who seek out religion *only* at times of painful life transitions. By itself, this psychological function of religion says nothing about the reality of the Holy. Furthermore, religion-as-consolation should not be belittled; it is reasonable to expect the Holy to be comforting. But insofar as religion operates as an opiate, leading to the irresponsible negligence of real personal and social problems that in principle have solutions, it is inauthentic and outside the spirit of true religion. For this reason, we need the prophet Marx.

That religion has functioned historically as ideological justification of the social status quo is not questioned by any social scientist. Even those social scientists who are most favorably inclined toward religion do not deny that it functions all too often in this way. Peter Berger, for example, writes "that religion has been the historically most widespread and effective instrumentality of legitimation."[57] This claim, made earlier by Marx, is important for all who would see the world improved, which implies a need for change.

It is nevertheless obvious that at historical moments religion has also served revolutionary purposes, challenging social inequities and oppression. The Social Gospel movement in nineteenth- and early twentieth-century America is a historically recent example, and today's liberation, feminist, and African-American theologies are contemporary examples of religion taking a critical stance toward current social structures. Marx was simply too simplistic in viewing religion as purely ideological. I suspect we could say, when it came to religion, he was not true to his own dialectical method.

Again, though, the prophet needs to be heard. Those who are religious and would also be concerned for a humanity free (or at least freer) from inequality, poverty, oppression, and injustice have a spiritual responsibility to turn a critical eye on the religion they endorse and support. The early Christian church recalled Jesus teaching that the essence of true discipleship results in the hungry being fed, the thirsty receiving drink, the unclothed being clothed, the stranger finding welcome, the sick and the imprisoned being comforted.[58] The Qur'an suggests that the truly righteous give wealth to their "kinsfolk, to the orphans, to the needy, to the wayfarers and to the beggars, and for the redemption of captives."[59] I would suggest that wherever religion is justifying social institutions and practices that do not address or even render worse the real human deprivations of material want and lack of freedom, it works against the spirit of the Holy. If such religion were our only option, the holy would have to abandon religion.

Notes

1. Lillian Breslow Rubin, *Worlds of Pain: Life in the Working-Class Family* (N.Y.: Basic Books, 1976), 30.

2. Francis Wheen, *Karl Marx: A Life* (N.Y. and London: W. W. Norton, 1999), 299.

3. Ken Hovind, *Are You Being Brainwashed? Propaganda in Science Textbooks* (Pensacola, Fla.: Creation Science Evangelism, n.d.), 34; italics mine.

4. Ernst Bloch, *On Karl Marx* (N.Y.: Herder and Herder, 1971), 162.

5. See discussions in Wheen, *Karl Marx*, 122, 299-300, 323.

6. Terrell Carver, "Reading Marx: Life and works," in *The Cambridge Companion to Marx*, ed. Terrell Carver, 1-22 (N.Y.: Cambridge University Press, 1991), 13.

7. Ludwig Feuerbach, *The Essence of Christianity*, ed. E. Graham Waring and F. W. Strothman (N.Y.: Frederick Ungar, 1957 [1841]).

8. Hobsbawm, *Age of Revolution*, 141; also Peter N. Stearns, *1848: The Revolutionary Tide in Europe* (N.Y. & London: W. W. Norton & Co., 1974), 116.

9. Quoted in Franz Wiedmann, *George Wilhelm Friedrich Hegel: in Selbstzeugnissen und Bilddokumenten* Reinbek bei Hamburg: Rowohlt, 1965, 35 (translation mine).

10. Hobsbawm, *Age of Revolution*, 141; and Stearns, *1848*, 102.

11. Hobsbawm, *Age of Revolution*, 141; and Stearns, *1848*, 46-48.

12. Hobsbawm, *Age of Revolution*, 140.

13. See Stearns, *1848*, 6-7.

14. This section owes much to Wheen, *Karl Marx*, more than will be evident in the endnotes.

15. Quoted in Wheen, *Karl Marx*, 37.

16. Quoted in Wheen, *Karl Marx*, 270.

17. Lewis S. Feuer and David T. McLellan, "Marx and Marxism: Life and works of Marx," *The New Encyclopaedia Britannica*, 15th ed., vol. 23 (Chicago: Encyclopaedia Britannica, 1994), 535.

18. Quoted in Wheen, *Karl Marx*, 383.

19. Carver, "Reading Marx," 4.

20. Wheen, *Karl Marx*, 8-11.

21. Wheen, *Karl Marx*, 9-12.

22. Wheen, *Karl Marx*, 14, 16, 27, 33; Allen Wood, "Karl Marx," in *The Philosophers: Introducing Great Western Thinkers*, ed. Ted Honderich (N.Y.: Oxford University Press, 1999), 167.

23. Carver, "Reading Marx," 10.

24. See H. F. Peters, *Red Jenny: A Life With Karl Marx* (London: Allen & Unwin, 1986).

25. Wheen, *Karl Marx*, 160.

26. Wheen, *Karl Marx*, 233.

27. Wheen, *Karl Marx*, 262-264.

28. Carver, "Reading Marx," 11.

29. Wheen, *Karl Marx*, 359-361.

30. For quick-and-relatively-painless entry into Hegel's thought: Paul Strathern, *Hegel in 90 Minutes* (Chicago: Ivan R. Dee, 1997); Peter Singer, *Hegel* (Oxford and N.Y.: Oxford University Press, 1982); Stephen Houlgate, *Freedom, Truth and History: An Introduction to Hegel's Philosophy* (London and N.Y.: Routledge, 1991).

31. Peter Singer, "dialectic," in *The Oxford Companion to Philosophy*, ed. Ted Honderich (Oxford & N.Y.: Oxford University Press, 1995), 198.

32. Marx, *Writings of the Young Marx*, 477. See Allen W. Wood, "Dialectical Materialism," *Routledge Encyclopedia of Philosophy*, ed. Edward Craig, vol. 3, *Descartes to Gender and Science*, 53-58 (London & N.Y.: Routledge, 1998), 56.

33. See Karl Marx, *The Communist Manifesto*, ed. Frederic L. Bender. (N.Y. & London: W. W. Norton, 1988 [1848]), 60.

34. See Bloch, *On Karl Marx*, 128.

35. Karl Marx and Frederick Engels, *The German Ideology: Part One*, ed. by C. J. Arthur (N.Y.: International Publishers, 1947 [1845-46]), 64.

36. Marx, *Manifesto*, 56.

37. See Adam Smith, *An Inquiry Into the Nature and Causes of the Wealth of Nations*, vol. 39, *Adam Smith*, Great Books of the Western World, ed. Robert Maynard Hutchins et al. (Chicago: Encyclopaedia Britannica; William Benton Publisher, 1952 [1776]), 28.

38. Marx, *Writings of the Young Marx*, 363.

39. Marx, *Manifesto*, 59.

40. Marx, *Manifesto*, 57.

41. Marx, *Manifesto*, 61, 64.

42. Marx, *Manifesto*, 60.

43. Marx, *Manifesto*, 63, 65-66.

44. Marx, *Manifesto*, 65-66, 73-75.

45. See Karl Marx, *Economic and Philosophic Manuscripts of 1844*, trans. Martin Milligan, ed. Dirk J. Struik (N.Y.: International Publishers, 1964 [1844]), 106-119; also Ernest Mandel and George Novack, *The Marxist Theory of Alienation* (N.Y.: Pathfinder Press, 1970).

46. Karl Marx, *Capital*, trans. Samuel Moore and Edward Aveling, ed. Friedrich Engels, revised with additional translation by Marie Sachey and Herbert Lamm, vol. 50, *Marx, Engels*, Great Books of the Western World, ed. Robert Maynard Hutchins et al. (Chicago: Encyclopaedia Britannica; William Benton Publisher, 1952 [1867-1890]), 35.

47. Marx, *Writings of the Young Marx*, 250.

48. See Marx and Engels, *German Ideology*, 47.

49. Denys Turner, "Religion: Illusions and liberation," in *The Cambridge Companion to Marx*, ed. Terrell Carver (N.Y.: Cambridge University Press, 1991), 320-321.

50. Marx, *Writings of the Young Marx*, 250.

51. Marx, *Writings of the Young Marx*, 250-251.

52. Marx, *Writings of the Young Marx*, 251.

53. See Timothy Freke, *The Illustrated Book of Sacred Scriptures* (Wheaton, Ill.: Quest Books; Theosophical Publishing House, 1998), chap. 6.

54. The phrase is from Fromm, *Escape*, 197.

55. Marx and Engels, *German Ideology*, 53.

56. Billy Graham, "Young people practicing Satan worship are playing with fire," *The Kansas City Star*, 2 July 1994, E11.

57. Berger, *Sacred Canopy*, 32.

58. Matthew 25:31-46.

59. The Koran, trans. N.J. Dawood (Middlesex, England: Penguin, 1974), 2:177, p. 350.

Chapter 7

Whither Is God?
Modern Critics of Religion: Friedrich Nietzsche
(1844-1900)

Walter Kaufmann writes that when reading Nietzsche, two things should happen. One is the "sheer enjoyment of his writing."[1] Indeed, Nietzsche is a delight to read—for many reasons—but especially if you enjoy playfulness in the midst of serious concerns. What other serious philosopher saw himself as the "enemy of the spirit of gravity," or argued that "we should call every truth false which was not accompanied by at least one laugh," or that "we should consider every day lost on which we have not danced at least once"?[2]

The second thing that should occur when reading Nietzsche, according to Kaufmann, is the "harrowing experience of exposing oneself to his many passionate perspectives."[3] Indeed, Nietzsche relentlessly criticizes the major sources of meaning for human beings, insisting on radical openness and ruthless honesty. He writes: "To make the individual *uncomfortable*, that is my task."[4]

Reading Nietzsche is little like riding a roller coaster while looking into the abyss. "Truth is hard," writes Nietzsche.[5] And, unless you are one who enjoys the skeptical dismantling of humanity's alleged knowledge and faith, it can be disturbing to follow him through the relentless debunking of philosophical, religious, scientific, and social thought by which people live. He himself was aware of the danger: "Whoever fights monsters should see to it that in the process he does not become a monster. And when you look long into an abyss, the abyss also looks into you."[6]

Nietzsche celebrated life, or rather, he wanted to celebrate life. It was not easy for him, and he queried his readers (as he challenged himself) whether they were among the haters or the lovers of life. He confronts us with a doctrine he called eternal recurrence (also known as eternal return). It is the question whether we love life enough to will the life we have had—forever?

91

Nietzsche is a man who grew up, the lone male, in a household of pious women—doting, I'm sure, but also overbearing. Throughout his adult life he suffered from long-lasting headaches, pain around the eyes, stomach cramps, dizziness, nausea, insomnia, indigestion, and neurasthenia.[7] He was a writer with a tremendous ego and sense of mission whose work received very little attention during his life. His ailments made it almost impossible for him to stick with any activity, even reading or writing for any length of time.[8] He experienced permanent ruptures in all of his closest relationships. He was unable to marry the woman whom he truly loved because she was already married. He suffered terrible loneliness and despair. Yet he confronts himself and his readers with this test: Only those who are willing to live their entire lives, in every detail, over and over in an "eternal recurrence"—only these are truly lovers of life.

> What, if some day or night a demon were to steal after you into your loneliest loneliness and say to you: "This life as you now live it and have lived it, you will have to live once more and innumerable times more; and there will be nothing new in it, but every pain and every joy and every thought and sigh and everything unutterably small or great in your life will have to return to you, all in the same succession and sequence. . . . The eternal hourglass of existence is turned upside down again and again, and you with it, speck of dust!"
>
> Would you not throw yourself down and gnash your teeth and curse the demon who spoke thus? Or have you once experienced a tremendous moment when you would have answered him: "You are a god and never have I heard anything more divine."[9]

At some point in Nietzsche's own "loneliest loneliness" he may have had an experience of intense emotional liberation in which the concept of eternal recurrence, which was not an original idea with him, grasped him as the key to unlock the door to valuing a life he found difficult to endure. Nietzsche's "formula for greatness" in human beings, then, became that they must love their fate (*amor fati*). They must not want anything different, not in the past, not in the future, not in all eternity. And they are not to simply grin and bear it or hide or repress it; they must "*love*" it." [10]

Some Historical Context

In late nineteenth-century Western Europe the forces of nationalism had been gaining momentum for decades. Historian Norman Rich wrote that "it is not too much to say that the mystique of nationalism was the major ideological force making for change in European politics and society."[11] Nietzsche himself volunteered for military service in 1870 during the Franco-Prussian War. Later he would denounce the nation-state as the "new idol."[12] He would deride German nationalism and race hatred, adding that he was unable "to take pleasure in the national scabies of the heart and blood poisoning that now leads the nations of

Europe to delimit and barricade themselves against each other as if it were a matter of quarantine."[13]

Democracy and socialism were other forces competing for adherents and agitating for change. The failure of the revolutions of 1848 set democratic movements back, but liberals continued to lobby and organize for democratic reforms. Socialism received a boost by the revolutions, although it had played an insignificant role in those conflicts.[14] By the 1880s, when Nietzsche wrote his mature works, parliamentary reforms were making headway in numerous countries, and there were significant socialist and communist movements in most Western countries.

The ongoing march of economic liberalism, carried by the gains of capitalism and industrialization, was nurturing a society characterized by cultural and economic segmentation, class division, and the erosion of traditions and traditional forms of authority—much as Marx had observed in *The Communist Manifesto* but also as had the very non-Marxian Emile Durkheim in *The Division of Labor in Society* and in *Suicide*.[15] This would seem to imply movement toward a pluralistic culture of greater individuality and diversity. But most major critics, including Nietzsche, believed that just the opposite was happening as people were pressured by economic, political, and cultural forces into lives of uniformity and regimentation.

Social scientists coined the term "mass society" for this new modern culture manifesting tremendous pressure toward greater uniformity in lifestyles and ideas.[16] Norman Rich has written that in the last decades of the nineteenth century:

> Mass production, mass education, and mass ideologies all seemed designed to crush human individuality and the creative spirit, to reduce European culture to the lowest common denominator of mass taste. In various ways anarchists and artists, philosophers and poets, expressed their hatred for the contemporary world, but none did so more passionately or eloquently than the German philosopher Friedrich Nietzsche.[17]

Indeed Nietzsche wrote: "This is the age of the masses: they grovel on their bellies before anything massive."[18]

Religion remained a major force, even increasing its numbers, while, paradoxically, losing influence over government and the cultural mainstream.[19] A relentless challenge to religion's influence was fueled by philosophical developments in the wakes of the Enlightenment and scientific thought, particularly that of Darwinism. The latter half of the nineteenth century became a time of mass movements accompanied by intellectual doubt about ultimate truths. Nietzsche viewed it as an era of nihilism.

Some Biography[20]

Friedrich Wilhem Nietzsche was born in 1844 in Röcken, Saxony—a Prussian province. His father Ludwig was a Lutheran minister, and both of his parents were children of Lutheran ministers. Ludwig died at the age of 57 in 1849. In 1850 Nietzsche's younger brother died. Nietzsche grew up as the only male in a household of women—mother, sister, grandmother, and two aunts.[21]

Nietzsche's school years were characterized by a strong interest in poetry, literature, and the classics. He entered the university at Bonn in 1864, studying theology and classical philology but soon dropping the theological studies. He transferred to Leipzig to follow his favorite teacher, Friedrich Ritschl.[22]

Ritschl was exceptionally impressed with Nietzsche. Nietzsche, after publishing a little in professional journals but not having finished his doctorate, received a call to the University of Basel in Switzerland. In a letter of recommendation to the University Ritschl wrote that he had "never known a young man...to become so mature so quickly and at such an early age." Ritschl said Nietzsche is "some kind of prodigy" as well as "amiable and modest" and that "he will accomplish anything he puts his mind to."[23] Leipzig quickly awarded Nietzsche the doctorate, and he taught at Basel from 1869-1879, except for a brief time in the military.[24]

During his military service, caring for ill soldiers as a medical orderly, Nietzsche became quite ill. He went back to work at the university, but suffered ill health the rest of his life.[25]

He published his first book, *The Birth of Tragedy*, in 1872. It was so unorthodox an approach that, after its publication, Nietzsche found himself an outcast from philological circles, and philology students in Basel avoided him.[26]

Nietzsche resigned his position at the university in 1879, primarily because of his health. From that time on he moved from place to place, in accord with the changing seasons, probably in search of some relief from his painful afflictions.[27]

One of the most important relationships of Nietzsche's adult life was with the composer, Richard Wagner, including a series of visits to Wagner between 1869 and 1872 and extensive observations about Wagner's work.[28] Nietzsche was greatly impressed by Wagner's creative genius. "All things considered," Nietzsche wrote, "I could not have endured my youth without Wagner's music."[29] Wagner's wife, Cosima, was also especially important for Nietzsche. He seems to have secretly loved her.

Wagner was, however, self-centered, domineering, even ego-maniacal. Nietzsche sought his own independence and self-affirmation. When Nietzsche broke with Wagner, it was with considerable ferocity and criticism. Kaufmann suggested the break was like a late adolescent emancipation.[30]

The break developed over time and involved several explicit issues. Nietzsche saw Wagner's Christian opera *Parsifal* as disingenuous. Nietzsche abhorred dishonesty, and he felt *Parsifal* was a shameless exploitation of attitudes Wagner did not hold, merely for a theatrical performance. Another issue was Wagner's rabid German chauvinism and his anti-Semitism. Furthermore, Wagner published an attack on Nietzsche after reading Nietzsche's *Human, All-Too-Human.*[31] What Nietzsche saw himself breaking with, Kaufmann writes, was "a mass movement and a *Weltanschauung* with which he could not compromise."[32] Nietzsche, however, always conceded Wagner's genius; he simply felt Wagner had squandered his genius.

Nietzsche's sister Elisabeth loved him devotedly, but for Nietzsche it was a love-hate relationship. In 1885 she married an active anti-Semite and German nationalist. Nietzsche was thoroughly unhappy about this marriage. In his letters to her in Paraguay (where her husband had founded a Teutonic colony), Nietzsche identifies himself as an "incorrigible European and anti-anti-Semite."[33] Nietzsche deplored anti-Semitism and attacked it in his writings.

Nietzsche's life was enriched, complicated, and, in the end, burdened by a friendship with two people in whom he had great hope apparently of carrying on with his ideas and, more significantly, of deep friendship. Lou Salomé was a lively, intelligent, and nonconforming woman. Paul Rée was a psychologist and historian. The relationship between these three has been difficult to clarify because of conflicting accounts. Apparently Nietzsche loved them deeply, but a combination of factors—Rée's jealousy of Nietzsche's relationship with Salomé, things Rée and Salomé said about Nietzsche (and to Nietzsche although the correspondence is not available), and the meddling of his sister who hated Salomé—led to a break that caused Nietzsche great anguish.[34]

The wandering nine years from 1879 till 1888 were years of relative obscurity for Nietzsche, but they proved prolific. In those nine years he wrote *The Gay Science, Thus Spoke Zarathustra, Beyond Good and Evil, The Genealogy of Morals, The Case of Wagner, Twilight of the Idols, The Antichrist, Nietzsche Contra Wagner,* and *Ecce Homo*—the last five within six months in 1888.[35]

In January, 1889, Nietzsche collapsed on a street in Turin. After receiving an alarming note from Nietzsche, a friend came and took him to Basel. Nietzsche went from a clinic in Basel to an asylum in Jena. From there his mother took him home. Soon thereafter, his sister, back from Paraguay after her husband's death and the dissolution of the German colony, took Nietzsche to Weimar. His illness continued. There were fewer and fewer moments of lucidity, as darkness gradually enveloped "Nietzsche's mind in hopeless night."[36] Nietzsche's insanity may have been the result of syphilis, although this is uncertain.[37] He died August 25, 1900.

Nietzsche on Religion

In the 2001 fall premiere of Warner Brothers' television show *Smallville*, Superman, as a teenager, stumbles with an arm load of books near Lana Lang. As he picks up the books, she notices one of them is *The Portable Nietzsche*, and she says, "Clark, I didn't know you had a dark side."[38] Undoubtedly the scene is to suggest where Clark Kent will get his idea for the "Superman" identity. But Lana Lang's comment represents a widely shared misconception of Nietzsche. Nietzsche is "dark" only if you think a hyper-critical approach to life is dark. Nietzsche is actually remarkably playful—albeit also quite caustic—as he goes about his project of criticizing the philosophies, religions, ideologies, and practices of Western history.

We could argue that he is luminous. After all, he sought to illuminate the human condition in service to an ideal of an enhanced, creative, courageous, and powerful humanity. In a letter in 1882 Nietzsche wrote that his books, beginning with *Human, All-Too-Human*, "are meant to erect 'a new image and ideal of a free spirit.'"[39]

The free spirits, for Nietzsche, would be independent individuals who embrace life with courage, honesty, joy, discipline, and creativity. They would not resort to the false illusions of religion or grand philosophical systems that distort life by forcing it into imaginary systems of logic and speculation. They would not surrender themselves to collective identities, such as nationalism, socialism, liberalism, or racism. They would not reduce themselves to mere members of the masses preoccupied with buying and selling in the marketplace or distracted by the imitative arts of popular culture. In a quest to overcome themselves, to perfect themselves, they would be their own critics, their own authorities, their own priests. The free spirits are those individuals who, with Nietzsche, would aspire to the status of *höhere Menschen* (higher humans). (Nietzsche also used the concept *Übermensch*, translated *superman* by early English translators, but now typically *overman* because of the popularity of the comic book hero.)

The higher humans are those who can live with the radical criticism that shows that all "truth" is "false." Nietzsche is known for his *perspectivism*. This simply means that he promotes the argument that all perspectives on reality are only that—perspectives; that is, views from people in particular times and places and with particular interests in seeing the world in that way. There are no facts, argues Nietzsche, "only interpretations." The world is not really "knowable"; it is only "interpretable"; this is "perspectivism."[40]

"What, then, is truth?" asks Nietzsche. He answers that truth is a "mobile army of metaphors, metonymns, and anthropomorthisms"—that is, words, symbols, and images taken from everyday life to give structure and meaning to human existence. They are "embellished poetically and rhetorically," and over time they take on a reality of their own. They become fixed, unchallenged, and obligatory. Being truthful, he continues, is a matter of "using the customary metaphors." Morality then becomes "the obligation to lie according to a fixed convention."[41] Some social scientists would say that all "truths" are true, in the sense that they manifest the truly existential and psychological realities of the perceivers. But, for Nietzsche, who wants to shake things up, it is essential to notice their falsehood: they are false, he suggests, because they say more about the perceivers (their motivations and life circumstances) than they do about reality.

On the other hand, in other places Nietzsche suggests there is truth. In *On The Genealogy of Morals* he argues that "truths do exist." They might be "plain, harsh, ugly, repellent, unchristian, immoral truth[s]"; nevertheless, they are truths.[42] Furthermore, to make the argument, as Nietzsche does, that some things are false implies also some standard of truth, which, I'm sure was not lost on Nietzsche. There are many such "inconsistencies" in Nietzsche, and scholars argue over whether they are truly inconsistencies or something like moments in a dialectical movement that, when rightly understood, turn out to be resolved.

In any case, what seems important to Nietzsche is that human beings create truth and assign meaning to life. For Nietzsche, this is the glory of humanity, and any attempt to locate the source of truth and meaning of reality outside human beings (as religion does!) is alienating, dehumanizing, and therefore an enemy of life.

Nietzsche recognizes this insight of perspectivism as a potentially terrifying reality for human beings. With no ultimate truth that can be trusted, there simply is no place on which to stand, and yet we must stand somewhere. The honest person faces life, then, as an abyss that needs to be filled. Nietzsche calls on his readers to give up their illusions. However, he recognizes that human beings cannot live without illusions since all perspectives are illusions. He is too honest himself to suggest he could find the illusionless existence.

So he calls for creating one's own illusions—having the courage to cut loose from all those social forces that would tell people what to believe and how to act, and live one's life freely and creatively. In other words, approach one's life as artists approach the materials for their works. Such a burden, Nietzsche argues, could be borne only by the higher humans who can laugh and still passionately affirm life—*their* lives in all their individuality and creativity. They would need playfulness and laughter to tolerate the burden of terror in the unmasked existence, and they would need courage to affirm life by living fully in spite of the absence of any external, objective reality to give life meaning. They would need exceptional strength. "Independence is for the very few; it is a privilege of the strong," writes Nietzsche.[43] The higher humans would embrace life by exercising their natural powers to live with passion and freedom. They would not require for their meaning and motivation any force such as the party ideology or the nation or religion.

Nietzsche believed most people would not be able to do it. Most will do as most have done in the past; they will surrender their individuality, their freedom, and their creativity to some collective identity—religion, nationalism, liberalism, socialism, *et cetera*. They will do this out of fear and resentment. *Fear* and *resentment* (Nietzsche uses the French *ressentiment*) are central and frequently occurring concepts in Nietzsche's thought. Fear and resentment are seen in those who surrender their lives to forces external to themselves. Out of fear of suffering and death, most people give up their autonomy, abandon intellectual honesty, and reject responsibility for their own self-realization. Because they themselves are weak and fearful, out of resentment they support causes that would restrain others from self-realization. Such causes typically promise to redress wrongs and promote justice, but Nietzsche views them as merely attempts to restrain stronger, more courageous types from realizing themselves, from overcoming themselves, from authentically fulfilling life's will to power.

Nietzsche posits as fundamental to life what he calls the "will to power." He clarifies this concept by contrasting it with the competing claim that life is a struggle for survival. "It can be shown most clearly that every living thing does everything it can not to preserve itself but to become *more*."[44] Life is at bottom not a drive for existence; rather life wants to gain and grow. "Life wants to climb and to overcome itself climbing," says Nietzsche.[45]

It follows, then, that only the courageous and adventurous—those who will venture into the new and the unexplored—the higher human beings—are those who positively affirm life's will to power. "O my brothers," writes Nietzsche, "I dedicate and direct you to a new nobility: you shall become procreators and cultivators and sowers of the future."[46] Such sowers of the future will not look for self-justification in their past, in buying and selling, in association with the high and the mighty, or in former accomplishments. They keep on keeping on, always seeking to overcome themselves. "For that I bid your sails search and search," says Nietzsche.[47]

The higher humans will also have to be those who can discipline their passions and tolerate suffering. Nietzsche does not promote anything like a licentious, devil-may-care, let-it-all-hang-out life of impulsiveness. Nor does he encourage the pursuit of pleasure. In fact, he distrusts indulgence in pleasure. The higher human is rational and self-controlled and willing to pay any price to achieve "independence of the soul."[48] The higher humans even value difficulties and obstacles because it is in the process of overcoming them that they overcome and perfect themselves. Nietzsche asks: "The discipline of suffering, of *great* suffering—do you not know that only *this* discipline has created all enhancements of man so far?"[49]

All human beings are imbued with the will to power, according to Nietzsche, even the fearful and resentful who do not take the path of self-realization.[50] The difference is that the fearful and resentful have shrunk from risk and danger, thereby betraying life and themselves. In fact, their resentment is a sign of their fear and consequent weakness, and it leads them to do things that harm life and stifle the strong—which, according to Nietzsche is typical of any form of collectivism.[51] Any cultural force that discourages people from courageous lives of individuality and creativity is an enemy of life, a promoter of hatred for life, argues Nietzsche. And he names socialism, democracy, nationalism, and, above all, religion as just such forces.

Nietzsche wrote a great deal about religion, about God, and particularly about Christianity. There are sympathetic theological interpreters of Nietzsche who suggest Nietzsche was not so much denying the reality of God as criticizing the distortions of religion and struggling with his own repressive religious up-bringing.[52] Certainly Nietzsche's level of vehemence against Christianity, espe-cially in his later writings, could be a sign of a deep-seated psychological strug-gle, but Nietzsche is both unequivocal and forceful in his denunciation of religion from early on in his writings. I think we should take seriously and not misrepresent a thinker who wanted to be taken seriously and not misunderstood. Simply stated, Nietzsche did not believe in God, and he thought religion was basically alienating and dehumanizing. He was a thoroughgoing secularist.

One important qualification to make is that on occasion in his writings he does promote a kind of alternative "faith," but it is a faith in nature, in nobility, in human individuality, in the cosmos—not something that would be practiced in any social institution typically recognized as religion. Another qualification needs to acknowledge that he praises the religion of the ancient Greeks in which, as he saw it, people use their divinities "to ward off the 'bad conscience,' so as to be able to rejoice in their freedom of soul."[53] So while Nietzsche denied any reality beyond empirical nature, his primary target was Christianity more than it was religion itself. He amassed a great deal of critical observations of it, includ-ing one whole book. I will highlight certain observations while trying to get at the core of his criticism.

In one of his early works, *Human, All-Too-Human*, he criticizes numerous orthodox, Christian doctrines:

> A god who begets children with a mortal woman; a sage who bids men work no more, have no more courts, but look for the signs of the impending end of the world; a justice that accepts the innocent as a vicarious sacrifice; someone who orders his disciples to drink his blood; prayers for miraculous interventions; sins perpetrated against a god, atoned for by a god; fear of a beyond to which death is the portal; the form of the cross as a symbol in a time that no longer knows the function and the ignominy of the cross—how ghoulishly all this touches us, as if from the tomb of a primeval past! Can one believe that such things are still believed?[54]

And in *The Wanderer and His Shadow* he goes after the Calvinist doctrine of the sovereignty of God:

> *The persecutor of God.* Paul thought up the idea, and Calvin re-thought it, that for innumerable people damnation has been decreed from eternity, and that this beautiful world plan was instituted to reveal the glory of God: heaven and hell and humanity are thus supposed to exist—to satisfy the vanity of God! What cruel and insatiable vanity must have flared in the soul of the man who thought this up first, or second.[55]

In *The Dawn* Nietzsche analyzes St. Paul as one who struggled with the law because he could not keep it. So Paul, says Nietzsche, got the remarkable idea of annihilating it as a great revenge. He embraced Jesus and founded Christianity. Nietzsche suggests the same psychological thing happened for Luther. Both of them got free from the law by vengefully turning against it and its representatives.[56]

Nietzsche felt that Christianity had debased natural human passions. "The passions become evil and insidious when they are considered evil and insidious. Thus Christianity has succeeded in turning Eros and Aphrodite—great powers, capable of idealization—into hellish goblins." Nietzsche says that one of the very rare realities in nature whereby people give each other pleasure is sexuality. But Christianity has taken this natural pleasure and turned it into corruption with a "bad conscience." So what has happened—ironically but psychologically understandably—is that Eros has become all interesting to humanity, rendering the love story the favorite pursuit of all.[57]

Nietzsche, as a philologist and a scholar, comments on the absurdity of typical Christian biblical interpretations. He argues that dishonesty is clearly manifest in the writings of Christian scholars. They give little evidence of any perplexity from their own biblical interpretations, he notes. "Again and again they say, 'I am right, for it is written,' and the interpretation that follows is of such impudent arbitrariness that a philologist is stopped in his tracks, torn between anger and laughter, and keeps asking himself: Is it possible? Is this honest? Is it even decent?"[58]

Even early in Nietzsche's writings he is contemptuous of commitment that did not come from a position of honesty, integrity, courage, and a love for life. This is particularly true of his view of faith. "To accept a faith just because it is customary, means to be dishonest, to be cowardly, to be lazy," he wrote in *The Dawn*.[59]

Nietzsche realized that modern philosophical and cultural developments had rendered religious faith problematic for thinkers in general. He saw himself as beyond faith by instinct.

> I do not by any means know atheism as a result [of a bad conscience]; even less as an event [of culture]: it is a matter of course with me, from instinct. I am too inquisitive, too *questionable*, too exuberant to stand for any gross answer. God is a gross answer, an indelicacy against us thinkers—at bottom merely a gross prohibition for us: you shall not think![60]

The world was moving past belief, he believed. He proclaimed that God is dead. "Whither is God?" he has a madman ask in *The Gay Science*. "I will tell you. *We have killed him*—you and I."[61] While he saw the decline of belief as a sign of nihilism, he hailed it as necessary for human liberation and sought to nail the coffin shut with extravagant criticism of Christianity.

Nietzsche on occasion talks about other religions, Judaism, Islam, Buddhism, Hinduism. He even gives Buddhism and some elements of Hinduism unusual praise in *The Antichrist*, but his focus remains primarily on Christianity.

Nietzsche believed that Christianity generated fear and resentment, and turned people into haters of themselves and of life. By positing a reality outside themselves that judged them ever in the wrong, they came to feel in the wrong and to despise life. "The Christian resolve to find the world ugly and bad has made the world ugly and bad," he writes.[62]

> All preachers of morals as well as all theologians share one bad habit; all of them try to con men into believing that they are in a very bad way and need some ultimate, hard, radical cure. Because humanity has listened to these teachers much too eagerly for whole centuries, something of this superstition that they are in a very bad way has finally stuck. Now they are only too ready to sigh, to find nothing good in life and to sulk together, as if life were really hard to *endure*.[63]

Nietzsche argues that Christianity also allowed the herd mentality to triumph over an aristocratic world in which higher human beings could thrive. The herd's resentment of the strong and its concern to protect itself from the powerful fit in well with the Christian ethos that denigrated power, egoism, and passion, and exalted weakness, selflessness, and distrust of the self. He writes, "Christianity has been the most calamitous kind of arrogance yet." Christianity allowed domination of Europe by people with little creativity, no sense of vision, no experience of self-conquest, and no capacity to recognize the great differences between the quality of individual human beings. Such people have so promoted the notion of "equal before God" that they have bred a smaller, ridiculous, sickly, mediocre type—the "herd animal."[64]

Christianity's triumph in the West meant the triumph of weakness and hatred of life, according to Nietzsche. He argues that ironically and deviously Christianity's resistance to domination allowed its own leaders to control and dominate. The religious leader is "a parasitical type of man," taking the name of God in vain because he calls circumstances in which he rules and dominates "the kingdom of God," and he calls it "the will of God" to maintain these circumstances. Furthermore, "with cold-blooded cynicism" these leaders evaluate peoples, individuals, and eras by the degree to which they have supported or resisted this domination.[65] In fact, the whole Christian history shows a concern to control and dominate in spite of all its preaching about humility, service, and care. Clearly it lies, argues Nietzsche. It betrays the will to power because of fear and distrust of nature, but comes to power through revenge and resentment—a colossal historical irony.

> 'Thou shalt not rob! Thou shalt not kill!' Such words were once called holy; one bent the knee and head and took off one's shoes before them. But I ask you: where have there ever been better robbers and killers in the world than such holy words?[66]

Although Christianity came to dominate a whole civilization, it failed, by its own standards, to establish the kind of world it claimed to promote. Nietzsche says this should tell us something about its motivations. It was doomed to failure because it was never truly driven by love and mercy; it was driven by revenge and resentment—a hatred of life. "Christianity has sided with all that is weak and base," and taught that the "supreme values" of the strongest spirits are sinful.[67]

Nietzsche is ambivalent about Jesus, praising him at one time, criticizing him at another. Yet he seems to think Jesus would not have promoted the Christianity that developed after his death, claiming at one point that had Jesus lived longer, he would have recanted his teaching and at another point identifying Jesus as the "only . . . Christian."[68] In any case, Nietzsche notes that "Christians have never put into practice the acts Jesus prescribed for them."[69]

For Nietzsche, Christianity is hostile to life and thus also the enemy of the higher human beings. The higher humans have no need for revenge or resentment. They don't need to control or dominate others. They don't lie to themselves about a better life in some beyond. They live beyond good and evil in an embrace of life—all of life—however demanding and difficult.

Some Reflection

Nietzsche was an atheist, "from instinct," he said. Again, as with Marx and with the other critics to come, this is where believers find themselves irreconcilably separate. It is no trivial difference. I suspect Nietzsche would agree with theologian Schubert Ogden, although with a different conclusion, that the question of God's reality is not the most important question; it is "the only question."[70] Nietzsche's view of life has no room for anything other than the natural—the empirically available existence. The religious sentiment, though, includes some sense of another transcendent reality—sacred or not, conscious or not, supernatural or not—a sense of something more that is seen as of ultimate importance. This is perhaps the basic division between believers and spiritual seekers on the one hand and atheists on the other.

In spite of his many detailed observations, Nietzsche caricatured historical figures and religion, especially Christianity, with broad and crude brushstrokes. Nevertheless, Nietzsche offers us a call to ruthlessly honest and critical examination of motives. If our faith is a flight from life, if it is a kind of misery-driven groveling before a hoped-for redemption we may or may not really believe in, if it is a manifestation of an unwillingness to shoulder responsibility for growth, creativity, exertion of effort, if it is a fear of the never-easy struggle to grow and mature in community with others—then it might not be faith at all. It could be an infantilism that has never come to grips with the break from the safety of childhood. I think of Dag Hammarskjöld's journal entry: "Your cravings as a human animal do not become a prayer just because it is God whom you ask to attend to them."[71]

It is true that religion, especially Western religion, promotes practices of humility, dependence on the divine, submission to God. "Islam" means submission. "Obedience" is a thoroughly common concept promoted by religious leaders, and, of course, how this gets translated into practice typically is obedience to some religious authority. Nietzsche can lead us to some critical awareness of the dangers from this theme of servility and obedience. In so far as believers are discouraged from any trust in their own reason, perception, and experience, and encouraged to uncritically accept some religious tradition or theological current, they are vulnerable to demagoguery and authoritarianism.

The experience of the Holy comes with a sense of awe and humility. Such awe and humility, however, are categorically different from docile submission in hierarchical social structures. A reverence for God or Life does not require suspension of one's critical faculties. It does not require the subversion of human autonomy. I think Nietzschean critique is useful wherever religion, in its historical forms, has channeled sacred awe into fearmongering, affirmations of servile helplessness, and legitimation of domination.

Nietzsche can be viewed, in some ways, as the culmination of the Western, humanistic tradition of individualism and self-affirmation. Certainly this tradition has its own problems, but the idea of relatively autonomous individuals—creative and rational, passionate but disciplined, courageous and responsible—is an important element in the world's cultural heritage. At their best, religious traditions recognize and affirm this. Perhaps few of us are able to be the kind of higher human Nietzsche envisioned—even if we could get a clear fix on what that would mean—but we can develop a faith-practice of critical rationality, of affirmation of the goodness of nature, of life, of individuality, of creativity, of stretching ourselves. I see no reason for religion to fear this, although its acceptance could transform religion itself. Nietzsche may not have been correct in his wholesale, absolute condemnation of religion, but he is uncomfortably insightful regarding some of its psychological dynamics.

Nietzsche wrote that his "formula for an act of supreme self-examination on the part of humanity" is the "revaluation of all values."[72] His insights and challenge could inspire some serious re-evaluation of our faith traditions to sort out those elements that denigrate and diminish life and humanity from those that have a healthy life-and-earth affirmation. Some less-than-healthy strands of thought in religious traditions may need to be jettisoned or transformed. For example, the concept of *obedience* is one such possibility. Of what use can an uncritical application of such a concept be in a modern world of religious pluralism, freedom of choice, and individual responsibility? (Religious researcher David Barrett says there are "nine thousand and nine hundred distinct and separate religions in the world, increasing by two or three new religions every day"!)[73] In the Christian gospels Jesus is seen as consistently rejecting attempts to make him some kind of king or infallible lord, and he warns his disciples not to seek domination over others. It seems to me we are in greater need for some concept of reflective, critical, responsible, and passionate decision-making instead of obedience. Obedience, even to God, cannot escape from obedience to some interpretation by "authorities" or from obedience to some impulse of one's own which may or may not be a rationalization of one's own desires.

While religions of the East and West warn against excessive attachment to mundane realities, they still endorse the goodness of creation and natural life, as well as the capacity of human beings to take responsibility for themselves and their world. In ancient mythologies this is a matter of recognizing and valuing the necessary role of mother earth in the primeval pair (sky god and earth mother).[74] Nietzsche's embrace of life is not unlike the spiritual embrace of mother earth. His will to power is not unlike the spiritual yearning of humanity for transcendence. Indeed, the religious sentiment, at its best, is also a sentiment that values something higher than survival. For these reasons, I'm guessing, Nietzsche has found appreciation among many theologians.

There is far more that could be said in reflecting on Nietzsche's critique of religion than I have space for. I would add just this: It seems to me that for the believer and the seeker one of the most important insights of Nietzsche is captured in a paragraph from *Thus Spoke Zarathustra.*

> Truthful I call him who goes into godless deserts, having broken his revering heart. In the yellow sands, burned by the sun, he squints thirstily at the islands in abounding wells, where living things rest under dark trees. Yet his thirst does not persuade him to become like these, dwelling in comfort; for where there are oases there are also idols.[75]

Life is hard—no matter what one's circumstances. If you are fortunate enough to not be among the millions of human beings for whom survival itself is the first and last task of every day, you still must negotiate the complex labyrinths of modern life. Just growing up has plenty of perils. Functioning well in the configurations of kinship and friendship is perpetually demanding, and in them there are minefields for everybody I know. Finding adequately rewarded and satisfying work is more difficult than all the self-help columns and books imply. There are challenges of community and citizenship, especially as manifested in the many competing lifestyles, philosophies, ideologies, and religions of a modern, pluralistic culture. And no one is spared the realities of tragedy and suffering. The temptation is therefore great, on the one hand, to latch onto some authoritarian leader or rigid religious orthodoxy that will tell us what to think and do or, on the other, to seek out a pandering religion that will "bless" whatever we are by withholding any critical judgment of the dominant culture and its lifestyles.

It takes courage, honesty, discipline, and, undoubtedly, a sense of humor to resist homesteading in the oases of dogmatic orthodoxy or lackadaisical culture religion. And any religious system is potentially another idol. We are not likely to follow Nietzsche in a wholesale rejection of religion and faith. Nor should we. But we can hear his insightful call to the importance of being hard on oneself and risk going into the "godless deserts"—those places where we can gain a critical perspective on ourselves, where we can confront our desire for certainty, comfort, and ease over uncertainty, challenge, and growth. Theologically speaking, this is the issue of living without idols. Proclaims the Koran:

> Allah! There is no god
> But He — the Living,
> The Self-Subsisting, Eternal.[76]

Psychologically speaking, it is a matter of growing up. Psychotherapist Sheldon Kopp writes: "Growing up often means facing the anguished isolation of no longer belonging as we wander in exile through a strange world that makes no sense."[77]

There may or may not be a divine power that helps us live with such courage, but in either case there is in our own humanity, as Nietzsche points out, a resource not to be forgotten—the ability to dance and laugh. *Thus Spoke Zarathustra*:

> You higher humans, your worst is: you have not learned at all to dance, how one must dance—to dance over yourselves! What does it matter that you went wrong or failed!
>
> How much is yet possible! So *learn* how to laugh at yourselves! Lift up your hearts, you good dancers, high! higher! And also do not forget the good laugh!
>
> This crown of the laughing, this rosary-crown: to you, my brothers [and sisters], I throw this crown! I have pronounced it holy to laugh; you higher humans, learn from me—laugh![78]

Notes

1. Walter Kaufmann, introduction to *The Portable Nietzsche*, by Friedrich Nietzsche (Middlesex, Eng.: Penguin Books, 1968), 1.

2. Friedrich Nietzsche, *Thus Spoke Zarathustra: A Book for All and None*, in *The Portable Nietzsche*, ed. Walter Kaufmann (N.Y.: Penguin, 1968 [1883-85]), 304, 322.

3. Kaufmann, introduction, *Portable Nietzsche*, 1.

4. Note from 1874, in Friedrich Nietzsche, *The Portable Nietzsche*, ed. Walter Kaufmann (N.Y.: Penguin, 1968), 50.

5. Friedrich Nietzsche, *Beyond Good and Evil: Prelude to a Philosophy of the Future*, trans. Walter Kaufmann (N.Y.: Vintage; Random House, 1966 [1886]), 201, §257.

6. Nietzsche, *Beyond Good*, 89, §146.

7. This list of ailments is from Ronald Hayman, *Nietzsche* (N.Y.: Routledge, 1999), 11.

8. Hayman, *Nietzsche*, 11.

9. Friedrich Nietzsche, *The Gay Science: with a prelude in rhymes and an appendix of songs*, trans. Walter Kaufmann (N.Y.: Vintage, 1974 [1882, 1887]), 273-274, §341.

10. Friedrich Nietzsche, *Ecce Homo*, trans. Walter Kaufmann (N.Y.: Vintage; Random House, 1967 [1888]), 258.

11. Norman Rich, *The Age of Nationalism and Reform: 1850-1890*, 2nd ed. (N.Y. & London: W. W. Norton, 1977), xi.

12. Nietzsche, *Thus Spoke Zarathustra*, 160-161.

13. Nietzsche, *Gay Science*, 339, §377.

14. Stearns, *1848*, 181, 244-246.

15. Emile Durkheim, *The Division of Labor in Society*, trans. George Simpson (N.Y. and London: The Free Press, 1933 [1893]); Emile Durkheim, *Suicide: A Study in Sociology*, trans. John A. Spaulding and George Simpson, ed. George Simpson (N.Y.: The Free Press, 1951 [1897]).

16. Alan Wells, "Mass Society," in *Encyclopedia of Sociology*, (Guilford, Conn.: The Dushkin Publishing Group, 1974), 172. See also Peter Glasner, "Mass," in *Fifty Key Words: Sociology*, ed. David Martin, 44-45 (Richmond, Va.: John Knox Press, 1970).

17. Rich, *Age of Nationalism*, 47.

18. Nietzsche, *Beyond Good*, 174, §241.

19. See Rich, *Age of Nationalism*, 27-31.

20. This brief biography follows Walter Kaufmann, *Nietzsche: Philosopher, Psychologist, Antichrist*, 4th ed. (Princeton, N.J.: Princeton University Press, 1974), chap. one.

21. Kaufmann, *Nietzsche*, 22-23.

22. Kaufmann, *Nietzsche*, 23-24.

23. Quoted in Karl Jaspers, *Nietzsche: An Introduction to the Understanding of His Philosophical Activity*, trans. Charles F. Wallraff and Frederick J. Schmitz (South Bend, Ind.: Regnery/Gateway, 1965), 28.

24. Kaufmann, *Nietzsche*, 25-26.

25. Kaufmann, *Nietzsche*, 26.

26. Jaspers, *Nietzsche*, 29.

27. Jaspers, *Nietzsche*, 29.

28. See especially Friedrich Nietzsche, *The Birth of Tragedy*, trans. Walter Kaufmann (N.Y.: Vintage; Random House, 1967 [1872, 1886]); Friedrich Nietzsche, *The Case of Wagner*, trans. Walter Kaufmann (N.Y.: Vintage; Random House, 1967 [1888]); Friedrich Nietzsche, *Nietzsche Contra Wagner*, in *The Portable Nietzsche*, ed. Walter Kaufmann (N.Y.: Penguin, 1968 [1888]).

29. Quoted by Kaufmann, *Nietzsche*, 31; from *Ecce Homo* II 6.

30. See Kaufmann, *Nietzsche*, 33-34.

31. Walter Kaufmann, introduction to *The Case of Wagner*, by Friedrich Nietzsche (N.Y.: Vintage Books; Random House, 1967), 149-150.

32. Kaufmann, *Nietzsche*, 39.

33. Quoted by Kaufmann, *Nietzsche*, 44.

34. Kaufmann, *Nietzsche*, 47-64.

35. Kaufmann, *Nietzsche*, 65-66.

36. Kaufmann, *Nietzsche*, 70.

37. Kaufmann, *Nietzsche*, 69.

38. Perhaps not an exact, word-for-word quotation. Alfred Gough and Miles Millar, writers, "Premiere," *Smallville*, prod. Gough, Millar, Mike Tolin, Brian Robbins, and Joe Davola; dir. David Nutter. Warner Bros. Television. KSMO, Kansas City. October 26, 2001.

39. Quoted in Kaufmann, *Nietzsche*, 52.

40. Friedrich Nietzsche, *The Will To Power*, trans. Walter Kaufmann and R. J. Hollingdale, ed. Walter Kaufmann (N.Y.: Vintage; Random House, 1967 [1901]), 267, §481.

41. Fragment from 1873, in Nietzsche, *Portable*, 46-47.

42. Friedrich Nietzsche, *On The Genealogy of Morals*, trans. Walter Kaufmann and R. J. Hollingdale (N.Y.: Vintage; Random House, 1967 [1887]), 25, I 1.

43. Nietzsche, *Beyond Good*, 41, II:29.

44. Nietzsche, *Will to Power*, 367, §688.

45. Nietzsche, *Thus Spoke Zarathustra*, 214.

46. Nietzsche, *Thus Spoke Zarathustra*, 315.

47. Nietzsche, *Thus Spoke Zarathustra*, 314.

48. Nietzsche, *Gay Science*, 150, §98; see also discussion in Kaufmann, *Nietzsche*, 244-246.

49. Nietzsche, *Beyond Good*, 154, §225.

50. See Nietzsche, *Beyond Good*, 48, II:36; 123, III:14.

51. See Nietzsche, *Genealogy*, 45-48, I:13-14.

52. See, for example, William Lloyd Newell, *The Secular Magi: Marx, Freud, and Nietzsche on Religion* (N.Y.: The Pilgrim Press, 1986), 142-143, 179; but see also pp. 183-185.

53. Nietzsche, *Genealogy*, 93-94, II:23; see also Friedrich Nietzsche, *Twilight of the Idols*, in *The Portable Nietzsche*, ed. Walter Kaufmann (N.Y.: Penguin, 1968 [1889]), 554.

54. Nietzsche, *Portable*, 52-53.

55. Nietzsche, *Portable*, 68.

56. Nietzsche, *Portable*, 76-77.

57. Nietzsche, *Portable*, 52-53.

58. Nietzsche, *Portable*, 80.

59. Nietzsche, *Portable*, 81.

60. Nietzsche, *Ecce Homo*, 236-237.

61. Nietzsche, *Gay Science*, 181, §125.

62. Nietzsche, *Gay Science*, 185, §130.

63. Nietzsche, *Gay Science*, 256, §326.

64. Nietzsche, *Beyond Good*, 75-76, §III:62.

65. Friedrich Nietzsche, *The Antichrist*, in *The Portable Nietzsche*, trans. Walter Kaufmann, (Middlesex, Eng.: Penguin, 1968 [1888]), 596, §26.

66. Nietzsche, *Thus Spoke Zarathustra*, 314.

67. Nietzsche, *Antichrist*, 571, §5.

68. Nietzsche, *Thus Spoke Zarathustra*, 185; Nietzsche, *Antichrist*, 612, §39.

69. Nietzsche, *Will to Power*, 113, §191.

70. Schubert M. Ogden, *The Reality of God and Other Essays* (N.Y.: Harper & Row, 1966).

71. Dag Hammarskjöld, *Markings*, trans. Leif Sjöberg & W. H. Auden (N.Y.: Alfred A. Knopf, 1964), 11.

72. Nietzsche, *Ecce Homo*, 326, IV 1.

73. Quoted in Toby Lester, "Oh, Gods!" *The Atlantic Monthly*, February 2002, 38.

74. See Mircea Eliade, *Patterns in Comparative Religion*, trans. Rosemary Sheed (N.Y.: New American Library, 1958), chapters 2 and 7.

75. Nietzsche, *Thus Spoke Zarathustra*, 215.

76. *The Meaning of The Holy Qur'an*, trans. 'Abdullah Yusuf 'Ali (Beltsville, Md.: Amana Publications, 1422 AH/2001 AC), 3:2 [hereafter *Holy Qur'an*].

77. Sheldon Kopp, *An End To Innocence: Facing Life Without Illusions* (Toronto: Bantam, 1978), 4.

78. Friedrich Nietzsche, *Also Sprach Zarathustra: Ein Buch für Alle und Keinen*, in *Friedrich Nietzsche: Werke in Zwei Bänden*, Band I (München: Carl Hanser Verlag, 1967 [1883-85]), 753-754 [translation mine].

Chapter 8

Society Is the Soul of Religion
Modern Critics of Religion: Emile Durkheim
(1858-1917)

Emile Durkheim was enormously influential on the cultural life of France, especially on the development of the social sciences.[1] Outside France, he is not widely known except among scholars, mainly social scientists and students of religion.

Of the six modern thinkers we're examining, Durkheim is different from the others because he displayed no hostility toward religion. He did not share the negative evaluation of religion manifested in the writings of Voltaire, Marx, Nietzsche, Freud, and Russell. In fact, he seemed quite sympathetic to religion, even though he himself was not a believer. He viewed the mythologies of religion as incorrect interpretations. He writes that, while religion is always a true reflection of its culture, still it is "mistaken in regard to the real nature of things: science has proved it."[2]

Although he did not share the antipathy toward religion that our other Enlightenment humanists manifested, he supported quite actively policies in the Third Republic of France that challenged the hold of religion on the culture. In particular, he supported removing public education from under church control and putting it under a secular state. Durkheim desired the security and stability of the Third Republic of France. The Catholic church was largely aligned with the reactionary monarchical interests who preferred a return to the *ancien regime*—the old regime of the French monarchy. His political sympathies were with liberal, republican government. He also believed religion could no longer be a solidifying force in modern societies. The future development of modern societies, Durkheim believed, would have to be secular and guided by science, particularly a science of society. Durkheim believed that "scientific thought is only a more perfect form of religious thought," and it would be "natural," then, to anticipate religion progressively giving way to science.[3]

Some Historical Context[4]

Most European countries saw a lot of change in the nineteenth century, but probably no country experienced more tumult and upheaval than France. Historian, Albert Guérard, writes: "For eight centuries," until the French Revolution, "the French had been obstinately loyal to the same dynasty," even "under the most tragic circumstances, when the king was a child and when he was a prisoner, when he was a wastrel and when he was a madman."[5] But for the next hundred years, every generation of the French would witness major political upheavals that changed or threatened the governments under which they lived.

The French Revolution began in 1789, resulting in explosive change, including the dethronement of the monarchy in 1792 and the Reign of Terror in 1793-1794. The popular General Napoleon Bonaparte took supreme power in a coup in 1799 and was made emperor of the first French empire in 1804. In 1815 after the decisive defeat of Napoleon, the Bourbon Monarchy was restored by the Congress of Vienna. The revolutionary upheavals of 1830 led to the establishment of a constitutional monarchy. The Second Republic arose out of the revolution of 1848. The Second Empire was established in 1852 when Louis-Napoleon, nephew of Napoleon (Napoleon III), engineered a Coup d'État. When the French were defeated in the Franco-Prussian War of 1870-1871 and Napoleon III was captured, "the Second Empire collapsed."[6] The Third Republic was established and would last until World War II.

The Third Republic seemed particularly fragile.[7] Lewis Coser notes that the "constitution of 1875 was framed by monarchists who expected the Republic soon to give way to a return of the Bourbons."[8] An attempt by the president to establish a strong, central presidency largely independent of parliament was defeated in 1879 by moderates and the left. France was controlled for the next two decades by a "moderate Republican left." Probably its most significant accomplishment was to wrest control of public education away from the Catholic Church. The government remained deeply divided by the radical right, the radical left, and moderates—none with a majority. Conflict and scandal tended to shake the public's confidence in its political leaders. The famous Dreyfus affair broke out in 1896. An innocent military captain, Alfred Dreyfus, was falsely accused of treason. The accusation, trial, and sentencing were all tinged with elements of anti-Semitism; Dreyfus was Jewish.[9]

> By 1898 almost the entire educated elite of France was committed to one side or the other. The Dreyfus affair shook French society to its very foundations. It pitted the liberal anticlerical defenders of the Republic against the Church and the army, the left-wing intellectuals against the nationalists, the Sorbonne

against the traditionalist judiciary, and the local school teacher against the resident priest. Finally the defenders of Dreyfus won their case, and the Republic survived.[10]

Underlying the political struggles were, of course, ongoing geo-economic changes. France was industrializing and urbanizing. The Third Republic of "France was Europe's third and the world's fourth industrial power."[11] Although fifty-five percent of the population was still rural in 1914, forty-four cities had over 50,000 inhabitants, and 7.5 million French lived in these cities, "as compared with 2.5 million in 1870."[12] Workers were beginning to organize. Socialist groups of varying stripes were developing, but their own fragmentation inhibited their influence. "The Third Republic continued to be operated by the middle class, and despite pious proclamations to the contrary, it remained devoted to the furtherance of middle-class aims and interests."[13]

Some Biography[14]

Emile Durkheim was born April 15, 1858, in Épinal in Lorraine, a northeastern region of France. Thus he was twelve and thirteen years of age during the Franco-Prussian War of 1870-1871, when part of Lorraine came under the control of the German Reich.

His father was an important Rabbi, and it was thought that Emile, too, would become a rabbi. He even attended rabbinical school for a while. But he broke with family expectations and traditions, eventually declaring himself an agnostic.

At eighteen, Durkheim went to study at the *Ecole Normale Supérieure*. While there, he became a member of an important group of intellectuals. He developed strong political attitudes in support of representative democracy and progressive social reform.

He spent the years from 1882 to 1887 teaching in provincial public schools (*lycées*), with the exception of a few months in 1885-1886 when he did some study in Germany. Not long after returning to France, he married Louise Dreyfus, about whom little is known.

Durkheim's intellectual and political concerns led him to view sociology as the discipline best suited to deal with those concerns. At the time, sociology was not established as a discipline; in fact, it was viewed with some suspicion. Part of the reason was that the creator of the term *sociology*, Auguste Comte (1798-1857), had wanted to turn sociology into a new kind of religion of humanity. It became one of Durkheim's goals and, in many ways, his accomplishment to establish sociology as a distinct and respected academic discipline in its own right.

Durkheim acquired a position as lecturer in social science and education at the University of Bordeaux—a position created for him because the director of

French higher education liked Durkheim's ideas and political views. In his inaugural lecture Durkheim held up sociology as the discipline with the potential of overcoming many of the nagging problems of philosophy, history, and law. His efforts to establish sociology as the first among equals in the study of human society was met with considerable controversy among elements of academia.

As a social philosopher in the intellectual and political context of the time, Durkheim had to come to terms with Marxism and laissez-faire capitalism. He rejected both, endorsing a reforming socialism. In other words, he steered a course between the political extremes and promoted use of the state as the vehicle for reform, especially "through furthering equality of opportunity."[15] He promoted the development of what we today would call the welfare state and the mixed economy.

Durkheim concentrated his energy and efforts primarily on education and sociology. Although not a political activist himself, he remained in personal contact with many of the people who were—"politicians, industrialists, journalists, even military men."[16] And he involved himself in two political disputes—the Dreyfus affair and the struggle over control of public education in France.

In 1898 Durkheim founded *L'Année sociologique* (Sociology Annual), probably the first sociology journal. The journal sought "to provide a comprehensive yearly review of sociological literature and related works in the 'specialized social sciences' of economics, demography, geography, ethics, and law."[17]

In 1902 Durkheim took a position in education at the Sorbonne, becoming a full professor in 1906. His chair was renamed in 1913 as a Chair in Education and Sociology. His influence was greatly enhanced by the fact that he taught a course in the history of education in France that every student who would teach in the public schools was required to take.

After 1914, Durkheim immersed himself in activities related to World War I, which hampered his own work. He died at 59 in 1917, brokenhearted because his only son, a promising intellect in his own right, was killed in the war.

Durkheim on Religion

A sociological approach by its very nature views religion as a social product; that is, as something largely constructed by people in interaction in particular times and places. Sociologists, since their approach is scientific, will talk about studying religion from a perspective of "methodological atheism." What this means is that for the purposes of research and study, they will make no assumption about the reality or unreality of God. Probably it is better termed methodological agnosticism, but a sociological approach does mean viewing religion as a social product. This does not mean that sociologists of religion are without religious faith; only that they must do their research and studies while suspending their own theological beliefs, if any. When Durkheim studied religion, he himself was not a believer. Apparently he claimed to be an agnostic.[18]

Guiding Durkheim's work was his concern to provide sociological understanding that would help modern societies threatened by the disintegrating forces of industrialization and secularization. He was particularly concerned about nation-building for his beloved France and the Third Republic.[19]

Durkheim argued that early societies (called *primitive* in his day), were relatively small and held together by widely shared values and perceptions that were based on an elementary division of labor. With smaller societies, without many different social roles, with a great deal of day-to-day, face-to-face interaction people tended naturally to think and feel alike. In other words, there was great similarity from one person to another, so maintaining social cohesion was not so very difficult. In such societies, claimed Durkheim, the individual person is entirely a part of the whole. There is little or no sense of individuality because "the individual personality is absorbed into the collective personality."[20] Such a society reaffirmed its collective sense of self and reinforced its social relations and norms through its religious ideas by the regular enactment of religious ritual.

In the large, modern, industrialized societies it is different. There are different levels of class; people work many different kinds of jobs; they participate consequently in various subcultures. They are interrelated with most others in society in anonymous, sometimes even distant, ways. Consequently individuals tend to experience the world differently from one another. The very fact that individuals living in the same society have vastly different daily life experiences means that they become different in their feelings and ideas about life. This is the nature and source of modern individualism. Durkheim thought that such a society is held together by the interdependence of individuals filling diverse roles.[21] For example, when I get up in the morning, I drink coffee grown and produced by coffee growers, processed by coffee processers, delivered by truck drivers, to grocery stores run by a staff of grocers, where I purchased it by driving there in a car manufactured by automakers on streets maintained by road maintenance crews; furthermore, the coffee manufacturing, the grocery stores, and the roads are all governed by rules developed by legislators and regulators, and enforced by various kinds of policing authorities. Any single activity of the day can be viewed as such a locus of intersecting roles that spread out to include almost everyone.

Durkheim recognized, however, that the phenomenon of interdependent roles was not enough to hold modern societies together. Societies were not based only on their daily interactions of cooperation and competition; they were also based on an emotional sense of belonging and thus a willingness to fill one's roles and play by the rules. Durkheim was concerned that as the realm of the individual personality grows, the hold of the collective becomes weaker.[22] This carries a threat to the social order that the interdependence generated by the division of labor by itself cannot handle.

Durkheim believed that modern societies need something like the religious rituals by which "primitive" societies re-enacted their communal narrative. However, in the modern world religion is losing its hold as a unifying force for society. We cannot imagine, he writes, what the "feasts and ceremonies of the future" will be. "The great things of the past which filled our fathers with enthusiasm do not excite the same ardour in us . . . ; but as yet there is nothing to replace them." In other words, "the old gods are growing old or already dead [sic], and others are not yet born."[23]

Durkheim's concerns led him to undertake a study of religion by which he hoped to identify its earliest forms in human history. Published in 1912 as *Les Formes élémentaires de la view religieuse* (*The Elementary Forms of Religious Life*), it was a second-hand study primarily of Australian aboriginal tribes' and clans' religious beliefs and practices, but including also those of some of the North American native tribes.

Social scientific critics of Durkheim's study of religion have highlighted many problems with *The Elementary Forms*. They have raised good questions particularly about the reliability of his sources and whether his research supports his conclusions.[24] It seems to me, though, that Durkheim's study is better viewed as an illustration of his theory of religion. In other words, he was marshalling evidence to support his hunch and presumption that religion is the embodiment of society's collective sense of self. By that standard, there is prima facie evidence that Durkheim's insights have much going for them, even if his study does not always meet the strict principles of scientific methodology.

The Australian clans' religious practices were identified by researchers as totemism, which was thought by many, in Durkheim's day, to be the earliest form of religion. In totemism human groups are paired mythologically with animals, plants, and sometimes inanimate objects in nature. These pairings are fundamental for the identity and distinctiveness of each group. There is a historical echo of totemism in the United States where individual states have their own state bird and state flower. A relationship of greater similarity to totemism holds between modern nations and their flags. In totemism, just as in flag-waving nationalism, various rituals function to reinforce the identification of a group with its totem.[25]

Durkheim felt that the Australian tribes were "primitive" enough that they would be close to the kind of society human beings developed at the dawn of human history—at least as close as we could obtain. They would also be easier to study because, so Durkheim believed, primitive societies are characterized by uniformity and simplicity.[26] By studying their religious practices, then, we could be confident of discovering religion's basic reality; i.e., its "elementary forms."

The aim of *The Elementary Forms of the Religious Life*, according to Durkheim, is to explain the essential nature of humanity.[27] He argues that religion is the most basic human social reality—the reality from which everything else important and essential to human beings arose.[28]

Durkheim points out that social systems are, as wholes, greater than the sum of their parts.[29] This means that society is more than a collection of individuals, and society has a reality of its own, over and above individuals. "Religious representations are collective representations which express" this social reality.[30]

For this reason, says Durkheim, human beings experience themselves as double—two beings in one. One is the individual organism that needs rest, food, water, and so on. The other is the social being, which is shaped and defined by the cultural reality of the society. So individuals come to feel that the rules of society and its ideas exist both inside and outside themselves.[31] This is how people come to have a sense of transcendence beyond their individual selves.

Religion is made up of two basic categories, according to Durkheim: beliefs and rites. Religious belief classifies all things into the categories of sacred or profane. (By *profane*, Durkheim means what today we call *secular*, which I will use to avoid confusion.) People can pass from one to the other, but the two are opposed to each other. Religious rites are the prescribed behaviors for being in the presence of sacred realities.[32]

Religion also requires a community. It is, says Durkheim, "inseparable from the idea of a Church." Individual members will have their own take and twist on things sacred and secular, but this does not change the reality that religion is basically a social reality that is shared with others.[33] Durkheim writes: "Thus we arrive at the following definition: *A religion is a unified system of beliefs and practices relative to sacred things, that is to say, things set apart and forbidden—beliefs and practices which unite into one single moral community called a Church, all those who adhere to them.*"[34]

Through his analysis of totemism, Durkheim argues that society has everything necessary to generate the idea of the divine: a force superior to individuals, a force on which individuals are perpetually dependent, and one that requires of them the disciplines and sacrifices for social life. "Since it is in spiritual ways that social pressure exercises itself, it could not fail to give men the idea that outside themselves there exist one or several powers . . . upon which they depend."[35] In other words, the society projects its own collective sense of self onto the universe, and misinterprets it as a sacred force (god).

Our experience of the mundane realities of everyday life gives rise to the form of consciousness that is secular, and the felt influence of the collective gives rise to the sense of the sacred. Society consecrates particularly loved individuals, objects, and ideas, and by doing so, generates feelings and attitudes of sacredness toward them. This consciousness of a sacred reality, set apart from everyday secular life, is generated through the practice of tribal ceremonies. The collective rituals of society give birth to the religious idea and endow it with emotional power, says Durkheim. It is this process by which individuals come to have strong emotional attachments to the symbols of religion and thus also to the community.[36]

Religion is not hallucination or illusion, says Durkheim. Indeed, a force, external to the individual exists; "it is society." Religion "is a system of ideas with which the individuals represent to themselves the society of which they are members, and the obscure but intimate relations which they have with it." Whatever other functions religion may fulfill, this is primary.[37]

Durkheim notes that religions typically include some idea of spiritual beings, especially an idea of the soul. We can see then, says Durkheim, that the soul comes from the internalized sense of one's group, particularly in the form of the conscience. The body is sensed as a part of secular reality, while the soul is seen as part of sacred reality. But, of course, the body is the house of the soul. In this way, the individual, the group, and the religious symbol are all related in a sacred way.[38]

Individual souls come to be seen as surviving the death of the body for the obvious reason that, although the individual may die, the clan continues to exist. The sacred force, the sense of the social collective, transcends the life of the individual, and the soul, seen as a part of that force, is then viewed as immortal.[39]

Once the idea of spiritual beings has "been established, it naturally spreads to the higher spheres of the religious life, and thus mythical personalities of a superior order are born." The individual clans realize they are part of a larger tribe, so the idea of a god greater than the clan evolves. In this ongoing mythological expansion, religious beliefs historically have tended to flow over the boundaries of any one society to include others. In this way more complex religions develop until ultimately we get the great monotheistic and universalistic religions.[40]

It is also easy to see, says Durkheim, how society maintains itself in the specific religious rites. In rites of initiation, for example, young men are initiated into the culture typically through practices of abstinence, privations, and suffering. These practices of discipline and self-denial prepare them for participating in social life since the welfare of the community requires moral and social discipline.[41] Rituals typically also include some sense of sacrifice; some of them are primarily sacrificial rites. What is actually happening is that individuals are surrendering ("sacrificing") themselves to the "higher" authority of the society, represented in the beliefs as the divine.[42] There are also rites of mourning that help society deal with death. There are commemorative rites in which the society rehearses the mythical past of the group. All rites serve, in one way or another, to intensify individuals' sense of identification with the group as a whole.[43]

It is important, says Durkheim in his conclusion, that we recognize that religion is then an idealization of society. It is not a mere reflection of the social order; it is a higher consciousness—the collective consciousness and conscience of the society.[44] Religion is how society represents itself to its individual members.

Some Reflection

In some ways Durkheim's approach is more challenging to people of faith than are the anti-religion philosophers. Certainly Voltaire, Marx, and Nietzsche made acute observations about the historical conditioning of religion, but they did not pursue it in nearly as thorough or systematic a manner as did Durkheim. Although Voltaire was highly critical of religion, he may have been a believer and did not reject religion entirely. Marx and Nietzsche, both hyper-critical of religion, identified serious problems of religion, but by and large the person of faith could accept the gist of their criticisms without rejecting religion, per se. Durkheim was not hostile to religion, and he was the first, or certainly one of the first, to display brilliant social analysis that sought to show precisely how religion arises among humanity and how its origin is found in the interactions and rituals of society itself. As we have seen, he also offered a particularly thorough analysis, trying to explain all the basic elements of religious life. While some of Durkheim's sociological assumptions and the way he used his evidence are vulnerable to criticism,[45] his basic argument about religion is a powerful one that challenges believers to question whether the "God" they worship is anything more than the "spirit" of their own community.

Furthermore, Durkheim agrees with religion's own claim that the idea of the holy cannot be entirely reduced to psychological states of fear or desire, nor to awe before the forces of nature, nor to a tool for political manipulation. For both, religion and Durkheim, there is a transcendent source for religious sentiment. But whereas for religion, it is the reality of the Divine, for Durkheim this transcendent force is society itself. Durkheim believed that religion had "given birth to all that is essential in society . . . because the idea of society is the soul of religion."[46]

Durkheim was talking about society as a whole and specifically the ideal, moral force of the social collective. A significant problem for social scientists is that society is not a thing. Society is a collection of individuals who share a location and a culture. We can sense or feel it through what we call social pressure, so it is real. However, it is not a thing we can see or touch or measure. What is seen are, as Durkheim pointed out, only its representations—language, law, ritual, artifacts, symbols, etc. We infer the reality of a moral force outside ourselves from our feelings of its presence and from the cultural signs and symbols that express it. Durkheim's argument here is an important and essential anthropological insight, but to also say that this moral force felt in society is entirely identical with the cultural reality of society is an inferential leap of faith. Actually Durkheim acknowledges this in an earlier essay thereby implicitly exposing the arbitrariness of his anti-theistic argument in *The Elementary Forms*:

> In the world of experience I know of only one being that possesses a richer and more complex moral reality than our own, and that is the collective being. I am mistaken; there is another being which could play the same part, and that is the Divinity. Between God and society lies the choice. I shall not examine here the reasons that may be advanced in favour of either solution, both of which are coherent. I can only add that I myself am quite indifferent to this choice, since I see in the Divinity only society transfigured and symbolically expressed.[47]

By Durkheim's logic, since this social totality is available to us only inferentially and indirectly, the theist could just as easily turn Durkheim's argument on its head and make it a justification for belief in a transcendental divine reality. The argument could go something like this: If even the earliest, most "primitive" people sensed a sacred and moral power, even without the benefit of an institutional superstructure of priests and rituals and sacred scriptures, it implies the existence of a transcendent reality that could be divinity.

The apologist for traditional Christianity, C. S. Lewis, made just such a case in his *Mere Christianity*. He argues that human beings are "haunted by the idea of a sort of behaviour they ought to practise, what you might call fair play, or decency, or morality, or the Law of Nature." It appears to be a law of nature because it is universal, and nobody in particular seems to have created it. "It begins to look as if we shall have to admit that there is more than one kind of reality, that...there is something above and beyond the ordinary facts of men's behaviour, and yet quite definitely real—a real law, which none of us made, but which we find pressing on us." Because of this, among other reasons, there seems to be "a Something which is directing the universe, and which appears in me as a law urging me to do right and making me feel responsible and uncomfortable when I do wrong."[48]

Of course, C. S. Lewis's argument is no sure proof for the reality of God. This is demonstrated by the plausibility of Durkheim's argument. But Durkheim's argument, as we have seen, is also no sure argument that Lewis is wrong.

There is simply an unbridgeable gap between the limited view of science and the unlimited views of theism. It seems to me that whenever thinkers try to bridge that gap, they end up inflating science into something more than it is or reducing religion to something less than it is. While C. S. Lewis seems to me to have not always been so good at seeing the limitations of his own arguments, he was good at seeing the limitations of others. He writes:

> Supposing science ever became complete so that it knew every single thing in the whole universe. Is it not plain that the questions, 'Why is there a universe?' 'Why does it go on as it does?' 'Has it any meaning?' would remain just as they were?[49]

In other words, as Ian Barbour writes, "science and theology ask fundamentally different sorts of questions, even if they interact at some points."[50]

Nevertheless, Durkheim is on to something correct and important. Once we have acknowledged the limitations of empirical science saying anything about the reality or unreality of the Holy, we can still recognize that religion is fundamentally a product of human culture. While Durkheim's argument cannot conclusively reduce the source of religious faith to culture, it does underscore rather powerfully that religion is all mixed up with the culture in which it is found. If one is not convinced of this by a casual look around at religion operating in one's culture, there is a great deal of social research since Durkheim that confirms it.[51] It has been and is quite common for religious adherents to lose sight of this rather mundane linkage of their own religion. Religion is typically much more "worldly" than its culture despisers imagine.

Durkheim's perspective points us to the importance of critically evaluating the cultural captivity of religion. This involves the possibility of seeing how religion manifests specific, historically conditioned ideas and practices which are themselves in conflict with either the higher ideals of the religion itself or the humanistic ideals of human decency and social justice or both. I once heard a Bible Church pastor say, "We make no apology. We do equate Americanism and Christianity." Such a sentiment would have dismayed Durkheim, as it did me, but Durkheim could have said, "See, I told you so."

Does this mean that religion is not divinely ordained? Is Durkheim correct that we must choose between God and society? Not necessarily; at least not logically. As long as one presumes divine presence or activity, the divine can be perceived quite logically operating in historical and natural formations, which is what most religions claim. But what does seem irrational and fairly incoherent is any claim that one's religion is somehow infallibly protected from "contamination" by culture. What Durkheim's work shows and what lots of subsequent social scientific research demonstrates is that religions manifest extraordinary influence from their time and place in history and culture. This challenges any claim to infallibility or eternal certainty for a particular religion. This should serve the cause of humility as well as tolerance of faith perspectives other than one's own.

To take Durkheim seriously is to recognize that our religious sentiments get all mixed up with our cultural, collective sense of self. One of the more obviously egregious examples—one about which I think everyone would today agree—was seen in the religious justification of American slavery.

James Henry Hammond was a governor of South Carolina and a United States Senator prior to the Civil War. But what he's most remembered for now in accounts of American history are his well-reasoned, cogent, clear defenses of slavery. And one of his most reasonable defenses of slavery, written in about 1858, defends it on biblical grounds.[52]

Hammond writes that "the first question we have to ask ourselves is whether [slavery] is contrary to the will of God as revealed to us in his Holy Scriptures—the only certain means given us to ascertain his will." Hammond recites the seventeenth verse of the twentieth chapter in Exodus: "Thou shalt not covet thy neighbor's house, thou shalt not covet they neighbor's wife, nor his manservant, nor his maidservant, nor his ox, nor his ass, nor any thing that is thy neighbor's." This is the tenth commandment. And Hammond points out that the plain meaning is that you should not "disturb your neighbor in the enjoyment of his property," and, furthermore, this sacred scripture recognizes manservants and maidservants as "consecrated property."

Then Hammond says it cannot be denied that the Hebrews were authorized by God to own slaves, and he refers to Leviticus, chapter 25. In that chapter the Hebrews are permitted to acquire slaves from the nations around them and from the aliens resident among them, and to keep those slaves as property that can be inherited by their children.[53]

Furthermore, Hammond continues, in biblical times, including the New Testament period, slavery even "in its most revolting form was everywhere visible," and it is not spoken against in any way in the Bible, even to suggest it should be less cruel. Rather, slavery seems to be regarded "as an established . . . inevitable condition of human society," and "they never hinted at such a thing as its termination on earth." Why, even "St. Paul actually apprehended a runaway slave and sent him [back] to his master!" Hammond concludes his argument with these sentiments:

> It is impossible, therefore, to suppose that slavery is contrary to the will of God. It is equally absurd to say that American slavery differs in form or principle from that of the chosen people. *We accept the Bible terms as the definition of our slavery, and its precepts as the guide of our conduct.* . . .
>
> I think, then, I may safely conclude, and I firmly believe, that American slavery is not only not a sin, but especially commanded by God through Moses and approved by Christ through his Apostles. And here I might close its defense; for what God ordains and Christ sanctifies should surely command the respect and toleration of man.

Hammond's argument is disturbingly clear, adequately logical, and "biblical." The kind of transhistorical, transcultural sociological perspective Durkheim displays so well in his analysis of religion helps us see the immorality and inhumanity in such perspectives.

In *Der schwarze Obelisk* [*The Black Obelisk*], Erich Maria Remarque's novel about Germany in the 1920s, the main character is in the business of selling tombstones and other stone monuments. He's also a veteran of World War I, watching with considerable dismay the rise of fanatical, right-wing nationalism in the midst of the stagflation and social upheaval of Weimar Germany. One day he starts thinking about a religious service surrounding the dedication of a monument he'd delivered:

> The pastors bless the monuments; each for his God. I often thought about that when we were ordered to attend worship while we were in the field [of battle], and the pastors from various denominations prayed for victory for the German weapons, just as likewise the English, French, Russian, American, Italian and Japanese spiritual leaders prayed for victory for their weapons of their lands, and I would imagine God as some kind of harried club president in a great predicament, especially when two opposed countries of the same faith were praying. For which one should he decide? For the one with the greatest population? Or the one with the most churches? Or where was his justice when he let one land win, and the other lose, although in the other they too prayed earnestly?[54]

Notes

1. See Henri Peyre, foreword to *Montesquieu and Rousseau: Forerunners of Sociology*, by Emile Durkheim (Ann Arbor: University of Michigan Press, 1975), v-vii.

2. Emile Durkheim, *The Elementary Forms of the Religious Life*, trans. Joseph Ward Swain (N.Y. and London: The Free Press, 1915 [1912]), 102.

3. Durkheim, *Elementary Forms*, 477; see also Robert Alun Jones, *Emile Durkheim: An Introduction to Four Major Works*, Masters of Social Theory, vol. 2 (Newbury Park, CA: Sage Publications, 1986), 150.

4. This section is informed by Lewis A. Coser, *Masters of Sociological Thought: Ideas in Historical and Social Context*, 2nd ed. (N.Y.: Harcourt Brace Jovanovich, 1977); Albert Guérard, *France: A Modern History* (Ann Arbor: The University of Michigan Press, 1959); Hobsbawm, *Age of Revolution*; Arno J. Mayer, *The Persistence of the Old Regime: Europe to the Great War* (N.Y.: Pantheon Books, 1981); and Rich, *Age of Nationalism*.

5. Guérard, *France*, 233.

6. Rich, *Age of Nationalism*, 184.

7. This discussion of the Third Republic follows closely Coser, *Masters*, 156-160.

8. Coser, *Masters*, 156.

9. Coser, *Masters*, 157-158.

10. Coser, *Masters*, 158-159.

11. Mayer, *Old Regime*, 71-53.

12. Mayer, *Old Regime*, 71-72.

13. Coser, *Masters*, 160.

14. The sources for the biographical information are primarily Anthony Giddens, *Émile Durkheim* (N.Y.: Penguin Books, 1978), 18-24; and Coser, *Masters*, 129-176.

15. Giddens, *Durkheim*, 21.

16. Coser, *Masters*, 171.

17. Giddens, *Durkheim*, 22.

18. Henri Peyre, "Durkheim: The Man, His Time, and His Intellectual Background," in *Essays on Sociology and Philosophy*, ed. Kurt H. Wolff, 3-31 (N.Y.: Harper Torchbooks; Harper & Row, 1960), 8.

19. Peyre, "Durkheim," 29.

20. Durkheim, *Division of Labor*, 131.

21. Durkheim, *Division of Labor*, 131.

22. Durkheim, *Division of Labor*, 131.

23. Durkheim, *Elementary Forms*, 475.

24. See Giddens, *Durkheim* and Jones, *Durkheim*.

25. For a clear discussion of totemism, see Noss, *Man's Religions*, 21.

26. Durkheim, *Elementary Forms*, 18.

27. Durkheim, *Elementary Forms*, 13.

28. Durkheim, *Elementary Forms*, 21-22.

29. See especially Emile Durkheim, *The Rules of Sociological Method*, trans. W. D. Halls, ed. Steven Lukes (N.Y.: The Free Press, 1982 [1895]).

30. Durkheim, *Elementary Forms*, 22.

31. Durkheim, *Elementary Forms*, 29-30.

32. Durkheim, *Elementary Forms*, 51-56.

33. Durkheim, *Elementary Forms*, 60-61.

34. Durkheim, *Elementary Forms*, 62.

35. Durkheim, *Elementary Forms*, 237, 239.

36. Durkheim, *Elementary Forms*, 243-252.

37. Durkheim, *Elementary Forms*, 253-257.

38. Durkheim, *Elementary Forms*, 273, 281-297, 299.

39. Durkheim, *Elementary Forms*, 304.

40. Durkheim, *Elementary Forms*, 320-333.

41. Durkheim, *Elementary Forms*, 348, 351, 352-355, 356.

42. Durkheim, *Elementary Forms*, 366, 377, 384, 388.

43. Durkheim, *Elementary Forms*, 366, 377, 389-390.

44. Durkheim, *Elementary Forms*, 468, 471.

45. See Jones, *Durkheim*, 152-155.

46. Durkheim, *Elementary Forms*, 466.

47. Emile Durkheim, "The Determination of Moral Facts," in *Sociology and Philosophy*, trans. D. F. Pocock (N.Y.: The Free Press, 1974 [1906]), 52.

48. Lewis, *Mere Christianity*, 26, 30, 34.

49. Lewis, *Mere Christianity*, 32..

50. Barbour, *Religion and Science*, 29.

51. For a few of the "classic" studies, see Weber, *Protestant Ethic*; Liston Pope, *Millhands & Preachers: A Study of Gastonia* (New Haven and London: Yale University Press, 1942); H. Richard Niebuhr, *The Social Sources of Denominationalism* (N.Y.: New American Library, 1957); Will Herberg, *Protestant—Catholic—Jew: An Essay in American Religious Sociology*, rev. (Garden City, N.Y.: Doubleday, 1960); Gerhard Lenski, *The Religious Factor: A Sociological Study of Religion's Impact on Politics, Economics, and Family Life* (Garden City, N.Y.: Doubleday & Co., 1961); Robert N. Bellah, "Civil Religion in America," *Daedalus*. 96, no. 1(winter 1967): 1-21.

52. Hammond, "Slavery Defended."

53. Leviticus 25:44-46.

54. Erich Maria Remarque, *Der schwarze Obelisk: Geschichte einer verspäteten Jugend* (Frankfurt/M: Ullstein, 1956), 104 [translation mine].

Chapter 9

Longing for a Father
Modern Critics of Religion: Sigmund Freud
(1856-1939)

Time magazine's 1999 series on "the 100 most influential people" of the twentieth century showed Sigmund Freud on the cover and featured him among the "century's 20 most influential scientists, thinkers, and inventors."[1] In the lead article, on Freud, Peter Gay wrote that "for good or ill, Sigmund Freud, more than any other explorer of the psyche, has shaped the mind of the twentieth century."[2]

Freud founded psychoanalysis almost single-handedly. Freudian depth psychology became the stack-pole from which most other psychologies had to define themselves; although psychology was older than Freudian thought. In *Pioneers of Psychology*, Raymond Fancher argues, "In fact, there is probably no area of research in personality or abnormal psychology that is untouched by the Freudian influence."[3] Much of Freud's thought has also inspired and challenged historians, philosophers, sociologists, and others.[4] His stress on the role of sexuality in human development scandalized a Western culture in many ways still heavily under the influence of Puritanical and Victorian norms against open discussion of anything sexual. That same stress on sexuality made Freudian thought both a popular target for jokes and easily dismissed by the sexually squeamish.

Within the social sciences no single theory is fully dominant. It is common today to identify any given social scientific field (economics, sociology, psychology, political science) as multi-paradigmatic. The competition between the adherents of various paradigms can be fierce. Furthermore, the social sciences deal with human social reality which is, of course, characterized by personal and political conflicts over values, priorities, and goals. So social scientific thought is quickly appropriated by combatants in culture wars.

Freud's theories certainly remain controversial among scholars and thera-
pists.[5] Freud's defenders and detractors, like those of Marx, manifest at times
excessive passion, probably for the usual reasons—the success of the psychoanalytic movement, psychoanalytic abuses, some of Freud's own personality
quirks and professional practices, the magnetic draw of creative and controversial pioneering thought, professional competition, and the reality of competing
theories. What is funny to the outside observer but infuriating to the critics of
psychoanalysis is that psychoanalytic theory itself contains the abusive potential
for dismissing its critics. It is possible to claim that the critics are in denial,
manifesting psychological resistance, even displaying an Oedipal-wish to kill
their fathers (of psychoanalytic thought, of course). And psychoanalysis's foun-
ders and defenders have at times been undisciplined about applying such arm-
chair diagnoses to critics.

Whether Freudian psychoanalysis will hold up in the long run of human history is impossible to say, but psychoanalytic theory has been a powerful current
of thought in modern culture. Peter Gay suggests, "The very fierceness of his
detractors are a wry tribute to the staying power of Freud's ideas."[6]

Some Historical Context[7]

To judge from the work of European historians, Vienna was the place to be in
1900. Turn-of-the-century (*Fin-de-Siècle*) Vienna was an unusually culturally
rich city, a place of surprising political developments, a crossroads for many of
the intellectual currents of Western civilization. Its artists and scientists were
giving birth to ideas and movements that would continue to generate interest and
debate for the rest of the twentieth century. Vienna was also the capital of the
Austro-Hungarian Empire, whose cultural and political conflicts would set the
stage for and finally spark the conflagration of World War I. *Fin-de-Siècle* Vienna is also associated with Freud not only because that is where he lived and
worked but also because his most famous work, *The Interpretation of Dreams*,
was published in November 1899.

Vienna, like other European capitals, was changing rapidly in the latter half
of the nineteenth century and the early years of the twentieth. The Habsburg
emperor Franz Josef razed the old fortifications around the city and built boule-
vards and magnificent public buildings, still standing today. The population of
Vienna increased rapidly. The Habsburg court was generous in sponsoring talent, skill and ambition. "To Vienna flocked Czechs and Magyars, Rumanians
and Croatians, Poles and Slovenes, representatives of every class and profession,
all with a desire to make a name in the world."[8] This included thousands of Jewish immigrants. They came to Vienna "as a refuge from persecution and a haven
of opportunity."[9] Freud's family was among them.

Jews entered many professions—those to which they were permitted—in
large numbers, but they were always aware, sometimes painfully, of anti-

Semitism. Freud's entire life was punctuated by acts of anti-Semitism—resulting eventually in emigration and exile. In Austria after 1867, with a new constitution of liberal reforms, Jews ceased to experience legal discrimination. In part, this was due to the dominance of liberal thought in Austrian politics. Freud, himself, like most Austrian Jews, was politically liberal. But social ostracism remained a reality. Even though they were "disproportionately important not only in bank-ing but in commerce, manufacture, and industry, as well as in the professions and the arts," Jews were still barred from the upper echelons of Austria's class system and remained largely politically impotent.[10]

Norman Rich has written: "The wealth of talent that poured into Vienna, the crosscurrents of culture, the competition among the nationalities, made the Habsburg capital a lively and exciting place, a rival to Paris as an intellectual and artistic center."[11] This intellectual and artistic center has come to be seen as an important birthplace of the fragmented and unmoored postmodern world. Carl Schorske offers up *Fin-de-Siècle* Vienna as the epitome of the fragmenta-tion of modern culture—a post-Nietzschean "whirl of infinite innovation, with each field [of high culture] proclaiming independence of the whole, each part in turn falling into parts."[12] The cultural innovations and permutations by Vienna's intelligentsia had tremendous influence on Western culture, but they also put more players on the field of cultural debate and included revolutionary chal-lenges to established traditions.

These radical changes of culture were taking place at the dawn of an era of political cataclysm. Austria, as a historical entity, began modestly during the 900s CE and developed over the centuries into an empire of power and influ-ence. It was retitled Austria-Hungary in 1867 when it came to an agreement with the Hungarians to be a dual monarchy. Austria-Hungary was an empire of multi-ethnic division, dissension, and conflict. It was broken up after defeat in World War I, with Poland, Czechoslovakia, Hungary, and Yugoslavia (a union of Serbs, Croats, and Slovenes) going their own way in newly independent states.

The first Austrian Republic was established in November 1918. It would last until the *Anschluss* (annexation) by Nazi Germany in 1938. Three months after the annexation, the Jewish Sigmund Freud and his family made their escape into exile in England.

Some Biography[13]

Sigmund Freud was born May 6, 1856, in Freiberg, Moravia (now Príbor in the Czech Republic). His parents were Jewish. However, they were not practicing, although his father would read the Bible, and Freud remained fascinated with the Old Testament throughout his life. His father was a wool merchant. Freud was given the name Sigismund Schlomo; later he shortened it to Sigmund and avoided using Schlomo entirely.[14]

Freud's immediate family was confusing for a young child. His mother was the third wife of and twenty years younger than his father. This meant Freud had a half brother older than his mother and a nephew older than Freud himself.[15] He was to have five sisters and a brother.

They were poor when he was born. They moved to Leipzig in 1859 and then to Vienna in 1860. Freud always had mixed feelings about Vienna, declaring his distaste for it frequently.[16]

As a child, Sigi, as he was called, was quite gifted. His parents expected great things from him and indulged him accordingly. Peter Gay writes: "From his childhood days on, an assertive display of intellectual independence, controlled rage, physical bravery, and self-respect as a Jew coalesced into a highly personal, indestructible amalgam in Freud's character."[17]

Even as a child Freud had been very studious. He entered medical studies at the University of Vienna in 1873 with tremendous ambition. He was "outwardly self-assured, brilliant in school and voracious in his reading."[18] While a student, Freud became enamored with science, especially for its potential and promise, in his view, for enlightening and helping humanity.

At the university he encountered anti-Semitism. He said, "I never understood why I should be ashamed of my descent or, as one was beginning to say, my race." Freud had great appreciation for his professors, among other reasons, because, in their liberalism, they were fairly intolerant of anti-Semitism. [19]

His university studies were interrupted by a required year in military service, which he found boring.[20]

In 1882 he left the confines of the university laboratories for a position at Vienna's General Hospital. He stayed there for three years.[21]

Also in 1882 he met Martha Bernays with whom he fell in love. They became engaged two months after meeting. Their engagement lasted for four years while Freud tried to establish himself in a practice lucrative enough to support them comfortably. Most of that time they were apart since she lived with her mother near Hamburg, Germany. At that distance, Freud struggled with his romantic attachment and was burdened by bouts of jealousy. These disturbed him greatly, in part, because they tended to undermine his self-confidence.[22]

As an impoverished physician with his love many miles away in Germany, he read widely. This included Nietzsche. He continued researches in anatomy and neurology, but he was increasingly preoccupied with the human mind. He began "to concentrate on psychiatry, with an eye to the income."[23]

He spent much of the fall and winter, 1885-1886, in Paris on a travel-study grant. There he found himself dazzled by the work of Jean Martin Charcot. Charcot was doing groundbreaking studies of hysteria and the use of hypnosis as a cure. Back in Vienna Freud sought to emulate Charcot's use of hypnosis in his own professional study and work.[24] Most of his colleagues in Vienna were not very receptive to this use of hypnosis, viewing it as a kind of charlatanism. Later he himself would abandon it in favor of the technique of free association—the "talking cure."

In 1886 he resigned from the hospital, and set up private practice. He had wanted to pursue pure research, but the lack of financial resources made that prohibitive. Piecing together various income sources, including wedding gifts, he and Martha were married in September. They would have six children. He was always busy and quite preoccupied with his therapy, research and writing, but he remained an attentive and devoted father and husband.[25]

Freud made his practice also a matter of research and the source of his developing theory of psychoanalysis. By 1892 he had developed the basic outline of his psychoanalytic practice. He realized that psychology had become his passion in life. He developed the wish to found and develop a fully scientific psychology[26]—which is, of course, what he did.

It began with publication of *Studies In Hysteria* in 1895, co-authored with Josef Breuer. Freud proceeded—through publications and lectures, the cultivation of followers and colleagues, the founding of professional societies and journals—to establish psychoanalysis as a theory of the mind, a therapeutic practice, and a framework for analyzing human culture and history. By the time he died in 1939, in England, his name and his theories were of world-renown. Many of his concepts—such as slip of the tongue, the unconscious, repression, id, ego, and superego—were known by people who never read him, as were such popular phrases as the "Freudian slip."

Freud on Religion

Freud's thought changed over time, and there is excellent record of those changes because Freud wrote and published prolifically. The changes are significant enough that many accounts of his work take a chronological approach. Even though Freud was quite dogmatic about the basic principles of psychoanalysis, he tried to be a good scientist by regularly pointing out that his views were not finally and ultimately complete. He typically presented his views as the current state of understanding, still needing further research. I will not try to trace Freud's development. Rather, I include here an admittedly sketchy account of his psychological theory as the framework for his interpretation of religion.[27]

Human beings are born as organisms of instinctual drives and needs. However, they are entirely dependent on their environment for the satisfaction of their needs. This environment is that of human culture, and, for the infant, it is mediated typically by parents. Unfortunately, for human beings, life is not a simple matter of exercising their instincts for satisfaction. They must grow up in a context that requires that their instincts be inhibited and disciplined in order to function more or less cooperatively with others. In other words, human development is inherently conflictual.

The fully developed human personality is made up of three systems or provinces. In his last summary of psychoanalysis, Freud calls them "mental provinces or agencies." The first and basic province is the *id*. The id is our genetically inherited constitution, including our instincts. The id is the driving force of the biological organism, seeking "the satisfaction of its innate needs."[28] From it come the basic biological needs for nourishment, love, comfort, sexual gratification, and whatever else may be biologically built in for human beings.[29]

"Under the influence of the real external world," the id undergoes a change. A "portion of the id" develops into a special agency that "acts as an intermediary between the id and the external world." This agency is called the *ego*. The ego is concerned with "the task of self-preservation." In its experience of the external world, it learns how to cope with and modify the world, so the organism (person) can be safe and still get its needs met. The ego controls the instincts, determining at what times and place they can be indulged and in what ways. The ego is "concerned with discovering the most favorable and least perilous method of obtaining satisfaction, taking the external world into account."[30]

During childhood and within the ego, another agency develops. This is the *superego*. The superego is the function of the mind whereby individuals internalize the demands of culture, transmitted primarily through one's parents. But it is shaped also by "later successors and substitutes" including teachers, admired figures, even high social ideals. Whereas the id represents the influence of heredity, the superego represents the influence of culture. The superego's "chief function remains the *limitation* of satisfactions" in the interests of human community.[31]

For Freud human development is inherently conflictual because the satisfaction of individual needs conflicts with the social need for the restriction of drives. However, according to Freud, development is also biologically inherently conflictual. There are two basic instincts, he argues. One is Eros, a life instinct (also called libido) that seeks the preservation and reproduction of life. It is tied up with sexuality. Love is rooted in the libido. The second is a death instinct, associated with aggression, which works "to undo connections and so to destroy things." These two basic instincts interact, working against each other and in combination.[32]

The complicated challenge for the ego is to mediate between the conflicting demands of the id (especially the libido and death instinct), the superego, and the realities of the external world. Some kind of acceptable balance is typically achieved by the functioning adult. Whether that balance includes neurotic tendencies depends on how well the individual has been able to cope with life traumas, usually from childhood.[33]

Freud argued that human beings growing to adulthood pass through five stages of psycho-sexual development. Each stage corresponds with experiencing pleasure primarily from a particular portion of the body. The first is the oral stage, wherein infants get their primary sensation of pleasure through the mouth. The second is the anal stage, connected with the pleasure of defecation and the stimulating activity of the anus. The third he called the Oedipal stage, named after the Greek mythical figure, Oedipus. These stages operate concurrently and overlap.[34]

It is in the third stage, the Oedipal stage, that the young boy has fantasies of sexual pleasure with his mother, but discovers that he cannot have her without eliminating his father—generating tremendous anxiety and ambivalence. This Oedipal crisis must be maneuvered through successfully in order to avoid neurotic development. "The girl, after vainly attempting to do the same as the boy, comes to recognize her lack of a penis or rather the inferiority of her clitoris, with permanent effects upon the development of her character."[35]

At about the age of four or five, the sexual instinct enters a period of latency. It reawakens again at the time of puberty—the genital phase. At that time it takes on the form that will largely dominate one's adult sexual life. "This process is not always carried out perfectly." This is manifest in sexual disturbances, connected with experiences from the earlier stages, and results in what is commonly called "perversions."[36] This is also the time when neuroses will manifest themselves as a result of traumas in the pre-latency periods.

Basically Freud's argument is that in the interactions of the id, ego, superego, and external reality, full satisfaction is not possible. Compromises have to be made. So defense mechanisms are used to reconcile the competing demands. Some of these mechanisms are healthier than others. They almost always involve a certain amount of repression. Repression involves relegating anxiety-producing memories of earlier traumas to the unconscious. Undesirable feelings and thoughts are repressed under the impact primarily of the condemning superego. The energy behind these feelings and thoughts is still operative, so it must find other outlets for satisfaction. Some of these compromises involve neuroses that make it hard for the individual to function as a normal adult.

Like Marx, Nietzsche, and Durkheim, Freud operated in that nineteenth- and early twentieth-century intellectual context that was characterized by philosophical materialism and included a strong anti-religion bias.[37] Philosophical or scientific materialism is a view that sees all facts of human life, action, and history as ultimately attributable to physical causes.[38] It represents the view that only what is empirically available, directly or indirectly, is true. Views that posit something real beyond the world of the senses are metaphysics, superstition, or religion. These are only the imaginative projections of psychological and social needs. The disciplined pursuit of science, so many believed, would ultimately prove religions wrong by identifying their natural causes.

Also like Marx, Nietzsche, and Durkheim, Freud studied with considerable approval Ludwig Feuerbach, who argued that religious ideas are merely human projections of humanity's own characteristics.[39] "Among all the philosophers," Freud said, "I worship and admire this man the most."[40]

Freud's atheism was not *merely* unbelief; it was also driven by "a bitter antagonism to religion and all forms of religious authority."[41] This was the most serious difference between him and his wife who, at the time of their wedding, was a pious, orthodox Jew. Although, by Austrian law, they had to have a religious ceremony to legitimate their marriage, Freud made it clear to her that there were not to be any religious rituals in their home.[42]

Freud's view of religion was unmistakably clear: religion is illusion. This most definitive claim is in his little book titled *The Future of An Illusion*, published in 1927. According to Freud, the book is an attempt to offer up commentary regarding the likely future of human culture or civilization.[43] In fact, it is an attempt to destroy the illusion of religion. Here I will largely follow his argument as presented in *The Future*.

In that work Freud begins by positing that civilization is possible only at the expense of the human sacrifice of instinctual needs and desires. In other words, the collective life of humankind—so essential for coping with the threats of nature—is built on psychological frustration. Simply put, as Freud was wont to do, people were unable to sleep with whomever they want, kill whomever they want, and take whatever they want from someone else. If people were totally free to exercise their wishes, though, Freud admits, the situation would be even worse than the compromises we must make for living in society.[44] The maintenance of civilization, then requires forces of coercion and measures that both reconcile and compensate people for the sacrifices they must make for civilization. These measures of reconciliation and compensation Freud suggests could be identified as "the spiritual properties of culture."[45]

Among these spiritual properties are the superego (discussed above). Two additional important possessions of culture are its ideals and art. The cultural ideals are the most highly valued achievements, to which people are to aspire.[46] These are the aspirations for achievement and accomplishment that any culture places on its individuals to keep them working at being fully competent and cooperative members of society.

Art, according to Freud, heightens identification with the collective through the incentive for "commonly experienced and highly valued sentiments." In this way it offers "substitutionary satisfactions" for the sacrifices people make for the sake of civilization.[47]

Another cultural asset, and most important historically, is religion. Religion, says Freud, is "perhaps the most important element in the psychological inventory of a culture."[48]

Freud argues that human beings came together and created civilization because of the dangers of nature. Only by working together, could we protect ourselves from the much more powerful and destructive forces of nature. Freud argues that culture's "main task" is "to shield us from nature." And, by and large, it seems to work.[49]

Nevertheless, everyone realizes there still are numerous ways that nature shows itself dominant. There are elements positively derisive of human attempts at control; "the earth that heaves and tears," the water that floods and drowns, the storm that destroys, illnesses, and "in the end the painful riddle of death."[50] Early in human history, culture compensated for these realities by personifying the forces of nature. By giving them personality, they could be viewed as beings like humans who could be influenced and appeased. Even though this did not eliminate all of life's precariousness, it rendered it less strange, more familiar—a home for living beings.

Essentially, says Freud, humanity did the same thing with the universe that it must do in individual psychological development. As infants, we face an all-powerful father who is experienced both as threat and as guardian. In the process of growing up, we have to maneuver through the maze of family complexity to establish our own selfhood in relation to others.[51] The same is true for humanity as a whole in its relation to the external forces of nature.

Over time, humanity came to recognize that natural forces are not living beings. But our helplessness before those forces remained. The gods were altered accordingly. They were turned into beings themselves, first as animals, then as persons, no longer identified with natural forces.[52] However, they maintained their "threefold task of dispelling nature's terror, reconciling people to fate, especially death, and compensating for the misery and deprivations imposed on people as a result of sharing a collective culture."[53]

Eventually God came to be a single father who created nature to act as it does and prescribe a system of morality to guide human relations. In this conceptual scheme, death was no longer final; rather it became a new life in another form of existence, a kind of reward and/or punishment for one's faithfulness to the divine decrees during one's earthly life. Freud argued that psychologically, then, this was a matter of recovering one's infantile relationship to one's father.[54]

The historical development of religion also manifests a pattern that is strikingly similar to the development of the individual.[55] The child is born into helplessness, and the infant is driven by self-love (narcissism). The helplessness and self-love combine to create a powerful bond to whatever object assures one a sense of safety and satisfies one's needs. So the mother is, above all, one's first love object, one's "refuge from *angst*."[56]

The stronger father soon displaces the mother, and remains dominant throughout childhood. But the child has deeply ambivalent feelings toward the father who is both feared and admired. The child needs the father for protection, but the father was the threat heretofore. Essentially this is the Oedipus complex. Every religion, says Freud, manifests the same deep ambivalence toward its god or god-object as is found in the Oedipus complex. What has happened is that people have projected onto the gods they have created the very characteristics they desired and feared in the father.[57]

Religious ideas become highly valued, argues Freud, because they offer us "information about that in life which, for us, is most important and of greatest interest."[58] And adherents are discouraged from critically evaluating them for any rational or empirical justification.[59] What gives religious ideas their great emotional power, says Freud, is that they offer protection, compensation, and justification in light of our fears and suffering. They help allay the anxiety from childhood helplessness by providing a more powerful father than the original father. The "gracious rule of a godly providence," then, eases the fear of life's dangers. A moral world order is established that makes up for the injustices so much a part of real life, and one's existence is extended into a future life where everything can be made right.[60]

Freud calls religious ideas *illusions*. By this, he says, he does not mean that they are wrong. Rather, they are wish-fulfilling beliefs that cannot be proven. Science and reason cannot determine whether such ideas are ultimately true or not. For Freud, of course, this is the problem. It would be very surprising indeed, he says, if our ancient ancestors had solved the most problematic riddles of the universe, and the solution just happened to satisfy our deepest psychological wishes.[61]

At this point in his argument in *The Future*, Freud takes up a different angle of analysis, subtly abandoning his idea of religion as an illusion that may or may not be true, in order to expose it as a collective neurosis.

Freud observes that, although religion has dominated human society for much of human history, it has not created a world of admirable morality or justice. Furthermore, it is also doubtful whether people were happier in earlier, more religious times. So there is no reason to fear greater immorality or cruelty and injustice from the growing influence of science and the consequent retreat of religion among the educated and the intellectuals.[62] In fact, says Freud, such prohibitions, as those against murder, serve useful social functions, allowing human beings to live in community with a modicum of security. Societies will have their rules and laws even without having to view them as God-given. Furthermore, by approaching them in a more rational and practical manner, the rules and laws can also be changed as needed to serve humanity in new circumstances.[63]

The origin of religion and morality, for Freud, was not rooted merely in wish-fulfillment. Freud believed he had shown through psychoanalytic study of religion at the dawn of history that the concept of God and the prohibition against murder were rooted also historically in an actual murder of a dominant father by his sons in a primitive horde. This was one of his arguments in his earlier *Totem and Taboo*. So the development of religion consists not only of wish-fulfillments but also of memories of historical significance.[64]

Therefore, religion is a collective counterpart to individual obsessional neurosis. (Freud had identified similarities between religion and obsessive-compulsive neurosis in earlier essays.)[65] In other words, religion is a dysfunctional collective defense mechanism. Liberating humankind from the illusion of religion and reconciling them to their culture is a matter of unveiling the distortions of religion, just as psychoanalysis seeks to unveil the uncomfortable truths of repression with neurotics.[66]

Freud, thus, reveals the larger purpose of his work on religion. It is to help liberate humanity from the neurosis of religion toward freer and more rational living. Religion inhibits this development, he believes, by suppressing critical thought and thereby keeping people in a kind of infantilism. Human beings have to grow up sometime and deal with the adversities of life. This is a matter of coming to grips with reality. They need to recognize their own helplessness and give up the notion of being the center of a universe where they are the object of providential care.[67]

Toward the end of his book, Freud ponders whether humanity will be able to withstand such liberation. In doing so, he articulates a vision that insofar as human beings give up their expectations for life in the hereafter and concentrate their energies on life on earth, they are likely to get to a place wherein "life is tolerable for all and culture not oppressive for anyone."[68] This remarkably hopeful and optimistic statement contrasts strangely with the pessimism expressed two years later in *Civilization and Its Discontents* where Freud returns to his own contention that individual development in human society is inherently conflictual, requiring more-or-less satisfactory compromises.[69] Here, though, in *The Future* he is angling the best light onto a world potentially without religion.

Having made his case for religion as neurosis, Freud returns to his first argument that religion is an illusion, and entertains the potential objection that he is simply offering up another illusion to replace religion and one that will not be as functional. He says he realizes how susceptible we are to illusions. But he disagrees that the goal of a future humanity living in the primacy of the intellect is an illusion. Freud even offers a name for the new God: *Logos*, the Greek word for reason. (While appropriate within the history of philosophy, Freud's use of *logos* may have been also playful because he surely knew that the Christian Gospel of John begins with an identification of Christ as the Logos.)[70] Religion is a lost cause anyway, he argues, because its contradictions will give way under the incessant work of the rational mind. Science is the method of *Logos*, and science is not illusion because it is open to correction. So in light of new experiences and experiments, a humanity guided by intellect will at least have the potential of correcting its errors. Certainly new errors will be made, he says, and there is plenty of reason to wonder whether humanity can ultimately create a truly fulfilling and gratifying society. But under the rule of *Logos*, it can progress in light of empirical information and cool reflection without regression to the infantile neurosis of religion.[71]

He concludes *The Future of An Illusion* with the claim that "our science is no illusion. An illusion, however, it would be to believe that we could get from somewhere else what science cannot give us."[72]

Some Reflection

There is an interesting difference between Durkheim and Freud. Durkheim too anticipated science undermining religion, but because, for him, religion served the function of social cohesion, he thought it was simply a matter of finding secular substitutes for it. Religion was not an illusion; rather it was the manifestation of the very real collective spirit of society. It was a matter, then, of finding another vehicle for this spirit. For Freud, coming from a psychological perspective, religion functions to compensate individuals for the inevitable sacrifices and costs, including death, built into nature and human culture. Since religion was an illusion, there could be no substitute put in its place that would not also be an illusion. So there was only the option of living with a kind of gritty determination in the face of life's hardships and ultimate extinction.

Certainly Freud saw the important role of religion in the psyche of his patients. In one celebrated case, he suggested it was a better coping mechanism, even a "higher method," than some of the alternatives.[73] In a work published seventeen years before *The Future of An Illusion*, he acknowledged that religion offers "protection against neurotic illness" because it disposes of the "parental complex" with its "sense of guilt."[74] But overall he did not seem to give much consideration to the possibility that religion could promote mental health, coming to see it, as we have seen, as a kind of obsessional neurosis.

To work up his psychological explanation for the origin of religion, Freud drew on many of the same anthropological accounts as did Durkheim—accounts since largely discredited. Except for the coloring of the psychoanalytic framework, Freud's argument in *The Future of An Illusion* is a good summary of the typical materialist anti-religious sentiment of many thinkers in the nineteenth and twentieth centuries. (We will see it again in different form in Bertrand Russell.) His own presumptive atheism and his psychoanalytic perspective led him to reduce religion to psychological, even psychopathological, wish-fulfillment. This involved him in a philosophy of religion that went beyond the boundaries of empirical science in its claims. Essentially he offers a metaphysical atheism, claiming empirical justification.

Erich Fromm identified Freud's *The Future of An Illusion* as "one of his most profound and brilliant books."[75] It seems to me, though, that Freud's critique of religion in *The Future* is little more than an unfriendly caricature. It is really unworthy of him. He reduces religion to childhood psychology and links it with an imagined primitive childhood of humanity. With this framework, of course, one can perceive religion only as immature dependence and collective neurosis. It shows he did not take religion seriously—at least not as a scientist. His was no open, empirical, dispassionate examination. William Newell is correct in saying that Freud's treatment of religion, although systematic and meticulous, "is false and amateurish."[76] I think it is thus also a trivialization of psychoanalysis. It allows sociologists of religion to snidely counter that "the vision of a religionless future is but illusion."[77]

At the time of the publication of *The Future of An Illusion*, one of Freud's closest followers, Oskar Pfister, who happened to be also a Protestant pastor, . wrote a thoughtful point-for-point rebuttal. Freud, to his credit, saw that it was published in a journal devoted to psychoanalysis.[78] Other psychoanalytically trained thinkers, such as Carl Jung and Erich Fromm, to mention two, have also written about religion in a much more sympathetic way.[79] They point out, rightfully, that there is no inherent conflict between psychoanalysis and religion. Jung, in particular, is noted for exploring religion as a positive factor in mental health. I have pointed out in earlier chapters that a claim of atheism cannot logically be grounded in empirical science. It is also worthwhile to note, in the context of discussing Freud, that human desire or need for the divine does not prove or disprove the existence of God. Hans Küng says it well:

> It does not follow—as some theologians have mistakenly concluded—from man's profound desire for God and eternal life that God exists and eternal life and happiness are real. But those atheists who think that what follows is the nonexistence of God and the unreality of eternal life are mistaken too.[80]

Nevertheless, such a radical critique as Freud's, even though a caricature, is possible because it contains much that is true. Oskar Pfister acknowledged its truths in his critique. So did the Catholic theologian Hans Küng in *Freud and the Problem of God*.[81] And the Jesuit scholar, William Newell, writes:

> To explain religion as a function of a neurotic urge to create gods against the frights of the night is both correct and a slander: correct, since so much of religious experience and religious expectations among peoples' lives is infantile and neurotic, a dodge away from one's truth; a slander, since religion at its best is not such a dodge.[82]

Indeed, religion is often infantile and neurotic. At times it manifests an attempt to remain in a position of dependence and subservience wherein one need not take responsibility for one's life. This is seen, it seems to me, particularly in those relationships between an authoritarian religion and its adherents in which what one must believe and how one must act are laid out in detail and presented as ultimate truth not to be critically examined.

Religion often abuses its power in like manner by discouraging critical thought. Among the proofs for believing that have been given, Freud mentions two. One is the *Credo quia absurdum* argument (I believe because it is absurd). The second is that we must behave "as if" these things are true because it is so important for human society. Both of these obviously fail for the person of reason, argues Freud correctly. The former does not answer why these particular, absurd ideas and not others. The latter asks people to forego the need for confirmation of what is most important to them.[83] Indeed, anyone involved in religion or religious studies knows that in the popular practice of religion, one often finds the argument, sometimes not even very subtle, that critical evaluation is sinful disobedience.

Whenever religion discourages critical thought, it also inhibits individual autonomy and reinforces dependence. Religion's traditions and sacred writings must, of course, always be interpreted. Naturally, they are interpreted by the highly placed official leadership. Insofar as rational, critical evaluation of these traditions and writings is defined as wicked willfulness, laypersons remain in a position of submission to domination by religious elites. (It is interesting that

Feud said little about this aspect of religion, given the writings of Voltaire, Marx, and Nietzsche.)

No doubt, much of the obsessive nature of religious belief and ritual serves as defense against a bad conscience or repressed painful memories which threaten a person's sense of self. Küng notes that some "religious practices, which have become pointless or inadequately motivated, are often defensive and protective measures dictated by fear, guilt feelings, and tormented conscience, against certain—often unconscious—temptations and threatening punishments, just like the private ritual . . . of the obsessional neurotic."[84] Psychoanalysis is surely correct in arguing that it would be better to deal with these problems for what they are—problems of human behavior and attitudes that have tolerable solutions offering individuals a less burdened and more rational, thus also freer, life. Healthy religion, as Fromm implies, does not capitalize on sick souls; rather it seeks the cure of souls.[85]

Religion is also frequently a compensation for our sense of weakness in face of the overwhelming powers of nature and society. This function, in itself, is not a bad thing unless one believes, as Freud, that autonomous adulthood requires viewing reality as merely materialistic, devoid of sacred meaning. However, whenever religion is nothing more than such compensation, it would probably be better for the individual and the community, not to mention the religion, to abandon it and look for other ways to enhance one's sense of value and strength. I very much doubt that religion without some sense of the Holy and of the sacredness of life and of passionate care for others is genuine or beneficial. In this, surely Freud is right.

Notes

1. Walter Isaacson, "Thinkers vs. Tinkerers, and Other Debates," *Time*, 29 March 1999, 6.

2. Peter Gay, "Sigmund Freud," *Time*, March 29, 1999, 66.

3. Raymond E. Fancher, *Pioneers of Psychology* (N.Y.: W. W. Norton & Co., 1979), 248.

4. For several prominent examples, see Norman O. Brown, *Life Against Death: The Psychoanalytical meaning of History* (Middletown, Conn.: Wesleyan University Press, 1959); Herbert Marcuse, *Eros and Civilization: A Philosophical Inquiry Into Freud* (Boston: Beacon Press, 1966); Paul Ricoeur, *Freud and Philosophy: An Essay on Interpretation*, trans. Denis Savage (New Haven and London: Yale University Press, 1970).

5. See Frederick C. Crews, ed., *Unauthorized Freud: Doubters Confront a Legend* (N.Y.: Viking, 1998); Thomas Szasz, *The Myth of Psychotherapy: Mental Healing as Religion, Rhetoric, and Repression* (Syracuse, N.Y.: Syracuse University Press, 1988).

6. Gay, "Sigmund Freud," 66.

7. This section is informed by these works: Fritz Fellner, "Introduction: The Genesis of the Austrian Republic," in *Modern Austria*, ed. Kurt Steiner, Fritz Fellner, and Hubert Feichtlbauer, 1-22 (Palo Alto, Calif.: The Society for the Promotion of Science and Scholarship Inc., 1981); Peter Gay, *Freud: A Life for Our Time* (N.Y. & London: W. W.

Norton & Co., 1988); Rich, *Age of Nationalism*; Richard Rickett, *A Brief Survey of Austrian History* (Wien: George Prachner Verlag, 1966); Carl E. Schorske, *Fin-De-Siècle Vienna: Politics and Culture* (N.Y.: Vintage Books; Random House, 1979); Fritz Stern, "The Great World War: 1914-1945," in *The Columbia History of the World*, ed. John A. Garraty and Peter Gay, 981-993 (N.Y.: Harper & Row, 1972).

8. Rich, *Age of Nationalism*, 103.

9. Gay, *Freud*, 19.

10. Mayer, *Old Regime*, 115.

11. Rich, *Age of Nationalism*, 211-212.

12. Schorske, *Fin-De-Siècle*, xix.

13. This section leans heavily on Gay, *Freud*.

14. Gay, *Freud*, 4-7.

15. Gay, *Freud*, 5.

16. Gay, *Freud*, 7-9.

17. Gay, *Freud*, 12.

18. Gay, *Freud*, 13-14, 15, 22.

19. Gay, *Freud*, 30, quotation on p. 27.

20. Gay, *Freud*, 36.

21. Gay, *Freud*, 37, 41.

22. Gay, *Freud*, 37-38, 40.

23. Gay, *Freud*, 45-46, 46n.

24. Gay, *Freud*, 48, 49, 52.

25. Gay, *Freud*, 53, 54, 60, 74-76.

26. Gay, *Freud*, 73-74, 78-79.

27. This brief overview follows primarily Sigmund Freud, *An Outline of Psychoanalysis*, trans. James Strachey (N.Y.: W. W. Norton, 1949 [1940]).

28. Freud, *Outline*, 14, 19.

29. Fancher, *Pioneers*, 240.

30. Freud, *Outline*, 15, 19.

31. Freud, *Outline*, 16-17, 19; for Freud's strongest statement regarding the demands of culture, see Sigmund Freud, *Civilization and Its Discontents*, trans. Joan Riviere, in *The Major Works of Sigmund Freud*, in Great Books of the Western World, vol. 54, ed. Robert Maynard Hutchins et al. (Chicago: Encyclopaedia Britannica; William Benton Publisher, 1952 [1929]).

32. Freud, *Outline*, 20-21.

33. For a good summary of the "stabilized personality," see Calvin S. Hall, *A Primer of Freudian Psychology* (N.Y.: Mentor; New American Library, 1954), chap. 5.

34. Freud, *Outline*, 25-30.

35. Freud, *Outline*, 29-30.

36. Freud, *Outline*, 30-31.

37. See Newell, *Secular Magi*, 108.

38. See Ian G. Barbour, *Religion and Science: Historical and Contemporary Issues* (San Francisco: HarperSanFrancisco; HarperCollins, 1997), 78.

39. Feuerbach, *Essence*.

40. Quoted in Gay, *Freud*, 28.

41. Richard Wollheim, *Freud* (Glasgow: Fontana Paperbacks, 1971), 7.

42. Gay, *Freud*, 38, 54.

43. Sigmund Freud, *Die Zukunft Einer Illusion*, (bound with *Massenpsychologie und Ich-Analyse*) (Frankfurt am Main: Fischer Taschenbuch Verlag, 1993 [1927]), 109. See also Sigmund Freud, *Moses and Monotheism*, trans. Katherine Jones (N.Y.: Vintage Books; Random House, 1967 [1939]), 109. Freud acknowledges he is making no distinction between "culture" and "civilization"; see p. 110. Translations from *Die Zukunft* are mine.

44. Freud, *Die Zukunft*, 119.

45. Freud, *Die Zukunft*, 114.

46. Freud, *Die Zukunft*, 117.

47. Freud, *Die Zukunft*, 118.

48. Freud, *Die Zukunft*, 118.

49. Freud, *Die Zukunft*, 119.

50. Freud, *Die Zukunft*, 119.

51. Freud, *Die Zukunft*, 121.

52. Freud, *Moses*, 105.

53. Freud, *Die Zukunft*, 121.

54. Freud, *Die Zukunft*, 123.

55. An argument made earlier in Sigmund Freud, *Totem and Taboo: Some Points of Agreement between the Mental Lives of Savages and Neurotics*, trans. James Strachey (N.Y. & London: W. W. Norton & Co., 1950 [1913]).

56. Freud, *Die Zukunft*, 127.

57. Freud, *Die Zukunft*, 127.

58. Freud, *Die Zukunft*, 128.

59. Freud, *Die Zukunft*, 131-132.

60. Freud, *Die Zukunft*, 133.

61. Freud, *Die Zukunft*, 134, 136.

62. Freud, *Die Zukunft*, 140, 142.

63. Freud, *Die Zukunft*, 142-144.

64. Freud, *Die Zukunft*, 145.

65. See Sigmund Freud, "Zwangshandlungen und Religionsübungen," in *Der Mann Moses und Die Monotheistische Religion: Schriften über die Religion* (Frankfurt am Main: Fischer Tachenbuch Verlag, 1975 [1907]).

66. Freud, *Die Zukunft*, 147.

67. Freud, *Die Zukunft*, 151.

68. Freud, *Die Zukunft*, 152.

69. Freud, *Civilization*.

70. John 1:1; in English translations usually *word* is given for the Greek *logos*.

71. Freud, *Die Zukunft*, chapter X.

72. Freud, *Die Zukunft*, 157.

73. See Sigmund Freud, *Three Case Histories* (N.Y.: Collier Books; Macmillan, 1963), 308-309.

74. Sigmund Freud, *Leonardo Da Vinci: A Memory of His Childhood* (London: Ark Paperbacks; Routledge & Kegan Paul, 1957 [1910]), 74.

75. Erich Fromm, *Psychoanalysis and Religion* (New Haven: Yale University Press, 1950), 10.

76. Newell, *Secular Magi*, 88.

77. Quoted in William H. Swatos, and Kevin J. Christiano, "Secularization Theory: The Course of a Concept," *Sociology of Religion* 60, no. 3 (1999), 216.

78. Pfister, Oskar. "The Illusion of a Future: A Friendly Discussion with Prof. Dr. Sigmund Freud," appendix A in *Affirming the Soul: Remarkable Conversations Between Mental Health Professionals and an Ordained Minister*, by Jeffrey H. Boyd, trans. Ted Crump and Jeffrey H. Boyd, 177-215 (Cheshire. Conn.: Soul Research Institute, 1994 [1928]).

79. See, for examples, Fromm, *Psychoanalysis*, and Carl Gustav Jung, *Psychology and Religion* (New Haven and London: Yale University Press, 1938).

80. Küng, *Freud*, 79.

81. Küng, *Freud*.

82. Newell, *Secular Magi*, 131.

83. Freud, *Zukunft*, 131-132.

84. Küng, *Freud* , 97.

85. Fromm, *Psychoanalysis*.

Chapter 10

The Dragon That Guards the Door
Modern Critics of Religion: Bertrand Russell
(1872-1970)

There is widespread agreement with Russell biographer Ray Monk's contention that Bertrand Russell was "one of the very few indisputably *great* philosophers of the twentieth century."[1] Russell made original contributions to mathematics, logic, and philosophy. He was awarded the Nobel Prize for literature and the Order of Merit. He was unusual among creative thinkers in that he continued to critically reevaluate even his own thought, mercilessly exposing and admitting its shortcomings.[2] (This was also true with regard to his personal life.)[3] He worked hard at writing for a popular audience, which probably meant some disregard by professional philosophers. But he was very good at it, and many students have cut their first philosophical teeth on his *A History of Western Philosophy*.[4]

He also involved himself deeply in many of the social and political issues current during his life. He was not afraid to take unpopular stands, and he paid a price for them. He wrote and lectured widely on current issues, but much of this was not thought through or as carefully articulated as his work on science, philosophy, and mathematics. With only a little exaggeration, Monk claims, "The gulf in quality between Russell's writings on logic and his writings on politics is cavernous."[5]

Russell wrote about everything that interested him, and that was a great deal. Furthermore, he carried on an enormous correspondence. Russell's bibliography contains more than three thousand publications, and in addition there is a huge collection of papers and letters in the Russell Archives, the letters numbering over 40,000. Monk notes that this output, in Russell's long life, is equivalent to writing two or three thousand words a day.[6]

For public figures, Russell was unusual in his own candor about his struggle to philosophize and about his personal life which was unorthodox and offensive to traditional morality. Russell wrote that the desire for love, the quest for knowledge, and an "unbearable pity" for suffering humanity had blown him "hither and thither, in a wayward course, over a deep ocean of anguish, reaching to the very verge of despair."[7]

Some Historical Context

When Bertrand Russell was born, all major European powers had actively ruling royal houses; the British Empire extended around the world; and the first commercial typewriter was not yet on the market. When he died, only a few largely symbolic and ceremonial royal houses were left in Europe; Great Britain had lost its world empire; and the age of computers was dawning.

For someone who did not hold high political office, Russell was unusually involved in many of the major Western historical events during his life, and he met and knew a great many of the leading politicians, scholars, artists, and political activists of the twentieth century. He was—to use a phrase greatly popularized in the late twentieth century—*plugged in*. That Russell, in those decades of such phenomenal change, could involve himself in so much of its history is truly extraordinary—certainly a testimony to his aristocratic origins, but also to his own enormous passion, energy, brilliance, and literary output. Any biography of Russell reads also like a chronology of world historical events. I will note selected historical events correlating them with Russell's own sentiments.

The first major turning point in Russell's political views—indeed, in his views about all of life—occurred in 1901 during the Boer War (1899-1902) when Great Britain extended its reach in South Africa by conquering the Dutch settler republics.[8] It was a day on which he was feeling overwhelmed by the suffering of an ill friend. He had what he called a five-minute experience that left him temporarily possessed by "a sort of mystical illumination."[9] In his autobiography, he writes that in those few minutes he became "a completely different person." He stopped being an imperialist and became pro-Boer and pacifist. He was "filled with semi-mystical feelings about beauty" and with a driving desire to discover a philosophy that would "make human life endurable."[10] From that point on, he was to take consistently liberal and critical stands in relation to many of the political and cultural trends of Western history.

For many thinkers of the nineteenth and twentieth centuries, the Scotsman David Hume (1711-1776) and the Prussian Immanuel Kant (1724-1804) had conclusively shown that absolute and certain knowledge of objective reality was outside the reach of human beings.[11] But there were philosophers and scientists who continued seeking this holy grail of rational certainty, especially during the first half of the twentieth century. Russell was among them, and in his early intellectual endeavors he hoped to lay impregnable logical foundations for mathematics and for human knowledge.

Russell was also among those who came believe that this grail-quest was futile. It became widely accepted among philosophers and scientists that human beings could not acquire a fully objective and rational foundation for sure and unassailable knowledge. Simply put, Russell came to recognize, as did many other minds in search of undeniable truth, that no system of knowledge could be constructed without some fundamental assumptions that were themselves beyond empirical or logical justification. Since pure objectivity is unattainable, so is absolute knowledge—or, more precisely, the ability to know whether our "knowledge" is in any sense absolutely correct. It was this recognition, according to Ray Monk, that led Russell to abandon interest in mathematics.[12] In his autobiography Russell wrote that though the best years of his life had been dedicated to mathematical certainty, he had been left "in doubt and bewilderment."[13] In the postscript to his *Autobiography* he said that he had been "forced to the conclusion that most of what passes for knowledge is open to reasonable doubt."[14]

World War I ravaged Europe from 1914 till 1918. Russell opposed the war and spent six months in prison as a result of actions that were part of his opposition. Again in his autobiography, he writes that as the war approached he "became filled with despairing tenderness towards the young men who were to be slaughtered, and with rage against all the statesmen of Europe."[15] Nevertheless, he was "tortured by patriotism" because he had a deep love for England, and setting it aside had proven excruciatingly difficult.[16]

The Russian Revolution occurred in 1917. Russell was at first encouraged by the Revolution, and was pleased to have the opportunity to tour the Soviet Union with a British Labour delegation in 1920. "I went hoping to find the promised land," he writes.[17] On the tour, during which he met Leon Trotsky and interviewed Vladimir Lenin, he became disillusioned.

> I have not expressed the sense of utter horror which overwhelmed me while I was there. Cruelty, poverty, suspicion, persecution, formed the very air we breathed. Our conversations were continually spied upon. In the middle of the night one would hear shots, and know that idealists were being killed in prison.[18]

He wrote a book strongly critical of the Soviet experiment,[19] which earned him disapproval from many of his leftist friends, as well as praise from politicians and others on the right who had wanted him silenced during World War I. The Soviet Union, he concluded, made him feel there was little hope for progress by revolting against existing governments.[20]

Russell had become a peacenik during World War I with leanings toward pacifism, but he never became an absolute pacifist. He was alarmed by the rise of fascism, and it tested his pacifist leanings. He wrote that he "found the Nazis utterly revolting—cruel, bigoted, and stupid."[21] They were bereft of moral or intellectual integrity. He found it increasingly difficult to adhere to his pacifist attitudes. With ambivalence, then, he abandoned his pacifism during World War II and lent his support to the Allied cause, coming to believe that Nazi Germany must be defeated for the sake of civilization.

After World War II, the prospect of nuclear warfare greatly disturbed Russell. He was especially concerned about the nuclear arms race between the Soviet Union and the United States, which lasted from the end of World War II until the 1980s. Russell felt that it was urgent that he do all he could to alert the world to the perilous path it was on. He came to believe that the very existence of humanity itself was at stake.[22]

He had earlier and in a different mood and time said that he would prefer the horror of atomic warfare rather than that the world be ruled by Nazi-like governments.[23] But he seems to have changed his mind as the possibility of human extinction increased with the proliferation of ever more powerful weapons of mass destruction. Life under communism would not be a happy fate, but it would be better than human extinction, he came to believe.[24] He worked incessantly for nuclear disarmament, helping organize the Campaign for Nuclear Disarmament in 1958. He came to the conclusion that the only long-term hope for humanity was in some kind of world government that would regulate and control destructive nationalism.

The Vietnam War involved the U.S. and other nations from the 1950s until 1974. Russell became increasingly involved in opposition to the war from 1963 on. He resigned from the Labour Party, in part, over its policies regarding Vietnam. He and friends established the Vietnam Solidarity Campaign to show support for the North Vietnamese and the Liberation Front, and he established an unofficial International War Crimes Tribunal.[25] In his *Autobiography* he wrote that he and his colleagues became convinced that the attitude of the U.S. was not justifiable, and that the facts suggested the need for a quick end to the war, and "the only way to end it was to support the North Vietnamese and the Liberation Front unequivocally."[26]

The sexual revolution was a hot media topic during the 1960s and 1970s. One could say that Russell was a pioneer in breaking with Victorian sexual morality—having had numerous intimate liaisons including two long-term relationships with married women and four marriages. Upon first learning the facts of sex at twelve years of age, he later wrote, it seemed to him "at the time self-evident that free love was the only rational system, and that marriage was bound up with Christian superstition."[27] His book, *Marriage and Morals*, first published in 1929—which included criticism of traditional marital and sexual morality—probably added fuel to the sexual revolution.[28] In the book he suggests sexual exclusiveness is not necessary for the successful marriage. He argues: "Morality in sexual relations, when it is free from superstition, consists essentially of respect for the other person, and unwillingness to use that person solely as a means of personal gratification, without regard to his or her desires."[29] This was not strict enough, of course, for conservative views of the matter, but open marriage turned out later to be too difficult even for Russell. He discovered he could not really handle his second wife's intimate relationships with other men. He found that his "capacity for forgiveness" and "Christian love" was not up to the challenge. "Anybody else," he writes, "could have told me this in advance, but I was blinded by theory."[30]

Some Biography[31]

Christened Bertrand Arthur William, Russell was born in 1872 to an aristocratic family with a long heritage of involvement in public affairs. His mother's lineage went back to the Norman invasion of the eleventh century; his father was Lord Amberley, son of the First Earl Russell. Both of his parents died when he was quite young. To protect him from a religious upbringing, his father had appointed atheist guardians, but his grandparents went to court and gained custody of Bertrand and his older brother Frank.

So at the age of three, Russell went to live with his grandparents and came under the control of a politically liberal but religiously conservative and morally strict grandmother who kept him at home where he was taught by tutors. His grandfather died within two years. His older brother who was unhappy with the situation was sent off to boarding school. Ronald Clark writes: "Lady Russell's evangelical concern to press her younger grandson into a mould of her own choice stamped him physically, intellectually and emotionally with marks that lasted all his life."[32] In that childhood Russell acquired the introspective nature of a philosopher and an antipathy to religion. The comfortable but lonely isolation of his childhood, says Ray Monk, would leave Russell feeling cut off from humanity until he was nearly fifty when his first child was born.[33]

From 1890 to 1894 Russell studied mathematics and the moral sciences at Trinity College, Cambridge. He came under the tutelage and gracious care of Alfred North Whitehead who recognized Russell's remarkable gifts. They would co-author the classic work on mathematics and logic, *Principia Mathematica*, published in three volumes from 1910 to 1913.

In 1889 Russell met and fell in love with Alys Pearsall Smith, an American and a Quaker, five years older than he. Their courtship was vigorously opposed by Russell's grandmother. Nevertheless, they were married in 1894.

His wife was active in numerous socially progressive causes, including female suffrage, teetotalism, and free love. However, the free-love interest lasted only until Russell started practicing it.[34] Russell realized sometime between 1901 and 1903 that he was no longer in love with Alys. He experienced considerable guilt over this, suffering, as well, from the desperation of feeling trapped in a marriage he could no longer tolerate and from anxiety regarding the threat to his career that a broken marriage and scandal would mean. Their relationship deteriorated, and eventually they separated, but remained married until shortly before his son John's birth by his second wife, Dora Black, in 1921. In the meantime he had maintained long-term affairs with Ottoline Morrell and Constance Malleson, an actress known as Colette O'Neill. Other more temporary liaisons would punctuate his life until his senior years.

He became politically active and even ran unsuccessfully for Parliament in a couple of elections. In no election was he ever close to winning, but he was in fact more concerned to make political propaganda since his primary interest was in writing and lecturing. He joined the Labour Party in 1914 and remained loosely involved in the Party until he tore up his membership card and announced his resignation in 1965 because of the government's support of the Vietnam War.

His daughter, Kate, was born in 1923. Parenthood provided probably his greatest, if not his only real, sense of fulfillment in life. It also stimulated his interest in education and child psychology. With his second wife he opened a progressive, experimental school in 1927. It was to be a total institution maximizing freedom and creativity in a context of nurturing care. Beacon Hill School was a more or less successful attempt to apply principles of childhood education that would prevail more widely later. However, the financial and administrative demands were difficult for Russell. He had to keep writing and lecturing for money to keep the school afloat. It was apparently also hard on his own children and his relationship to his children. After Russell and Dora divorced in 1935, she ran the school until it closed in the mid-1940s.

Russell's anti-war activities during World War I had strained his relationship with Whitehead, but they managed to remain on good terms until Whitehead's death in 1947. Russell met Ludwig Wittgenstein in 1911, and their relationship was profoundly intellectually significant for both of them. Russell found Wittgenstein to be possibly "the most perfect example" of genius Russell had ever known.[35] Russell did much to help Wittgenstein's development and promote his career. Wittgenstein influenced Russell to see the futility of establishing absolute and certain knowledge. Nevertheless, it was a difficult relationship, in large part because of Wittgenstein's cantankerousness and his philosophical style. Russell writes: "I do not know anything more fatiguing than disagreeing with him in an argument."[36] As early as 1913 Wittgenstein's assaults on Russell's thinking led Russell to believe he (Russell) would never be able to do original philosophical work again, that he would have to leave that for younger thinkers. It filled him with despair.[37] Nevertheless, between them, Russell and Wittgenstein did much to lay the foundations for what came to be called analytic philosophy.

In 1936 Russell married Patricia Spence. She gave birth to a son, Conrad, in 1937. Feeling unloved, she left him in 1949, and they were divorced in 1952. In that same year he married an American, Edith Finch, whom he had known since 1925. This was a successful marriage during which he apparently acquired a sense of personal peace. He dedicated his autobiography in 1967 to her.

Although he continued to produce writings in philosophy, especially popularizations for wide audiences, the last two decades of his life were devoted primarily to working for nuclear disarmament, an end to the Vietnam War, and world peace. His political and organizational activity as well as most of his writings, lectures, and broadcasts dealt with these issues. He died in Wales in 1970, nearly ninety-nine years old.

Russell on Religion

Russell's philosophy was an empiricism that would maintain science and scientific method as the only path to anything we could rightly call "knowledge." He developed a philosophy that was influential in the developments known as logical positivism and analytic and linguistic philosophy.[38] This was essentially a view about the nature of reality and our capacity to know it.[39] Over time, he modified his views considerably, but he continued with a program of thought that analyzed language and presumed symbolic logic and empirical research to be the paths to human knowledge.[40] This perspective viewed metaphysical, religious, and ethical claims as outside the reach of what human beings could empirically verify. Religious and metaphysical thought was seen as speculative, and ethical claims as a matter of emotional preference and desire.[41] In *Religion and Science* (published in 1935) Russell writes: "Whatever knowledge is attainable, must be attained by scientific methods; and what science cannot discover, mankind cannot know."[42]

All empiricist philosophies came under sustained criticism in the twentieth century, and their inadequacies were exposed, sometimes even by their own, most creative adherents.[43] As noted above, Russell himself came to realize those inadequacies. Nevertheless, he doggedly stayed with the project, albeit with intellectual humility. Toward the end of *Human Knowledge: Its Scope and Limits* (published in 1948), he writes that "it must be admitted, empiricism as a theory of knowledge has proved inadequate, though less so than any other previous theory of knowledge."[44] He firmly believed that claims to knowledge outside scientific research and reasoning were always dangerous. They were intellectually dangerous as hindrances to new learning, and they were politically dangerous because the powerful were too often ready to enforce any new orthodoxy, sometimes with cruelty and brutality. In *A History of Western Philosophy*, he writes:

> Science tells us what we can know, but what we can know is little, and if we forget how much we cannot know we become insensitive to many things of very great importance. Theology, on the other hand, induces a dogmatic belief that we have knowledge where in fact we have ignorance, and by doing so generates a kind of impertinent insolence towards the universe.[45]

The logic of Russell's empirical philosophy allowed him to dismiss religious claims as lying outside the possibility of any meaningful discussion, and Russell took this approach in a celebrated debate with the Jesuit, Frederick Copleston, in

1948.[46] But his opposition to religion predated the development of his philosophy. Even as an adolescent, he took the view that theological claims to truth should require the same kind of evidence as scientific claims.[47] More significant than his scientific bias, he believed that religion was harmful. Consequently, his criticisms of religion, like his writings on all social and political issues, tend to be a blend of scientific reasoning and humanitarian concern. They are largely the typical science-and-humanism-versus-superstition arguments common to the eighteenth and nineteenth centuries—much in the spirit of Voltaire, Marx, Nietzsche, and Freud, and much of what Russell says echoes these earlier critics.

Paul Edwards collected a number of Russell's lectures, pamphlets and articles under the provocative title *Why I Am Not a Christian*, published in 1957. In the preface Russell makes a distinction between the truth and the harmfulness of religion. Nevertheless, he writes: "I think all the great religions of the world— Buddhism, Hinduism, Christianity, Islam, and Communism—both untrue and harmful."[48]

Russell's criticism of religion is based on his unbounded conviction of the importance of exercising one's rational mind in responsible evaluation of evidence. He believed, "A habit of basing convictions upon evidence, and of giving to them only that degree of certainty which the evidence warrants, would, if it became general, cure most of the ills from which the world is suffering." He is convinced, he argues, that religious faith tends to suppress doubt, resist recognition of contrary evidence, and encourage fanaticism.[49]

We might notice how very similar Russell is to Voltaire in his confidence in human reason while still recognizing the limitations of reason. (His lover, Ottoline Morrell once wrote: "Bertie loved to think he was treading in the paths Voltaire trod.")[50] We want to note as well the Voltairean passion for human welfare underlying Russell's perspective. Russell was indeed a scientific realist but a *humanistic*, scientific realist. In other words, although he objects to faith on grounds of credible evidence, his deeper concern is with the harm it causes people—a harm he experienced to some extent personally as a child under the over-protective guardianship of his grandmother.

It should also be noted that Russell's objection to faith is not limited to *religious* faith, as is evident in the quotation above including Communism. In reviewing some examples of harms of faith, he identifies the Catholic position on birth control, the Hindu stricture against remarriage for widows, and the "Communist belief in the dictatorship of a minority of True Believers."[51] In *Religion and Science* he says: "The newer creeds of Communism and Fascism are the inheritors of theological bigotry."[52] So it would seem that underlying his objection to religion is a still more fundamental opposition to absolute claims to truth accompanied by dogmatism and political and cultural repression. And at times he speaks more-or-less approvingly of modern religious thought that accommodates itself to science, and to the experience of mysticism except insofar as it gets associated "with false beliefs."[53] However, he remains more broadly opposed to religion as largely harmful and, when not, then unnecessary.

The first essay in Edwards' collection, "Why I am not a Christian," was delivered as a lecture in 1927 (the same year Freud's *The Future of An Illusion* appeared). He begins by stating what he means by a Christian. This is one who believes in God and immortality and that Christ was either divine or "the best and wisest of men."[54] These are what Russell addresses to show why he is not a Christian.

Russell offers up at first metaphysical critiques of the so-called proofs of God's existence. These are the proofs originally developed by St. Anselm, St. Thomas Aquinas, and Rene Descartes, essentially the same proofs debunked in the eighteenth century by David Hume and Immanuel Kant. Russell's criticisms of these proofs are on target and echo Hume's and Kant's earlier critiques. I mention them here just briefly since my concern is principally with the cultural critiques of religion.

Of the first-cause argument (reasoning backwards from cause to cause takes one to the inevitable first cause), Russell says there is no good reason to suppose that "the world could not have come into being without a cause" or that it could have always existed.[55] Of the natural-law argument which says surely someone (God) decreed the laws of nature, Russell says that this argument confuses human and natural laws. Natural laws do not require the assumption that someone decreed them.[56] Of the argument from design (the world appears designed just right for human life to exist), Russell points out that Darwin has demonstrated that life adapts to its environment, not the other way around, and that it is odd that people would think this world with all its defects could be designed by an omniscient and omnipotent being with millions of years to do the job.[57] Of the moral argument which says that there would not be any right or wrong without the reality of God, Russell reasons that if God decreed by fiat what is right and wrong, then God would be beyond right and wrong, so God's goodness comes into question. On the other hand, if God were conforming to some greater reality of good and evil, then God would not be the greatest reality.[58]

Then Russell shifts from the metaphysical critique to the cultural critique of religion. He claims, "Most people believe in God because they have been taught from early infancy to do it, and that is the main reason." A second powerful reason is that people "wish for safety, a sort of feeling that there is a big brother who will look after you."[59] In this latter reason, we can see an affinity with the Freudian view.

Russell takes on the claim that Christ was the best and wisest of all people. Russell says there is much in Christ's teachings he finds agreeable, but much of that Christians themselves do not follow. As examples, he mentions Christ's commands to not resist evil and turn the other cheek, to not judge others, to give to anyone who asks of you, and to sell all you have and give the proceeds to the poor.[60]

In addressing the question of Christ's wisdom, Russell sets aside the difficult issue of the historicity of Christ, saying he is dealing with the gospels as they stand. He points out Christ's claim that the second coming would come soon, within the lifetime of his listeners, which turns out to have been a less-than-wise claim.[61]

Russell finds objections to Christ's moral character because Christ believed in hell, spoke reproachfully to those who would not listen to him, and taught people to live in fear of damnation.[62] The doctrine of hell-fire as punishment for sin "is a doctrine of cruelty."[63] After reviewing a couple of other "curious" events in the gospels (casting evil spirits into a herd of swine and cursing a fig tree), Russell says he would place Buddha and Socrates above Christ for moral character.[64] In this evaluation of Christ's moral character and responsibility, Russell sounds a lot like Nietzsche.

Then Russell states that people accept religion on emotional grounds, not on rational argumentation. And he finds completely unconvincing the argument that people need religion to be virtuous. He notes examples of great brutality in the name of religion in the period when people believed most intensely, that is, in the Middle Ages. Russell goes on to claim that the Christian churches have been "the principal enemy of moral progress in the world."[65]

Religion is rooted primarily in fear, argues Russell, "fear of the mysterious, fear of defeat, fear of death." Fear gives birth to cruelty, so "it is no wonder if cruelty and religion have gone hand-in-hand."[66] We need to look fair and square at the world—its good facts, its bad facts, its beauties, and its ugliness; see the world as it is, and be not afraid of it.[67] Again, echoes of Nietzsche and Freud.

In the essay, "Has Religion Made Useful Contributions to Civilisation?" (published originally in 1930), Russell answers that any contributions have been precious few in number. Christians have not followed the benevolent teachings of Jesus. For that matter, the Buddhists, too, have neglected to follow Buddha's compassion. Both, in practice, have "been obscurantist, tyrannous, and cruel."[68]

Russell writes that his view of religion is the same as Lucretius. He regards "it as a disease born of fear and as a source of untold misery to the human race."[69] The leaders of religion have acted "like any other privileged class," using "their power for their own advantage."[70]

Christianity's "worst feature," says Russell, has been "its attitude towards sex."[71] It has resulted in pain, misery, and cruelty. This is true for women who have been viewed as temptresses and kept subservient to men and childbearing. And for countless people the anxiety about and ignorance of sexuality, imposed by the Church, have meant unnecessary suffering. Precautions against syphilis and unwanted births have been impossible in the face of Christian strictures regarding sexuality and particularly sexual knowledge as undesirable.[72] In this criticism, again, we hear echoes of Nietzsche.

Russell says there are two objections to religion—intellectual and moral. The intellectual objection is that religious beliefs are not subject to empirical evidence, "which produces hostility to evidence and causes us to close our minds to every fact that does not suit our prejudices."[73]

On the moral level, Russell suggests that in their powerlessness the early Christians came to stress the individual soul, personal righteousness, and immortality. This severe individualism encouraged egotism, and the doctrine of salvation became separated from social action altogether, except for warriors who fought the Muslims.[74] Furthermore, Christianity introduced levels of religious intolerance largely unknown historically except among the Jews.[75]

Religion leads to an abusive distinction between the righteous and the unrighteous. What happens is that "unrighteousness" comes to be whatever the herd dislikes. By developing systems of ethics around the righteous/unrighteous dichotomy, the herd becomes justified in punishing whomever it dislikes. Righteousness, then, is "an outlet for sadism by cloaking cruelty as justice."[76] Here Russell even seems to be paraphrasing Nietzsche.

While religion is rooted primarily in fear, it also appeals to human self-esteem. It allows people to feel "they are of interest to the Creator of the universe." It flatters us "to suppose that the universe is controlled by a Being who shares our tastes and prejudices."[77]

Since religion gives respectability to the passions of "fear, conceit and hatred," it becomes largely responsible for human misery and thus "a force for evil."[78] For all practical purposes, fear and hatred could be eliminated from human affairs by education and social reform, but religion stands in the way by providing institutional and traditional justification for the exercise of fear and hatred.[79] Common sense today tells us that "wicked" actions are largely the result of conditions and conditioning from the social environment. But Christianity is not interested in common sense.[80] As a result of scientific and intellectual advance, humankind could be "on the threshold of a golden age," says Russell. However, it would "be necessary first to slay the dragon that guards the door, and this dragon is religion."[81]

Some Reflection

As with Voltaire, Marx, Nietzsche, and Freud, much of what Russell lays at the door of religion contains uncomfortably much truth. Christians and other religious adherents have not lived up to the best in their ethical traditions. They have often persecuted and abused others. They have frequently opposed significant intellectual advances, especially the scientific. Religious leaders and secular leaders in the name of religion have abused power. Fear, self-importance, self-righteousness, resentment, and hatred have used religion often in destructive and cruel ways.

That Russell includes communism and fascism among his list of religions is telling, however. Furthermore, he found himself in the last two decades of his life combating the excesses of nationalism (nations' placing their own perceived interests above the welfare of humanity). One wonders if we are not here really dealing with something not so peculiar to religion, but some troubling human tendency to raise particular interests to universality, to view as absolute what is only contingent, and to justify it all with some ideology. Such ideologies take various forms—religion, nationalism, ethnocentrism, racism—depending on the historical circumstances. Although he did not explore it very fully, Russell seemed to realize in later years that his real concern was with the absolutizing of particular historical and cultural interests at whose altars the welfare and happiness of human beings can then be sacrificed. In a lecture in 1946, he said, "We are now again in an epoch of wars of religion, but a religion is now called an 'ideology.'"[82] Insofar as ideological absolutism is what Russell fought, religion needs to find common cause with this fight.

In contrast to religion, he suggests, science offers us a "temper of mind" that "is cautious, tentative, and piecemeal; it does not imagine that it knows the whole truth, or that even its best knowledge is wholly true." Science recognizes that all current, apparent "knowledge" will need correction and revision.[83] Russell is essentially correct about the spirit of science—at least, when at its best. At its best it manifests a built-in openness to correction and an intellectual humility often missing from theology and political ideology. We know, however, from historical and sociological studies of science that the practice of science often involves arrogance, self-aggrandizement, and political conflict as scientists jockey for advantage, influence, and notoriety.[84] And surely Russell goes too far in this extravagant generalization: "The spread of the scientific outlook, as opposed to the theological, has indisputably made, hitherto, for happiness."[85]

Strikingly, two pages after this paean to science for its contribution to happiness he expresses concern about the misuses of science. He identifies as problematic "the practical experts who employ scientific technique" and "the governments and large firms" that hire them, filling them with "a sense of limitless power, of arrogant certainty, and of pleasure in manipulation even of human material." This is not science, of course, "but it cannot be denied that science has helped to promote it."[86]

Later in his autobiography Russell stated what could be seen as a qualification to his hyperbolic praise of science when he writes "I do not believe that science *per se* is an adequate source of happiness, nor do I think that my own scientific outlook has contributed very greatly to my own happiness."[87] But the fact that acknowledging the misuse of science did not discredit science for him leads one to suspect he is applying a different standard, at least in part, to science than to religion. We can recognize, if Russell could not, that the misuse of religion does not necessarily discredit faith any more than the misuse of nationalism discredits patriotic pride or than the misuse of science discredits scientific inquiry. We might draw different conclusions if we compared religion at its best with science at its best and religion at its worst with science at its worst.

Certainly Russell is right that faith is not rooted in a thoroughgoing rational evaluation of empirical reality. Had he taken greater cognizance of that insight in his love affair with Lady Morrell, he could have saved himself a great deal of pain. With some naivete and a lot of pain for both of them, he labored fervently to convince her through rational criticism to abandon religious faith.[88] Of course, he was talking past her. Faith—for that matter, any of life's foundational projects—is rooted in deeply felt and complex existential realities of individuals. One suspects this was no less true of Russell with regard to his commitment to mathematics, logic, and philosophy. Furthermore, in spite of his continued opposition to religious faith, he conceded in *A History of Western Philosophy*: "science, unadulterated, is not satisfying; men need also passion and art and religion. Science may set limits to knowledge, but should not set limits to imagination."[89]

Paul Edwards identified Russell "as one of the great heretics in morals and religion."[90] I am tempted to call Russell the *last* great heretic in morals and religion. Russell's criticisms of religion were not new when he made them, and they seem even somewhat exhausted after reviewing some of the major critiques of the previous two hundred years. It seems to me that religion today is at a cultural crossroads, and the direction it takes will largely decide whether Russell's criticisms remain relevant or take a place in the museum of cultural history.

There are indications the world is shifting in its religious sentiment. Certainly Islamic terrorists have infused "infidel" with new twenty-first century meaning; and Christian fundamentalists battle evolution in America's schools; and some orthodox Jews assert Israel's divine right to all of Palestine. News headlines are often terribly discouraging: "Belfast schoolchildren caught in cross fire of religious hate"; "Religious violence flares in Nigeria"; "Religious rioting shakes India: Hindu reprisal attacks on Muslims kill 100."[91] Nevertheless, it is also widely accepted in the cultural centers of the world and among many (if not most) religious leaders and thinkers of all major faith traditions that the higher road is one of mutual respect and tolerance, if not acceptance. It is widely recognized that assertions of absolute and infallible truth can only be imposed on unwilling populations by political coercion and terror. "The nineteenth and twentieth centuries have given us as much terror as we can take," writes Lyotard in *The Postmodern Condition*, nine years after Russell's death.[92] Even traditions claiming infallible truth from sacred texts, creeds, traditions, and holy offices are exploring paths of peaceful co-existence with other competing faith-claims. Religious pluralism, diversity, and dialogue are the new currencies of a postmodern world.

It is true that reactions to this new age of diversity have included vitriolic culture "wars" and the growth of new fundamentalist religious movements.[93] And there is still plenty of arrogance and intolerance among all parties— orthodox and unorthodox alike—to make the path to tolerance and mutual respect painfully difficult. But it seems to me that leaders of orthodoxy—whatever the creed—increasingly recognize that coercion cannot substitute for persuasion. So they are resigned to, if not also celebrating, co-existence and dialogue. Among those outside orthodoxy—the philosophers, theologians, religious leaders, scientists, journalists, and people of letters—a great many are engaged in creative dialogue, finding common cause in concern about human social problems in our more diverse and complex world. It is this movement—of tolerance and co-existence, dialogue and respect—we need to join if we are to take Russell's critical insights seriously. He challenges us to slay the dragon of dogmatic and intolerant religion.

This essential human project is not made easier by postmodernism, but it might be made more possible.

Notes

1. Ray Monk, *Bertrand Russell: The Ghost of Madness, 1921-1970* (N.Y.: The Free Press, 2000), xi.

2. See especially his letter to Max Newman, published in Bertrand Russell, *Autobiography* (London and New York: Routledge, 1996 [1967-69]), 413-414.

3. See, for example, Russell, *Autobiography*, 429.

4. Bertrand Russell, *A History of Western Philosophy* (N.Y.: Simon and Schuster, 1972 [1945]).

5. See Monk, *Ghost*, 6.

6. Ray Monk, *Bertrand Russell: The Spirit of Solitude, 1872-1921* (N.Y.: The Free Press, 1996), xvii.

7. Russell, *Autobiography—1872-1914*, 3.

8. John P. McKay,; Bennett D. Hill,; John Buckler, *A History of Western Society. Vol. II: From Absolutism to the Present*, 4th edition (Boston: Houghton Mifflin, 1991), 838.

9. Russell, *Autobiography—1872-1914*, 220.

10. Russell, *Autobiography—1872-1914*, 220-221.

11. See especially David Hume, *An Enquiry Concerning Human Understanding*, in *Locke, Berkeley, Hume*, in Great Books of the Western World, vol. 35, ed. Robert Maynard Hutchins et al. (Chicago: Encyclopaedia Britannica; William Benton Publisher; 1952 [1758]) and Immanuel Kant, *The Critique of Pure Reason*, trans. J. M. D. Meiklejohn, in *Kant*, in Great Books of the Western World, vol. 42, ed. Robert Maynard Hutchins et al. (Chicago: William Benton, Publisher; Encyclopaedia Britannica, 1952 [1781]).

12. Monk, *Ghost*, 6-7.

13. Russell, *Autobiography*, 395.

14. Russell, *Autobiography*, 725.

15. Russell, *Autobiography*, 240.

16. Russell, *Autobiography*, 240.

17. In a letter to Ottoline Morrell, in Russell, *Autobiography*, 355.

18. Russell, *Autobiography*, 333.

19. Bertrand Russell, *The Practice and Theory of Bolshevism* (N.Y.: Simon and Schuster, 1964 [1920, 1948]).

20. Russell, *Autobiography*, 394.

21. Russell, *Autobiography*, 430.

22. Russell, *Autobiography*, 591.

23. Quoted in Ronald W. Clark, *The Life of Bertrand Russell* (N.Y.: Alfred A. Knopf, 1976), 520.

24. See Clark, *Life of Russell,*, 568.

25. Russell, *Autobiography*, 664-667.

26. Russell, *Autobiography*, 666.

27. Russell, *Autobiography--1872-1914*, 44.

28. Bertrand Russell, *Marriage and Morals* (N.Y.: Liveright, 1929, 1957).

29. Russell, *Marriage*, 153.

30. Russell, *Autobiography*, 431.

31. This brief biography is informed, besides Russell's *Autobiography*, by Clark, *Life of Russell*; Monk, *Spirit*; and Monk, *Ghost*.

32. Clark, *Life of Russell*, 27.

33. Monk, *Spirit*, 3.

34. Clark, *Life of Russell*, 58, 66.

35. Russell, *Autobiography*, 329.

36. Russell, *Autobiography*, 436.

37. Clark, *Life of Russell*, 205.

38. See Keith S. Donellan, "Western Philosophical Schools and Doctrines: Modern Schools: Analytic and Linguistic Philosophy," *The New Encyclopaedia Britannica*, 15th edition, vol. 25, 600-608 (Chicago: Encyclopaedia Britannica, 1994).

39. See Bertrand Russell, *The Philosophy of Logical Atomism* (La Salle, Ill.: Open Court, 1985 [1918, 1924]).

40. See Bertrand Russell, *An Outline of Philosophy* (Cleveland and New York: Meridian Books; World Publishing Co., 1960 [1927]); Bertrand Russell, *An Inquiry Into Meaning and Truth* (London: George Allen and Unwin, 1940); Bertrand Russell, *Human Knowledge: Its Scope and Limits* (London: Routledge, 1948).

41. See especially Bertrand Russell, *Religion and Science* (N.Y. and Oxford: Oxford University Press, 1997 [1935]).

42. See especially Russell, *Religion and Science*, 243.

43. See, for example, the fascinating discussion of Wittgenstein's development in relation to these twentieth-century empiricist philosophies in Allan Janik and Stephen Toulmin, *Wittgenstein's Vienna* (N.Y.: Touchstone; Simon and Schuster, 1973).

44. Russell, *Human Knowledge*, 527.

45. Russell, *History*, xiv.

46. "The Existence of God: A Debate Between Bertrand Russell and Father F. C. Copleston, SJ," in *Why I Am Not a Christian: And Other Essays on Religion and Related Subjects*, ed. Paul Edwards (London: Unwin Paperbacks, 1975 [1930]), 133-153.

47. Russell, *Autobiography—1872-1914*, 48.

48. Bertrand Russell, *Why I Am Not A Christian: And Other Essays On Religion And Related Subjects*, ed. Paul Edwards (London: Unwin Paperbacks, 1975 [1957]), 9.

49. Russell, *Why I Am Not*, 10.

50. Quoted in Monk, *Spirit*, 266.

51. Russell, *Why I Am Not*, 10.

52. Russell, *Religion and Science*, 173.

53. Russell, *Religion and Science*, 189.

54. Russell, *Why I Am Not*, 14.

55. Russell, *Why I Am Not*, 15-16.

56. Russell, *Why I Am Not*, 16, 17.

57. Russell, *Why I Am Not*, 17, 18.

58. Russell, *Why I Am Not*, 19.

59. Russell, *Why I Am Not*, 20.

60. Russell, *Why I Am Not*, 20-21.

61. Russell, *Why I Am Not*, 21, 22.

62. Russell, *Why I Am Not*, 22-23.

63. Russell, *Why I Am Not*, 23.

64. Russell, *Why I Am Not*, 23-24.

65. Russell, *Why I Am Not*, 24, 25.

66. Russell, *Why I Am Not*, 25.

67. Russell, *Why I Am Not*, 26.

68. Russell, *Why I Am Not*, 28.

69. Russell, *Why I Am Not*, 27.

70. Russell, *Why I Am Not*, 28.

71. Russell, *Why I Am Not*, 29.

72. Russell, *Why I Am Not*, 29-30.

73. Russell, *Why I Am Not*, 31.

74. Russell, *Why I Am Not*, 33-34.

75. Russell, *Why I Am Not*, 35.

76. Russell, *Why I Am Not*, 39, 40.

77. Russell, *Why I Am Not*, 39.

78. Russell, *Why I Am Not*, 40.

79. Russell, *Why I Am Not*, 42.

80. Russell, *Why I Am Not*, 36, 37, 38.

81. Russell, *Why I Am Not*, 42.

82. Bertrand Russell, "Philosophy and Politics," appendix to *Authority and the Individual*, by Russell, 81-101 (Boston: Beacon Press, 1949 [1946]), 97.

83. Russell, *Religion and Science*, 245.

84. See Thomas S. Kuhn, *The Structure of Scientific Revolutions*, 2nd ed. (Chicago: University of Chicago Press, 1962, 1970); Sal Restivo, "Critical Sociology of Science," in *Science Off the Pedestal: Social Perspectives on Science and Technology*, eds. Daryl E. Chubin and Ellen W. Chu, 57-70 (Belmont, Calif. Wadsworth, 1989).

85. Russell, *Religion and Science*, 244.

86. Russell, *Religion and Science*, 245-246.

87. Russell, *Autobiography*, 404.

88. Monk, *Spirit*, 226-219, 236-262.

89. Russell, *History*, 16.

90. Paul Edwards, introduction to *Why I Am Not a Christian*, by Russell, 5.

91. "Belfast schoolchildren caught in cross fire of religious hate," *The Kansas City Star* (The Associated Press), 4 September 2001, A7; "Religious violence flares in Nigeria," *The Kansas City Star* (The Associated Press), 9 September 2001, A20; Celia W. Dugger, "Religious rioting shakes India: Hindu reprisal attacks on Muslims kill 100," *The Kansas City Star*, 1 March 2002, A1, A10.

92. Jean-François Lyotard, *The Postmodern Condition: A Report on Knowledge*, trans. Geoff Bennington and Brian Massumi, Theory and History of Literature, vol. 10 (Minneapolis: University of Minnesota Press, 1984 [1979]), 81.

93. See, for example, the discussion in Akbar S. Ahmed, *Postmodernism and Islam: Predicament and Promise* (London & N.Y.: Routledge, 1992).

Chapter 11

Annoyingly Confusing
The Uncertain Path of the Postmodern

Modern societies have become notably fragmented and hotly contested in a confusing tangle of multiculturalism. In the United States this situation has been referred to as "culture wars."[1]

A most remarkable and confounding skirmish in the culture wars occurred in Liberty, Missouri, near Kansas City on June 24, 2002.[2] The occasion was a conference put on by the Colorado-based Focus on the Family at Pleasant Valley Baptist Church. Titled "Addressing, Understanding and Preventing Homosexuality in Youth," it was a "program based on the belief that homosexuality is not natural and is contrary to biblical teaching, and that with the help of loving family, friends and church, persons living the homosexual lifestyle can change." This was an Evangelical Christian event that promoted love for homosexuals in order to help them change. When protesters also showed up, things got interesting and confusing.

About thirty people "representing the area's gay, lesbian, bisexual and transgender community, including clergy members, lined a driveway and quietly conveyed another message, 'Love Welcomes All.'" Their message was basically that we should not try to change who we are; that being a practicing gay or lesbian is neither sick nor sinful—at least not inherently more so than being a practicing heterosexual.

But another group, more radically opposed to homosexuality, also showed up—about a dozen followers of the Topeka, Kansas, minister Fred Phelps who had achieved considerable notoriety in his campaign to oppose any toleration of homosexuality. They also carried signs with their usual message that God hates homosexuals.

So one group was saying we should love homosexuals, so they can change. Another group was protesting the message that homosexuals should change.

And a third group was protesting the message that homosexuals should be loved. But that was not the end of it.

Toward the end of the day two Nazi sympathizers showed up, and they seemed perplexed. "They had come there to protest the Love Welcomes All group, but they also didn't like the Phelps group's message." One of them said, "We're kind of standing here in the middle and we don't know what to do." The other, a member of a group called Blood & Honor, said "It's annoyingly confusing."

"Annoyingly confusing" is a mild description for a world in which the reality appears to be that reality is up for grabs. We find ourselves in a world of fragmentation, demystification, and disillusionment. We are increasingly aware that human knowledge is largely a "constructed" knowledge—relative to time and place in history and culture. Traditional belief systems, based largely on unquestioned authorities and tradition itself, have been challenged and found wanting by the developments of Western thought.

Since the Enlightenment, magnificent efforts have gone into the pursuit of a universal system of truth that could lead to the liberation of humanity from what has been perceived as the artificial shackles of the past. The heretofore failure of these various efforts—along with some of the most virulent tragedies in the twentieth century—have contributed to undermining the confidence of humanity that it could discover its rightful home in the universe. Nietszche's and Freud's labors challenged the very structures of reason itself. Now we stand before the frightfully awesome, but ironically liberating, truth that we have to create our own "home."

It is not entirely a new truth. A long time ago, some Hebrew editor, composing the book of Genesis, included this: "God said to [humankind], 'Be fruitful and multiply, and fill the earth and subdue it; and have dominion over the fish of the sea and over the birds of the air and over every living thing that moves upon the earth.'"[3] This idea of radical freedom (but note also domination!) lay for many centuries like a hidden kernel in grand edifices of religion and tradition. It was "liberated" from religion by the secular, rational thought of the modern mind. But to what?

Thus far, the subduing and dominating of the earth has had paradoxical consequences. On the one hand, it has led us to a deeply threatened ecosystem in a world of gross inequality and competing national, ethnic, class, and religious divisions that seem to keep every part of the globe on the edge of violent confrontation. On the other hand, democratic principles of political representation, equality before the law, human rights, and other communal values are operative in many countries and manifest themselves in international bodies, such as the United Nations and the World Court. Technological and economic developments have advanced to the point where a sizable minority of the world's population live in historically unimaginable affluence and where, in principle, no one in the world need do without life's necessities. On the other hand, gross inequality and desperate poverty are still widespread. These paradoxical results leave us uncertain and insecure about the future of the world.

Modernism to Postmodernism

The modern worldview that developed throughout the nineteenth century and much of the twentieth was characterized by the belief that there was a final true answer. It did not much matter what the question was. In economics the answer was, depending on your persuasion, laissez-faire capitalism, utilitarian liberalism, socialism, or communism. There were parallel perspectives on government. In the arts the quest was for what is truly art. And so on.

This belief in a single answer energized the search for foundational truth in the various realms of human endeavor. Where this foundation would be found was debated as well. Was it in the nature of human beings themselves (in their biology or psychology)? Was it in the nature of human society? Was it in the principles of social evolution as manifested in the history of humanity? Perhaps in the structure and practices of language? We have seen how some of the representative figures in the debates dismissed religion as a potential foundation.

In any case and whatever the answer, it was believed we could count on progressive evolution. Progress could be slowed by moving forward with the wrong answer at times, but progress there would be, sooner or later, toward an ever freer and more humane world. (Of the six major, modern thinkers discussed in this book, only Nietzsche did not embrace some hope for progress in this sense.) The confidence in progress was particularly evident in the West at the end of the nineteenth century. The historian Norman Rich writes:

> Thoughtful Europeans were fully aware of the gravity of the many problems still besetting their society and there was no lack of prophets of disaster among them, but the prevailing mood in Europe as the nineteenth century drew to a close was one of optimism. Human reason seemed to have demonstrated its capacity to cope with human problems. After three quarters of a century without a general European war, people had begun to count on the future.[4]

Sometime shortly after 1900, the quest for the final answer to truth and world community collapsed, as did the presumption of social progress; although the recognition of the collapse would not be widely evident till the latter half of the twentieth century.[5]

Throughout the first half of the twentieth century there continued Herculean efforts by many to pursue and promote particular systems of ideas as the roads to liberating truth. But these efforts were met and stalemated at every step by others who held opposing views—often backed by guns and bombs. Many factors contributed to the cacophony of voices: the expansion of the university system providing multiple centers of learning; the proliferation and fragmentation of political parties and social interests with access to various media; the spread of the media itself; government sponsorship of research and propaganda; the surplus wealth of the modernizing economy that could support the armies of thinkers, writers, artists, teachers, and propagandists. Technological developments in the media and cultural innovations in sports, entertainment, and recreation raised the level of noise and distraction to new levels. World War I, the Depression, World War II, the Holocaust, and the Cold War were, in part, manifestations of the competing visions. They were also major blows to the modern worldview. All these developments radically challenged the Enlightenment hope that human reason and sentiment, coupled with developments in science and organizational wisdom, would lead humanity through an ever more progressive evolution toward utopia.

The Enlightenment hope had been inspired, in part, by the recognition that if truth was a matter of believing some unquestioned authority, the world could hope for nothing more than warring factions and violent repression. But getting consensus on a humane and liberating substitute proved elusive. We can see now that all along the way there were signs that the quest for truth and emancipation had snares in its own logic and methods.

In hindsight we can see that the Enlightenment humanists themselves exposed the naivete of the Enlightenment hope. Voltaire suggested that the quest for ultimate truth was an intellectual's dance with no end. Marx exposed the reality that human consciousness itself was shaped by historical circumstances and social interests. Nietzsche drove home this insight particularly severely in his iconoclasm. Durkheim extended the sociological insight that understandings of reality were largely shaped by one's culture. Freud exposed the irrationality of rationality itself. Russell, in spite of valiant efforts to maintain the quest for incontestable truth, participated in a philosophical trend that came to recognize philosophy's inability to establish such truth. Many social critics even suggested that the worst, most brutal excesses of the twentieth century had their roots in Enlightenment thought itself—particularly in the very attempt to achieve a total answer.[6]

Other thinkers in the twentieth century exposed the crumbling of the quest for the emancipated new world order. The historian, A. J. P. Taylor, writing about cultural developments between World Wars I and II, said, "Many forces combined to end the reign of reason which had run since the Renaissance." Developments in physics challenged the old paradigm of a predictable universe. "Scientists cheerfully announced that they did not know what they were doing: 'indeterminacy' was now their basic principle."[7] Philosophers, Taylor suggested, "gave up the search for truth."[8] Others, Taylor observed, demolished reason with direct attacks. He mentioned the Freudians and Marxists.[9] The expansion of sociology as an academic discipline promoted the insight that human thought is socially relative. College and university students in the 1950s, 1960s, and 1970s learned their social relativism from numerous texts that celebrated the debunking power of the sociological analysis of knowledge.[10]

Many observers began pointing out that the engines of power politics and corporate bureaucracies—enhanced by the electronic media—were extending their reach and power over everyone. These engines had a logic of their own, suggesting the possibility that nobody could control them. These observers were often following the lead of Max Weber who, writing, early in the twentieth century, lamented the depersonalization of these forces. He felt that the modern "economic conditions of machine production" had come to so dominate humanity that everybody was doomed to coercive work in vast, inhuman bureaucracies—what he termed an "iron cage."[11] So by the 1960s individuals in the industrialized West and portions of the rest of the world found themselves increasingly isolated in a confusing world of competing philosophies and lifestyles, and they were to make a living somehow in an economy dominated by giant corporations and big government.

As the counter-cultural uprisings of the 1960s and 1970s ran out of steam, social observers began offering diagnoses of cultural transformation. Noteworthy among the many theses were those that suggested we had arrived at the time of the homeless mind, the end of ideology, the end of history, a post-liberal, post-capitalist, post-communist world characterized by culture wars.[12] These various arguments contributed to a growing sense that we were a world with ever fewer cultural moorings. In the 1970s scholars would begin identifying this new world as *postmodern*, a perspective that has gripped the imagination of journalists, scholars, and the reading public. It continues to fuel study and debate.

Postmodern thought is multi-faceted, involving countless esoteric interdisciplinary theses and debates about every aspect of life from the use of language to the content of film to the globalization of the world economy. For our purposes, there are several related and important themes central to postmodern analysis. The most basic is that there is no ultimate grounding for claims to truth. The modern world has made a significant cultural shift, so that it is a world wherein we *recognize* that ambiguity, constant change, complexity, and pluralism are the true state of humanity. Claims to truth are multiple, contradictory, and debatable. Traditional worldviews, such as religion, are subverted by the reality of competing perspectives. Modern worldviews, such as science and humanism, cannot establish a certain foundation of truth and knowledge. Elizabeth Ermarth writes, "Postmodernism denies absolute status to any truth or nature or reality. The question always remains—what truth, which nature, whose reality?"[13] The French philosopher Jean François Lyotard is most frequently cited for stating simply that the postmodern means "incredulity towards metanarratives."[14] By this, I think he means we are no longer convinced by any comprehensive view of the world—certainly not on a scale wide enough for the many competing interests to find common ground on which to build the human community of freedom and solidarity.

Furthermore, any given perspective on human affairs is tied to some social interest struggling for recognition, advantage, privilege, and power. The crucial question seems to be whether there is even the possibility for a universally shared worldview on which competing interests could build a free and just world. Obviously much—maybe everything—depends on whether this is possible. The Enlightenment thinkers themselves had a particular view of how the world should be. It was to be a secular and rational world of individual freedom guided by science. This vision proved to be naive in the face of powerful, collective forces and ideologies of capitalism, communism, socialism, and nationalism. It had some success against religion, but even this continues to be an ongoing struggle as manifest in increasingly militant religious fundamentalisms. Some thinkers, such as the German social philosopher, Jürgen Habermas, continue the valiant pursuit of the Enlightenment hope of finding a ground or process whereby the many competing interests can hammer out a democratic and humane world.[15] The only alternative seems to be a world in which whoever has the most power wins, with terrible consequences for the losers, or a world in which everybody loses either to incessant violent conflict or to massive inhuman social systems that nobody controls.

Another important theme in postmodern thought is that power and domination are exceedingly difficult to recognize. The way in which powerful groups dominate modern society through large and impersonal institutions of government, business, education, and law is subtle and complicated. Even in democratic societies there is a widespread sense of powerlessness and futility. The target of critique is, at best, always moving and, at worst, invisible. The globalization of the world economy; the complexity of the systems of information and finance; the ineffectiveness of governments at managing economic crises, protecting civil and democratic rights, maintaining national security, and avoiding ecological disaster; and the impotence of critical and reformist impulses in the face of mass consumption, entertainment, and media "noise"—all these make it all but impossible to find the pressure points to move modern societies toward creating social and cultural environments that are more livable and satisfying. Simply stated: we're caught up in impersonal and competitive systems of global scope still characterized by exploitation and gross inequality, and nobody seems to know what to do or even who is in charge, if anybody.

Postmodern thought is considerably more nuanced, varied, and conflicted than I have presented it. (Almost everybody who attempts to write about it has to make this qualification.) I think it is fair, though, to have identified these three themes as typically present in postmodern thought: (1) There seems to be no transcendental and ultimate grounding for claims to truth; (2) the world is fragmented by competing and conflicting interests with no universally accepted formula for mediating between interests; and (3) the power of domination is subtle and frequently "hidden."[16]

The question now seems to be whether we can hope for a humanized world of optimal security *and* optimal freedom *and* optimal justice: (1) without having any certain and uncontestable ground of truth and value; (2) recognizing that our own perspectives reflect the limited horizons and interests of the groups to which we belong; and (3) without a sure, predefined path for getting there. Clearly this requires individuals and groups with unusual mental capacity and moral courage. It involves the excruciatingly difficult task of groups asserting their own specific interests in dialogue and conflict with other groups, but without any group being able to claim dogmatic certainty. It means recognizing that one's own perspectives are not absolute and certain truth. It must include respectful tolerance of cultural and political competitors. And all the debate and conflict need to be in a context sensitive to the collective welfare of the planet. "Lacking modernity's iron fist," writes Zygmunt Bauman, "postmodernity needs nerves of steel."[17]

As I read them, the leading postmodernist thinkers are keeping alive the practice of unveiling and demystifying the ways by which personality is distorted, community is undermined, and power is hidden, but they have surrendered the quest for any total and universal blueprint for a solution. In this they carry forth the critical analysis of the Enlightenment humanists but without offering any new map toward a utopian future. Expressions of hope and despair vary with the social theorist and critic, but their work underscores an essential insight—one articulated repeatedly by the Christian theologian, Reinhold Niebuhr, in mid-twentieth century:

> The task of building a world community is man's final necessity and possibility, but also his final impossibility. It is a necessity and possibility because history is a process which extends the freedom of man over natural process to the point where universality is reached. It is an impossibility because man is, despite his increasing freedom, a finite creature, wedded to time and place and incapable of building any structure of culture or civilization which does not have its foundations in a particular and dated locus.[18]

The issues of social conflict and world transformation are beyond the modest concerns of this book, except in this important sense: if religion is to play a role in solving humanity's greatest problems, it will need to take seriously the legitimate and insightful critiques of the Enlightenment humanists and postmodern critics. It will need to seek healthful ways to embody the spiritual quest for individuals and society, as well as ways to criticize oppressive and dehumanizing social arrangements. Our concern, for the seeker's spiritual journey, is the postmodern recognition that as historical and cultural beings, we do not have access to infallible absolute truth. This insight presents a particularly difficult challenge to religious thinkers who wish to defend the "truths" of their religions and to reflective seekers who desire spiritual understanding. But this insight is extremely important because when we do believe we have access to infallible absolute truth, we tend to view others as lesser beings, and coercion as a proper means to deal with them.

Faith and Religion in the Postmodern World

It is no surprise, of course, that religious thinkers have used postmodern thought to buttress diametrically opposite positions. Some conservative religious thinkers have seen in postmodernism a confirmation of their claims regarding the worthlessness of human reason and the priority of revelation and tradition. More liberal religious thinkers have seen in the postmodern recognition of the limits of human reason a new point of origin for liberating faith.[19] Of course, between these two poles, there is a wide array of religious perspectives embracing and/or lamenting postmodern thought and our postmodern condition—a sign, I might add, of postmodernism itself.[20]

I would agree with the Christian theologian, Merold Westphal, though, that postmodern critiques "neither presuppose nor entail a godless world." They do not demonstrate "that there is no God, but simply that we are not God."[21] This is perhaps the important starting point for the spiritual seeker and, I would argue, the necessary cornerstone for all theological formulation. In other words, post-modernism brings to the table the re-affirmation of the traditional religious concern with images and idols and the dangers thereof. We have seen now that even secular ideologies can contribute to brutality, violence, and oppression. We are masters at idolatry, religious or secular. Murder is still murder whether it is done in the name of God or national security or capitalism or the party or the people or the one holy universal church. In this, postmodernism offers an understanding of religion better than religion often understands itself.[22] With this postmodern plank, religion can regain its memory.

The danger of dogmatic absolutism is only the first, albeit the most important, postmodern insight challenging religion. A second important offering (or confrontation, if you will) is this: The relative power of religion has declined and will continue to do so; and where it does have influence over public affairs, its own liberal and conservative manifestations will cancel each other out.

That religion in history could have been identified as oppressive (Voltaire), alienating (Marx), duplicitous (Nietzsche), socially legitimating (Durkheim), psychologically regressive (Freud), and harmful (Russell) points to the reality that it has had the power to do these things. This means, of course, that it also had the power to be liberating, reconciling, a critical voice of clarity, a challenge to the status quo, psychologically enabling, and constructive. Many of its defenders—in ongoing debate with Enlightenment humanists—continue to chronicle evidence for such. But today religion appears anemic next to the power of the giant capitalist dominated consumer society and the equally giant national and international governing bodies of the world. This is true in the West, much of the Orient, and, I suspect, will be increasingly so elsewhere.

This is true even though there seems to be currently a resurgence of interest in things religious. In a postmodern world religion is relegated largely to the private realm of the family and the individual. One aspect of secularization is that religion becomes a private affair. It means, paradoxically, that religious activity can increase, as it has in American history, while at the same time losing influence over the culture. Americans buying up the books on spirituality from New Age to Wicca to Buddhism to Christian fundamentalism are clearly seeking something, but apparently not a strategy for social and political influence.

In spite of some increasing interest in religion, most individuals in the most industrialized countries have little room in their lives for serious religion. Under corporate capitalism, between the demands of work, the unlimited consumer options for entertainment and recreation, the endless hustling of the unemployed and underemployed for some opportunity, and the preoccupations of interest-group partisanship—people have plenty to keep them occupied. In this context, religion for the individual tends to become the filler for those occasionally quiet moments when one wonders about ultimate meaning. For the family it becomes an institution where their own middle-class and patriotic values can be reinforced for the children, even in the name of God. Every American pastor has realized that church activity is not a robust competitor versus such things as soccer practice, Sunday football, or even more time in the office.

The religious struggles in Islamic countries and in India for influence and control over public affairs would seem to be evidence against a decline in the power of religion. These struggles are, I suspect, an historically temporary trend. So far in human history, such struggles have tended to discredit religion and contribute to its eventual decline in power. Since September 11, 2001, throughout the world Islam is laboring to show that it is not incompatible with modern social systems. As the relatively "new" nations, founded in the twentieth century, find ways to stabilize and develop without the use of religious ideologies, they will do as others did earlier—move toward toleration and disestablishment. The world no longer needs religion to legitimize the status quo or spur societies to change, and ruling groups will turn to other public philosophies when the fanatical wings of religion threaten to destabilize political arrangements.

Obviously major social problems and social conflict will continue to plague human relations. Religion will, through the activities of its social activists, exercise modest influence in the struggles over humanity's future, but its power to do this seems greatly diminished. In any case, its liberal and conservative wings will tend to cancel each other out, leading exasperated governments to alternately appease religious groups and drive a bigger wedge between religion and state. No doubt, religion will continue to comfort some number of people who do not feel at home in an alienating and dehumanizing world. And it should, but this is a meager offering in light of religion's grand vision of passion for human welfare and solidarity.

A third lesson postmodernism carries for religion is that no one religion can provide the world with a uniting and unchallenged faith. Each individual religion must itself recognize, no matter how dogmatically it holds to its doctrines, that it is one player among others. Historically, sociologically, and psychologically informed people can no longer adhere, in good faith, to the belief that those who do not accept their religion are, for that reason, guilty of sin or willfully disobeying God. Even from his own paternalistic and Christ-centered perspective, the head of the largest Christian body, Pope John Paul II, writing about the people in other religions, has said: "Christ came into the world for all these peoples. He redeemed them all and has His own ways of reaching each of them."[23]

No doubt, many religious groups will remain in a cultural space of isolated irrelevance—either ignoring or railing against the rest of the world. Postmodernism permits, even affirms, this option. However, those religious groups who understand their mission to include engagement with the world, will need the capacity to sit at table with people of other faiths just as sincere, just as smart, and just as passionately caring as they. To be able to do this, in good faith, religion will need to know itself better.

Underlying modern and postmodern thought is a basic human paradox. Even though, for a variety of reasons, we experience history as something that happens to us, we can see, as never so clearly before, that humanity collectively is the creative agent in its own history. This is what makes it so tragic. In cooperation, conflict, and struggle, we make our history, however much the social systems we create take on lives of their own. This is one place where the modernists and postmodernists diverge.

Postmodern thinkers, taking very seriously the irrational nature of humanity and the relative autonomy of social systems and the obvious lack of a common foundation of humanistic faith, are skeptical about our ever being able to create more intentionally a free and humane world. The intentional creation of an emancipated world was the Enlightenment hope and project, and it was naive, so it seems. At best, suggests postmodern thought, we can move in that direction only through partial and local struggles. If there is hope for significant social progress, it is not to be found in some grand scheme for everybody, but rather in the piecemeal advances fought for and won by the many disenfranchised and oppressed groups of the world. Among the modernists, there are still those who argue that we cannot give up the Enlightenment hope for a unifying worldview on which we can build human solidarity and freedom. But even they acknowledge the necessity of searching for creative ways of achieving this without falling into the totalitarian systems that have plagued human history—especially the bloody twentieth century.

For religion that does not just dig in its dogmatic heels and refuse to dialogue, the question is whether it will be reduced finally and completely to a private realm of occasionally comforting escape or whether it will engage the world in dialogue and confrontation, bringing to the table its own vision of tolerance, justice, and pluralism. Unfortunately, as noted above, when religion does enter the realm of public debate and discourse, the opposing political views among the religious tend to cancel each other out. I do not know whether this will ever change. But, if possible, it seems to me that the way for religion to get beyond authoritarian coercion, public irrelevance, and stalemated impotence is to recognize, in postmodern fashion, its own participation in constructing itself.

Another way of saying it is that for religion to exercise its voice in a spirit of authentic dialogue, religion needs to recognize itself as creative. In the history of religion there have been two fundamental views on how we arrive at "divine" truth: revelation and discovery. Western religion has emphasized revelation. The mainstream of Western philosophy emphasized rational discovery until, under the impact of science, it abandoned altogether any talk about the divine. Eastern religions have emphasized non-rational discovery. However, as we have come to see that human beings participate in constructing their cultures and consequently their perceptions and understandings of reality, we can see that that is true as well of the revelations and discoveries of religion. Religious "truth" cannot hide in a privileged space outside the boundaries of criticism because, to quote again Reinhold Niebuhr, "there is no historical reality, whether it be the reason of wise men or specialists, which is not involved in the flux and relativity of human existence; which is not subject to error and sin, and which is not tempted to exaggerate its errors and sins when they are made immune to criticism."[24] As long as religion remains convinced that its views of God, nature, and humanity are delivered infallibly from a reality outside history and culture, it cannot be adequately self-critical because it cannot recognize its own creative self in the encounter with the divine.

In the West it is not enough that we recognize theologies as humanly constructed interpretations of revelation. We must go back to the revelations themselves—mainly sacred texts—and recognize them, too, as creative constructions of the divine-human encounter. It makes all the difference in the world whether one says, "Jesus was the Son of God," or, "Jesus' followers experienced Jesus as divine." There is a significant difference between saying, "The angel Gabriel revealed the Qur'an to Muhammad," and "Muhammad wrote the Qur'an in response to mystical experiences he experienced as revelations from the angel Gabriel." The two latter statements recognize the human as creative agent and thus open the door for recognition of historical and cultural influence even over sacred texts. For fundamentalists, this is blasphemous, but it is the only way to embrace the historicity of human finitude. On a pragmatic level, I cannot see any other way for us to get beyond the historical impasse of competing absolutist monologues. The absolutism itself, as Bertrand Russell and others have pointed out, helps legitimate coercion and violence.[25] How else can we move from relationships that are antagonistic and exploitative to those of mutual respect and care—from, what the Jewish philosopher Martin Buber called, "I-It" relationship to "I-Thou"?[26]

I cannot, of course, predict the long-term historical consequences for religion in accepting the human as creative agent even in religion's most sacred traditions. We are talking about something that has shown itself as "higher criticism" in biblical interpretation, and two hundred years of such criticism among liberal Jewish and Christian scholars suggest it would not mean either the demise of faith or the collapse of religion. Such fears are undoubtedly what scares the orthodox. But this is the opportunity the postmodern condition offers us, and I, for one, would like to see us try.

Surely the world would not be worse off if Jews, Muslims, Christians, Buddhists, Hindus, Humanists, and others came to the common table of dialogue without assuming that their respective positions were the only correct and necessary truth. In a piece arguing for the superiority of love over knowledge, the Christian apostle Paul confessed that "we know only in part" and "we see in a mirror, dimly."[27] The Qur'an offers justification for mutual respect and tolerance: "To you be your Way, And to me Mine"; "Let there be no compulsion in religion."[28] If the religious—who affirm a compassionate and merciful "Sovereign" above all particular interests—could learn to dialogue with humility, respect, and openness, they would be in a better position to address the distortions and cruelties the Enlightenment humanists have called to our attention. They could also make greater contributions toward weakening the hold and destructive power of other particular "faiths" for whom the welfare of humanity is periodically sacrificed—such "faiths" as nationalism, racism, religious sectarianism, economic imperialism, and other loyalties one theologian has called "phony sovereignties."[29] The postmodern condition, writes Zygmunt Bauman, "makes possible—just possible—the long road . . . from tolerance to solidarity."[30]

Notes

1. James Davison Hunter, *Culture Wars: The Struggle to Define America*. N.Y.: BasicBooks, 1991).

2. This event is related in Tony Rizzo, "Event on homosexuality draws protests: Demonstrators represent wide range of views," *The Kansas City Star*, 23 June 2002, B4.

3. Genesis 1:28.

4. Rich, *Age of Nationalism*, 250.

5. See Harvey, *Postmodernity*, 28.

6. See, for example, Albert Camus, *The Rebel: An Essay on Man in Revolt*, trans. Anthony Bower (N.Y.: Vintage; Random House, 1956); Max Horkheimer and Theodor W. Adorno, *Dialectic of Enlightenment*, trans. John Cumming (N.Y.: The Seabury Press, 1972).

7. A. J. P. Taylor, *From Sarajevo to Potsdam* (London: Harcourt, Brace & World, 1965), 103-104.

8. Taylor, *From Sarajevo*, 106.

9. Taylor, *From Sarajevo*, 104.

10. Among which were Karl Mannheim, *Ideology and Utopia: An Introduction to the Sociology of Knowledge*, trans. Louis Wirth and Edward Shils, (N.Y.: Harcourt, Brace & World, 1936); Peter L. Berger, *Invitation to Sociology: A Humanistic Perspective* (Garden City, N.Y.: Anchor Books, 1963); Berger and Luckmann, *Social Construction*.

11. Weber, *Protestant Ethic*, 181. See also the chapter on bureaucracy in Max Weber, *Economy and Society: An Outline of Interpretive Sociology*, vol. 2, ed. Guenther Roth and Claus Wittich (Berkeley: University of California Press, 1978).

12. See Peter L. Berger, Brigitte Berger, and Hansfried Kellner, *The Homeless Mind: Modernization and Consciousness* (N.Y.: Vintage, 1973); Francis Fukuyama, *The End of History and the Last Man* (N.Y.: Avon, 1992); Hunter, *Culture Wars*.

13. Elizabeth Deeds Ermarth, "Postmodernism," in *Routledge Encyclopedia of Philosophy*, vol. 7, ed. Edward Craig, 587-590, (London & N.Y.: Routledge, 1998), 589.

14. Lyotard, *Postmodern Condition*, xxiv.

15. See Juergen Habermas, *The Theory of Communicative Action*, 2 vols., trans. Thomas McCarthy (Boston: Beacon Press, 1981).

16. The literature is enormous. For quick and painless entry, see Jim Powell, *Postmodernism for Beginners*, N.Y.: Writers and Readers Publishing, 1998). Other works of varying difficulty include: Perry Anderson, *The Origins of Postmodernity* (London & New York: Verso, 1998); Norman K. Denzin, "Postmodern Social Theory," *Sociological Theory* 4 (fall 1986):194-204; Ermarth, "Postmodernism"; Harvey, *Postmodernity*; Scott Lash, *Sociology of Postmodernism* (London and N.Y.: Routledge, 1990); Lyotard, *Postmodern Condition*; Joseph Natoli and Linda Hutcheon, eds., *A Postmodern Reader* (Albany, N.Y.: State University of New York Press, 1993); Steven Seidman, *Contested Knowledge: Social Theory in the Postmodern Era* (Oxford UK & Cambridge USA: Blackwell, 1994); Bryan S. Turner, ed., *Theories of Modernity and Postmodernity* (London: Sage, 1990).

17. Zygmunt Bauman, "Postmodernity, or Living with Ambivalence," in *A Postmodern Reader*, ed. Natoli and Hutcheon, 9-24, [from *Modernity and Ambivalence*, by Bauman 231-245, Cornell University Press and Blackwell, 1991], 24.

18. Reinhold Niebuhr, *The Children of Light and the Children of Darkness: A Vindication of Democracy and a Critique of Its Traditional Defense* (N.Y.: Charles Scribner's Sons, 1972 [1944]), 187.

19. See Ilse Bulhof, and Laurens ten Kate, "Echoes of an Embarrassment: Philosophical Perspectives on Negative Theology—An Introduction," *Flight of the Gods: Philosophical Perspectives on Negative Theology*, ed. Bulhof and ten Kate, 1-57 (N.Y.: Fordham University Press, 2000); John Caputo, *On Religion* (London and New York: Routledge, 2001); David Ray Griffin, William A. Beardslee, and Joe Holland, eds., *Varieties of Postmodern Theology* (Albany, N.Y.: State University of New York Press, 1989); Graham Ward, "Introduction, or, A Guide to Theological Thinking in Cyberspace," in *The Postmodern God: A Theological Reader*, ed. Ward (Malden, Mass.: Blackwell Publishers, 1997); Wolfe, "The Opening," 55-76.

20. Again, the literature is enormous, among which: Ahmed, *Postmodernism and Islam*; Walter Brueggemann, *Texts Under Negotiation: The Bible and Postmodern Imagination* (Minneapolis: Fortress Press, 1993); Ilse Bulhof and Laurens ten Kate, eds., *Flight of the Gods: Philosophical Perspectives on Negative Theology* (N.Y.: Fordham University Press, 2000); Ernest Gellner, *Postmodernism, Reason and Religion* (London and New York: Routledge, 1992); Griffin et al., *Varieties*; Graham Ward, ed., *The Postmodern God: A Theological Reader* (Malden, Mass.: Blackwell Publishers, 1997); Merold Westphal, *Overcoming Onto-Theology: Toward a Postmodern Christian Faith* (N.Y.: Fordham University Press, 2001).

21. Westphal, *Overcoming Onto-Theology*, 87.

22. A play on the hermeneutic concept of understanding authors better than they understand themselves; see Josef Bleicher, *Contemporary Hermeneutics: Hermeneutics as Method, Philosophy and Critique* (London: Routledge & Kegan Paul, 1980), 15, 122, 148, 208.

23. John Paul II, *Crossing the Threshold Hope*, ed. Vittorio Messori (N.Y.: Alfred A. Knopf, 1994), 83.

24. Niebuhr, *The Children of Light*, 70-71.

25. See Russell, "Philosophy and Politics," 94-95.

26. Martin Buber, *I and Thou*, trans. Ronald Gregor Smith, 2nd ed. (N.Y.: Charles Scribner's Sons, 1958).

27. I Corinthians 13:9, 12.

28. *Holy Qur'an*, 109:6, 2:256; cited in Ahmed, *Postmodernism and Islam*, 36.

29. Eugene M. Boring, "The Gospel of Matthew: Introduction, Commentary, and Reflections," in *The New Interpreter's Bible*, vol. VIII, ed. Leander E. Keck et al., 87-506 (Nashville: Abingdon Press, 1995), 415.

30. Bauman, "Postmodernity," 16.

Chapter 12

To Walk Humbly with Your God
A Case for Faith and Religion

In the meantime we, as individuals, have to get out of bed in the morning and make commitments. Furthermore, psychologically we require some ordering principle for personality and action. "There is nothing stable about the postmodern vision as a resting place for human consciousness," writes Patrick Glynn. Even though the mind insists on recognizing "these nihilistic propositions," the heart cannot tolerate them in the long run.[1] So we find ourselves now in a postmodern world faced with decisions about how to live our lives.

It seems that more people have more freedom than ever before. *Freedom* is an ambiguous term. There are problems, as some social critics have claimed, with viewing late capitalist society with its big government, giant corporations, and mass-consumer culture as a place of authentic freedom. However, as Albert Camus points out: "There is no ideal freedom that will someday be given us all at once, as a pension comes at the end of one's life." Rather, we have to win liberties "painfully, one by one, and" view those we already have as stages "on the way to total liberation."[2] Acknowledging the important debates about the authenticity of freedom, it is reasonable to argue that more people today have more options about what to think and how to live their lives than historically heretofore.

There is something both terrifying and comforting about this reality of greater choice. It means, on the one hand, all the uncertainty, insecurity, and agony of assuming responsibility for one's decisions and actions. On the other hand, it means all the thrill, challenge, and adventure of exploration and commitment. In either case, for the exercise of faith and religion, it means there is no longer the option of a naive, good-faith return to a pre-critical faith tradition. No matter one's choice, even if it is to opt for the most authoritarian and dogmatic religion, in today's global village it must be made in light of the awareness that there are other possibilities. In this, the Enlightenment project has succeeded—at least for much of the world—and, I believe, it is to our benefit.

A *caveat* is in order here. It has always seemed to me a little irresponsible to talk of individual freedom without acknowledging that the degree of such freedom depends on social, political, and especially economic factors largely beyond the control of individuals. This is, in part, why the term *freedom* is so ambiguous. While I am stressing the reality of choice and decision in the postmodern world, this does not mean that everybody has equal opportunity for movement. Unfortunately still too many of the world's population have few options. While a mark of postmodernism is the globalization of the world economy, this globalizing proceeds hand in hand with one of the most awesome maldistributions of wealth in human history. Millions in our shared world face stark problems of survival; other millions live with luxuries and options former monarchs could not even dream of; and a tiny minority in almost every country lives with opulence beyond any imaginative conception in history outside mythologies. We must concede that there are options really only for those whose lives are not an incessant struggle for day-to-day survival.

These are the people who have some freedom to reflect on their life commitments and the potential consequences for themselves and the world around them. It must also be acknowledged that the capacity of individuals to fulfill their commitments varies greatly depending on personalities and on circumstances which are often beyond their control. But there remains the possibility of choosing an outlook and a life-walk toward which one will strive—however far one might miss the mark. Given the intellectual heritage narrated in this work, it seems to me there are several options for thinking people today. I would call them faith-options.

Egoism is one possibility. This is simply the commitment to order one's personality and center one's life around the pursuits of one's own individual interests. In some ways it is possible to see Epicurus and Lucretius as founding fathers of egoism. Nietzsche exemplifies one way for the egoist; although his complexity means that categorizing him is easily disputed. Egoism is the philosophy of "to thine own self be true," and it is inherently secular since religious faiths typically posit at least an equivalent and altruistic caring connectivity to others. However, the egoist is not necessarily an isolated individual, for such a person will still have lovers, family, and friends who are held quite dearly. The point of reference, though, is the self.

I am not talking about people who are antisocial, unethical, unscrupulous, or criminal. Egoists typically respect the rights of others and conform to the norms of culture because this is usually the rational and civilized route to the good life, but they will at times also be the creative rebel or innovator, even contributing by their actions to new opportunities for other individuals.[3] The philosophy of capitalism is based, in part, on the insight that social order is still possible while individuals pursue their own interests in a context of open and good-faith competition.[4] What I am talking about is, I think, similar to what Ayn Rand means with her use of "selfishness" to refer to pursuing one's own interests and supporting oneself while not sacrificing the self or others.[5] The egoist may very well have strong political commitments because this position requires political, legal, and economic conditions that permit the practice of egoism.

Secular humanism is another option. Interestingly it is possible to see Epicurus and Lucretius as founding fathers also of secular humanism. Secular humanism is deeply rooted in Enlightenment philosophical traditions. This is the option exemplified in various ways by Voltaire, Marx, Durkheim, Freud, and Russell. It carries a principled commitment above all to the welfare of humanity, and it affirms certain ideals as best for humanity. "Secular humanism," claims Paul Kurtz, "is not a dogma or a creed." Nevertheless, Kurtz goes on to say that it involves a commitment to "reason, democracy, and freedom," and promotes additionally the ideals of free inquiry, separation of church and state, ethics based on critical intelligence, the importance of moral education, religious skepticism, and the practice of science, among other things.[6]

Secular humanists often involve themselves in activities and organizations in support of policies that advance secular humanist ideals. Frequently, this will be as part of some particular interest—such as feminism, racial justice, civil rights, economic justice, a cleaner environment, or whatever. But typically underlying these specific commitments is a broad commitment to transcending principles of humanism.

The third option in our postmodern world is religious faith.

Broadly speaking, there are two types of religious faith. Both are rooted in a stream of cultural religious traditions, involving sacred writings, ritual, and some community of fellow believers. But one type tries to remain exclusively within its tradition, accepting it uncritically and viewing everything outside it as friend or foe. It sees reality only in terms of its own assumptions and beliefs; everything else is measured and found wanting or acceptable entirely on its own terms. It is exclusive and not reflectively self-critical except when examining how it is winning or losing vis-à-vis other faiths. This is what I would call an authoritarian-and-exclusive faith, and it manifests itself in religious sectarianism. It is often identified, somewhat imprecisely, as fundamentalism or orthodoxy. Sometimes it is accompanied by withdrawal from mainstream society. Sometimes it comes with fanaticism, intolerance, and bigotry.

The second type of faith is what I would call, for want of a better phrase, *open and critical*. This is the way of orientation to a transcendent reality but without the spiritual arrogance of claiming absolutely correct or infallible truth that views other faiths as mistaken or even necessarily inferior. It is open to its own inadequacy and to new truth while still affirming the practice of faith. It is open to and gracious toward those of other faith traditions. Open-and-critical faith and its religious manifestations live in dynamic tension with other perspectives as well as other faiths. Open-and-critical faith is willing to experience influence from external views and practices while also exercising criticism of its own potential for distortion. It is willing to listen to the cultural critiques outlined in this book even when they come from humanists outside religious faith.

This dichotomy between authoritarian-and-exclusive faith and open-and-critical faith is an oversimplification. It is possible to see them as the poles of a continuum, at least as I have formulated it here. In reality the many denominations and schools of religions carry varying amounts of authoritarianism and openness, tolerance and intolerance, self-criticism and self-opacity. Nevertheless, it is accurate to say that the various schools and denominations within religions will tend to fall closer to one pole than to the other, and it is relatively easy to find good examples of each.

Of the world's major religions—what Huston Smith calls "the world's great, enduring religions"—I cannot identify one as more likely to offer open-and-critical options than another. In today's news Islamic fundamentalism is getting a lot of coverage; but there is plenty of fundamentalism in Christianity as well, and Islam is far more open than the media's sound bites imply. Some students of religion have suggested that Buddhism and Hinduism are the most inclusive and tolerant toward other religions. I do know that every major world religion has branches that are open and critical, so the spiritual seeker can find a room in somebody's inn.

Egoism, secular humanism, and open-and-critical religious faith—these seem to me to be the three basic options for reflective people today. There is, conceivably, a fourth that we could call the option of postmodernity. This would involve actually what most of us do—moving in and out of the various spheres of everyday life. There is the person, for example, who spends most of the work day in egoistic pursuit of career and income, a good portion of the afternoon voluntarily serving some non-profit community agency, the early evening in reciprocal care with family, and after dinner at choir rehearsal at church. This rather eclectic approach to lifestyle and life philosophy would have been seen as somewhat duplicitous in the traditional world of the Middle Ages, contradictory in the world of modernity, but quite understandable in a postmodern world. It is an option that deserves some serious exploration by someone, but I do not think we are ready quite yet to view it as an ideal to which we would consciously aspire.

Clearly I am excluding consideration of any authoritarian and tribalist option—such as the sectarianisms, nationalisms, racisms, and other creeds that elevate some historical and particular reality to godlike status. "One kills for a nation or a class that has been granted divine status," wrote Albert Camus in his essay, "Reflections on the Guillotine." And, he added, "Whoever thinks he has omniscience imagines he has omnipotence."[7] The isms and their absolutist creeds provide fuel for the conflicts and violence of our world. It is the absolutist, exclusive, and ethnocentric spirit among nations that helped turn the history of the twentieth century into a chronicle of successive bloodbaths. It is the absolutist, exclusive, and ethnocentric spirit in religion that did the same for earlier centuries.

Toward an Open-and-Critical Faith

Marx, in a lament of sorts, wrote that humanity has not been freed from religion; it has been given freedom of religion.[8] Indeed, it is true that for much of the world today people are free to explore their spirituality, and to do so in cultural contexts richly endowed with spiritual traditions. This is to be celebrated, and it is our point of departure for those who would continue the spiritual quest while not ignoring the insights of the Enlightenment humanists and postmodern thought.

I would confess that I love religion. The ritual, the theological struggles to understand the Divine and the relationship between the Divine and humanity, the piety of the devoted, the poetry of religious writing, the pageantry of religious ritual—I find religion exciting and inspiring, sometimes also boring and depressing, but almost always alluring. And I encourage others to involve themselves in religion. But for an open-and-critical faith, it is important to remember that the Divine-human encounter cannot be contained by religion. Any religion that suggests otherwise should be approached with suspicion.

From a theological viewpoint, religion itself can be a seductive substitute for any encounter with the Holy. Religion can be a way to avoid authentic relationship to God. And in so far as religion is a manifestation of a human attempt to reach God, grasp God, define God, it is also a ridiculous form of human pride. The terror of really facing the Divine, of dealing with the awesome sense of a potentially demanding sacred reality, of responding to the Holy Other without the protective shield of official religion is captured in that unique story about the Israelites who said to Moses, "You speak to us, and we will listen; but do not let God speak to us, or we will die."[9] They wanted somebody else to stand between them and God. Religion can be a buffer we place between us and any encounter with the Holy Other that would challenge us where it really matters—in our hearts, in our relationships, in the concrete reality of our everyday lives.

It has been common historically for religious leaders to sacralize religion itself—its ritual, its beliefs, its ethos. The external and internal, religious and secular critiques of religion reviewed throughout this book get much of their fuel from the tendency of particular religions to allocate absolute importance to themselves. In other words, religion's tendency to idolize itself makes it an easy target for religion's critics, and rightly so.

This is an essential insight for the spiritual journey. It is important to see that religion can be an idolatrous mask behind which we hide—from ourselves, from the world, from the Divine. An open-and-critical faith can, I believe, remember that the sense and reality of the Sacred Other cannot be contained by religion. I do not know any way to resist the powerfully seductive potential of religion for self-deception without an open-and-critical faith.

I would like to offer a number of claims—as humbly as I can—about religion and faith that might be helpful to some, frankly, because they have been helpful to me. These are, I must concede, theological claims. More precisely, I suppose, they are metatheological claims. By that I mean to imply that they are meant to be more general than any one specific religious tradition. They are meant to facilitate the decision to choose religious faith in an open-and-critical spirit. There are ten of them.

1. There is inherent in human experience a sense of the sacred. There seems to be inherently in human experience a sense of transcendental sacred reality beyond the immediately given that resists reduction to merely psychological or sociological explanations. I am talking about the experience commonly called *mystical*, which seems to be fairly universal, remarkably similar from one religion to another, and found even in secular contexts. Karen Armstrong writes that mystical experiences, although "culturally conditioned," seem to be "an incontrovertible fact of life. However we choose to interpret it, people all over the world and in all phases of history have had this type of contemplative experience."[10]

The experience involves a sense of feeling overwhelmed by the presence of something awesome and marvelous. That something is typically sensed as Holy Other. Early in the twentieth century Rudolf Otto, a German theologian, did a study of this fundamental human experience of transcendence and presence.[11] His book, *The Idea of the Holy*, has become a classic and the starting point for anyone who would take up the study of the human experience of the Holy. Otto described what he called the *mysterium tremendum*, a Latin phrase referring to a sense of awe-filled mystery, characterized by astonishment and humility. When this occurs, people are overwhelmed by the sense of an all-superior power and feel paradoxically both unworthy and cared for.[12] Otto called this a "feeling of the numinous," and he suggested it "is a primal element of our psychical nature" that "cannot itself be explained from anything else."[13]

If Otto is right, this is the definitive answer to the Enlightenment critics who would reduce religious faith to merely psychological expressions of misery, fear, or desire, or to sociological expressions such as the collective consciousness. The great many instances of this experience reported in human history, in a wide variety of circumstances, point to a unique sensibility—a sensibility that says, *There is something more.*[14]

This mystical experience of *something more*, of a transcendent Holy Other, is also characterized by a deep sense of connectedness and unity. W. T. Stace writes: "The most important, the central characteristics in which all *fully developed* mystical experiences agree, and which in the last analysis is definitive of them and serves to mark them off from other kinds of experiences, is that they involve the apprehension of *an ultimate nonsensuous unity in all things*, a oneness or a One to which neither the senses nor the reason can penetrate." In all religions, he says, "we find that the essence of the experience is that it is an *undifferentiated unity*, though each culture and each religion interprets this undifferentiated unity in terms of its own creeds or dogmas."[15]

There are even "secular" reports of experiences of this transcendent presence and wholeness. Dr. James Austin, while waiting for a train in London,

> suddenly felt a sense of enlightenment unlike anything he had ever experi-enced. His sense of individual existence, of separateness from the physical world around him, evaporated like morning mist in a bright dawn. He saw things "as they really are," he recalls. The sense of "I, me, mine" disappeared. "Time was not present," he says. "I had a sense of eternity. My old yearnings, loathings, fear of death and insinuations of selfhood vanished. I had been graced by a comprehension of the ultimate nature of things."[16]

Many scientists and naturalists have reported similar experiences while pursuing their own investigations. Peter Wylie, in an introductory essay to the study of the earth sciences, wrote that the development of an awareness and appreciation of the earth "brings us closer to nature, closer to an awareness of some transcen-dental power, closer to God if we choose to define God in these terms."[17] Stud-ies in brain imaging and mystical experience have led neurologists Andrew Newberg and Eugene d'Aquili to argue: "The human brain has been genetically wired to encourage religious beliefs."[18]

This is not to say that that experience proves the reality of God. No human experience can do that. It does, however, suggest that the sense of "Holy Other" is universal and inherent in human experience, and thus not easily dismissed or reduced to something else. William James wrote that the factual reality of mys-tical states "overthrows the pretension of non-mystical states to be the sole and ultimate dictators of what we may believe."[19] Alan Watts put it like this:

> No system of philosophy or theology, no precise intellectual structure, can ever fully embrace the mystical experience of God. Not only is the divine Spirit as living and ungraspable as the wind, but the experience itself contains paradoxi-cal elements which no ordinary logical procedure can reconcile.[20]

It is also reasonable to see the origin of religion as rooted in this experience, however much religion is also part and product of the mundane psychological and sociological factors rightfully identified by social scientists and critics of religion.[21]

2. The Holy is ultimately incomprehensible. Essential to an open-and-critical faith is the recognition that the Sacred Transcendental Reality is ultimately un-knowable in a cognitive sense, even according to religions themselves. Mystics have expressed this most forcefully. St. John of the Cross wrote: "One of the greatest favors bestowed on the soul . . . in this life is to enable it to see so dis-tinctly and to feel so profoundly that it cannot comprehend God at all."[22] But even the official sacred texts express such insight. In the Hebrew book of Job, Yahweh challenges Job's attempts to understand God, and Job replies: "I have uttered what I did not understand, things too wonderful for me, which I did not know."[23] The *Tao Te Ching* of Lao Tzu begins with this statement: "The Tao that can be told is not the eternal Tao. The name that can be named is not the eternal name."[24] The Christian New Testament stresses that God is "known" only in relationship and particularly in love. "Whoever does not love does not know God, for God is love," claims the letter of First John.[25] The Islamic Qur'an emphasizes that God is seen only in God's activities. "No mortal eyes can see Him, though He sees all eyes."[26]

This is why Western religions have emphasized the concept of revelation. The reasoning is that since humanity cannot "know" God, God must reveal God's own reality. However, no matter how much one religion has agreed on what the revelation is—the law and the prophets in Judaism, the Old and New Testaments in Christianity, the Koran in Islam—within each has been great diversity over how to read the revelation, over what it says, over what it emphasizes and de-emphasizes. God is experienced as many. Even if it were true that there is one true revelation of God, there cannot be any absolute certainty regarding the true interpretation. This is one of the places where religious fanaticism goes wrong. While religion's thinkers and its sacred texts recognize a profoundly indefinable "space" between finite human beings and the Infinite, spiritual pride and arrogance are often brought back in through the door of naive and uncritical interpretation of revelation.

What is spiritually liberating about the insight that the Holy Other is cognitively unknowable is that it allows us to shift from the impossible task of *knowing* God intellectually to the better possibility of "*knowing*" God personally. Experiencing God is not about knowledge in the traditional Western sense of grasping the essence of something. Rather, it is about relationship—a relationship of faith to the presence of the Divine.

A useful analogy would be the relationship in marriage. It is not uncommon for spouses to complain that they just do not understand each other. If any married person were to try with pen and paper to write an essay titled, "The Nature and Personality of My Spouse," it would typically be experienced as excruciatingly difficult if not impossible. The reality is that our relationship to spouses and lovers does not depend on our knowing them in the sense of having a complete or accurate cognitive grasp of them. Fidelity, mutual concern, love, affection, shared joys and sorrows—all the things that go into rich and meaningful relationships do not require such knowledge of our partners.

Our relationship to the Divine is like that. There are plenty of good reasons for trying to understand God. After all, misunderstandings, as with spouses, can lead to severely sad consequences. It is reasonable—as religions claim—to view the Holy Other as revealing or disclosing the Self to humanity in myriad ways, just as spouses attempt to enlighten one another regarding their personalities in the hope of being better understood and thus better loved. So in our pursuit of understanding we should use all the cultural, historical, and spiritual resources ("revelations") at our disposal. But in the last analysis, the joy and security and empowerment from "knowing" God is in the relationship and not in the theology. The Christian apostle Paul wrote: "O the depth of the riches and wisdom and knowledge of God! How unsearchable are God's judgments and how inscrutable God's ways!"[27]

3. Religion is a social institution. The concepts, *religion* and *faith*, are frequently used interchangeably. It is not necessarily harmful to do so, but it can be a little confusing, and I find it helpful to distinguish between them.

Any definition of religion tends to fit the frame of reference and purpose of the definer. This was obvious with some of the Enlightenment humanists' definitions, particularly those of Marx, Durkheim, and Freud. It is also true even in the so-called "value-free" definitions offered by social scientists in agonizing precision.

Psychologists' definitions tend to be oriented to individual experience—the typical focus of psychology. The psychologist Walter Clark defines religion "as the inner experience of the individual when he senses a Beyond, especially as evidenced by the effect of this experience on his behavior."[28] Sociologists, on the other hand, tend to emphasize the group nature of religion. Keith Roberts, for example, offers that "religion is a social phenomenon that involves the grouping of people around a faith perspective."[29]

My concern is not to arbitrate between various social-scientific definitions of religion, but to offer something helpful for believers and seekers. For that purpose, I would suggest it is better to keep a sociological angle in our definitions of religion because religion *is* an institution. But I think Otto's perspective on the experience of the Holy is also essential so that religion can be distinguished from other institutions. (Some social scientists, especially those sympathetic to religious faith, include in their definitions explicit reference to Otto's work.)[30]

The historian of religion, George Marsden, argued that, to avoid confusion, a definition of religion needs to involve "some faith in the transcendent" because religion is sometimes "used in a broader sense . . . to refer to a person's highest commitments, such as to nation, party, humanity, wealth, family, self, and so forth."[31] These other kinds of involvements are comparable to religion in the sense that they are also institutions, and they offer ritual, belonging, and meaning, but they themselves are not grounded in the experience of the Holy, which, by definition, transcends all particular attachments. Certainly people have religious-like experiences sometimes when they are caught up in the rituals of patriotism, the intensities of family relations, even perhaps in the glories of wealth. But none of these other institutions or elements of human life is seen as focused primarily on the Holy Other—at least not explicitly. In practice, they often substitute as the object of faith, which, from a religious perspective, is a form of idolatry. But no one, except in some poetic sense, would say that the nation or the family or money or even humanity is God.

It seems to me best to view religion as *the social expression of the sense of the Holy Other*. As such, it is the institutionalization of stories, symbols, and ritual designed to give voice to the collectively shared recognition of a transcen-

dent, sacred, and ultimate reality. Religion, like other institutions, manifests itself in culturally and historically conditioned forms. Also like other institutions
it develops layers of personnel who go about the process of building, justifying,
and defending it. Given enough time and personnel, it develops its own bureaucracy, ideological legitimation (i.e., theology), practices of recruitment and social
control. It is, then, part of what Jews and Christians call the fallen world, what
Buddhists and Hindus call *samsara*. In other words, it is finite, terrestrial, no
more inherently holy than other human institutions, never the proper object of
faith, and a phenomenon that must remain a target of critique.

4. Faith is a matter of ultimate concern. Although *faith* is commonly used as a
synonym for religion or a collection of beliefs, it seems to me best to view faith
as an orientation of one's life. The Christian theologian Paul Tillich offers an
understanding of faith as grounded in the existential reality of whole lives. Tillich argues that faith "is the state of being ultimately concerned"; that is, it is "an
act of total personality."[32] In other words, faith is the organizing principle of the
human personality. Faith involves centering one's self around some object of
faith. Faith gives our life direction and meaning. Most simply stated, it is an
issue of what is of ultimate importance to us.

In this view, then, faith cannot be reduced to belief in doctrines or to religious ritual or even to the experience of the Holy. Note, also, that in this view of
faith we can see that the object of faith can be anything—not only God, but religion, the nation, the self, etc. Therefore, Tillich even makes the point that we
are all polytheistic because in the actual practice of day-to-day living we give
ourselves over to ultimate concern about many things. However, true faith as
ultimate concern requires an ultimate object. "In true faith the ultimate concern
is a concern about the truly ultimate; while in idolatrous faith preliminary, finite
realities are elevated to the rank of ultimacy."[33] In other words, only God is God.
Thus this understanding of faith fits well with religions' spiritual insight that the
ultimate and the less-than-ultimate should not be confused. "I am the Lord your
God...: you shall have no other gods before me."[34]

5. Faith is a matter of *letting go*. There is a paradoxical reality to faith that is
important not to overlook. The language of "being ultimately concerned" and
"centering one's personality around God" is proactive, assertive language. It is
the language of grasping and attachment. Faith is also just as much a matter of
relaxing and letting go. That authentic spirituality involves letting go is a consistent theme among the great religions and spiritual leaders of the world.[35]

Letting go is the reverse side of the concept of centering one's personality
around God. *Letting go* is the passive side of faith. We can see, then, that *trust* is
better than *belief* as a synonym for *faith*. Without this sense of *letting go*, it becomes easy to forget that God is not to be grasped or controlled. It is a temptation, given the insecurity and discomfort of life's ambiguity, to grasp and attach
to a specific religion or doctrinal beliefs or religious rules. It is not easy, espe-

cially for Westerners with their aggressive traditions of philosophy and theology to realize that true spiritual security is not found in grasping and holding but rather in letting go of things. The importance of renunciation and non-attachment is more central to the Eastern religions of Hinduism, Buddhism, and Taoism. The four Holy Truths of the Buddha teach that desire is the source of ill in life, and true freedom depends on giving up all desire, all "craving for sensuous experience," even the "craving to perpetuate oneself" as well as the "craving for extinction."[36] In Western religious thought the sentiment of letting go, albeit not central, has been a consistent theme. After all, the Gospel of Mark quotes Jesus as saying:

> If any want to become my followers, let them deny themselves and take up their cross and follow me. For those who want to save their life will lose it, and those who lose their life for my sake, and for the sake of the gospel, will save it.[37]

6. Faith grows best in a community. By distinguishing between religion and faith above, I have implicitly reinforced the common claim of modern individuals that they can be spiritual without belonging to a religious community. Of course, this is true—strictly speaking. I suspect that almost everyone practices some kind of private spirituality. After all, the human heart longs for something more than the mundane world of everyday life. The psalmist's admission, "My soul thirsts for God," is a universal experience. Private individual practices, however, are typically spotty and impoverished when compared to participation in the cultural wealth of a religious community.

Furthermore, the human species is fundamentally social. A considerable body of social-scientific research has provided evidence that people who participate in a faith community tend to live healthier and happier lives than those who do not. Undoubtedly there are a lot of other factors involved in such correlations, and playing the odds for better health will not motivate people to join a church, but overall a vibrant faith requires a community. It is the rare individual who can maintain a worldview and strive for its realization without social support of some kind. Durkheim, who worried about the social consequences of the decline in religion, observed:

> A philosophy may well be elaborated in the silence of the interior imagination, but not so a faith. For before all else, a faith is warmth, life, enthusiasm, the exaltation of the whole mental life, the raising of the individual above himself. Now how could he add to the energies which he possesses without going outside himself?[38]

I believe it is important for spiritual seekers to join a faith community. The pluralism of the postmodern world means there is available a variety of religions and denominations from which to choose in most geographical areas. Not all of them will seek to coerce the individual into conformity to some approved set of doctrines and lifestyles. In fact, I suspect, most faith communities today, even conservative Christian, will offer some latitude for one's own development. It will, of course, be a little more difficult to find a community that truly encourages an open-and-critical faith, but there are such communities in every major religion.

7. Belief (i.e., theology) is a journey, not a destination. Of the six Enlightenment humanists we studied in previous chapters, only Voltaire remained more-or-less active in his religion. So it is not surprising that Voltaire's satires and critiques often zeroed in on the doctrinal disputes within religion.[39] From outside religious traditions, it is not so obvious how pervasive and how heated such disputes can be. Some of the people who drop out of religion do so because they are disgusted with the doctrinal in-fighting.

An open-and-critical faith will hang somewhat loose regarding doctrines. To reiterate what was said above, our relationship to God is more important than what we believe about God, just as our relationship to a spouse or friend is more important than the precision of our understanding of that person.

One thing that continues to characterize the misunderstanding that Christian fundamentalists carry to their debates with science is that a norm of science is a spirit of openness and learning. Scientific theory is not dogma, even though some scientists act like it is. So when fundamentalists deride such things as evolution by claiming that it is only a theory, the scientist can only shrug and say, "Of course." The norm of openness to new discoveries, ideas, and insights is one thing religion would do better to share with science.

The religious viewpoint is really much broader than the scientific. Science is restricted to what can be measured and tested. And because science can test its theories, it is conceivable that someday science could find its final paradigm; that is, a comprehensive understanding of the cosmos that could not be improved upon within the limits of human intelligence. (One of the most interesting questions for science today is whether that final paradigm will come at the expense of another norm of science: prediction.) A final, complete theology is inconceivable by its very nature. While theology is also concerned about nature and the cosmos, its main concern is about a Sacred Transcendent Reality that is more than the cosmos and that is not testable in a scientific sense. If it were testable, it would not be about the Divine.

This is not to say that beliefs are unimportant. What we believe about God, the universe, the nature of humanity—all these beliefs have consequences for our actions which have consequences for others, for society, and ultimately for the world. And there needs to be ongoing, mutually respectful debate within and between religions. Such debate sharpens our minds and helps us understand ourselves and others better. It is quite possible as well that this debate is essential for whatever insight is possible for understanding, what Huston Smith calls, "the Big Picture," by which he means ultimate reality. Combating the modern tendency to reduce all knowledge to only what science can know, Smith writes:

it would be foolish not to draw on every resource available. Inclusively, things are neither as science says they are nor as religion says they are. They are as science, and religion, and philosophy, and art, and common sense, and our deepest intuitions, and our practiced imaginations say they are. What all of these complementing resources—with the exception of modern science, which works with a limited viewfinder—have said about the Big Picture throughout human history has shaken down into a single, wondrously clear and inspiring worldview. This worldview, which I consider the winnowed wisdom of the human race, is found distilled in the world's great, enduring religions.[40]

I think it is better to view religious belief (i.e., theology, doctrine, dogma) as a journey rather than a destination. Spiritual humility means, among other things, recognizing the inadequacy of our beliefs. It is in this way that postmodernism resonates with spirituality. We are historical beings, which means changing beings, which also means change in our comprehension of things, both ultimate and less-than-ultimate. At any given point in one's life, it might be wiser, if not also healthier, to consider one's views as part of a process of life-long development in a particular historical time. This can ease the pressure from the doomed-to-fail quest to grasp *the* absolute truth of things.

Spirituality is also a matter of accepting one's humanity and finitude. In Western religions the distinction between God and humanity is a fundamental plank in the understanding of humanity's relationship to God. "Who is this that darkens counsel by words without knowledge?" asks Yahweh of Job in the Hebrew Bible.[41] Eastern religions are well known for their admission that there are limits to cognitive understanding. In the Hindu *Rig Veda*, as Annie Dillard points outs, it is "concluded that nobody—not even the gods—could understand the mystery of existence."[42] The *Rig Veda* says it playfully: "Whence this creation has arisen—perhaps it formed itself, or perhaps it did not—the one who looks down on it, in the highest heaven, only he knows—or perhaps he does not know."[43]

The spiritual quest is frequently referred to as a journey. In fact, it is quite common for people to think of life itself as a journey. Psychologists and philosophers, not to mention poets, have viewed individual human development as a life-long journey—an adventure, if you will, that is not finished until death, if then. John Caputo, in a fine little book about postmodernism and religion, poetically refers to the self as a question.[44] I suspect that whenever we settle for a "finished" answer, whenever we quit the journey and lock onto some set of dogmas claimed as absolute and final truth—something in us dies. In life's journey, if we close down one aspect of the personality, in this case the intellect, it is like ceasing to further exercise one of the body's limbs, resulting then in living the rest of life with a disability. Only some overly dogmatic bias would exclude one's intellect from the thrill of the pilgrimage.

It is good to remember, however, that engaging one's intellect has its own danger because the journey of faith is never without its mystery. Frequently spiritual sojourners—especially the more cerebral types—exit religion, in part, because of the logical inconsistencies of the religious tradition they have known. There does seem to be something about the human mind that is uncomfortable with logical discrepancy. Social scientists call it *cognitive dissonance*.[45] That very discomfort has been a driving force for scientific knowledge. It has also been a driving force in the richly embroidered philosophies and theologies of the world. I do not want to discourage the quest for logical consistency, but if it is one's primary or sole criterion for embracing or rejecting religion, one will never be able to enjoy the cultural wealth religion has to offer.

The reality seems to be that absolute logical consistency in religion or in life is outside the realm of human possibility. The philosophical developments of the last two hundred years have led over and over to this conclusion. Jean-François Lyotard writes that "it must be accepted that all formal systems have internal limitations." This is true, he points out, even of logic.[46] John Caputo writes: "In the wake of Nietzsche and many others . . . philosophers today have largely rejected the idea that there is some proud overarching thing called 'Reason' and they have settled instead for the humbler idea of 'good reasons,' in the plural and in lower case."[47]

I certainly want scientists, philosophers, and theologians to continue trying to make logical sense of life and the universe. However, when it comes to investing oneself in a religious tradition, one might want to avoid making logical consistency one's first principle, and find instead other "good reasons." There are clearly mysteries in the universe, in human existence, and, without a doubt, in the Divine that are and will remain outside the grasp of rationality and logic. This is why religious truth is best conveyed through stories. In Nikos Kazantzakis' novel, *Zorba the Greek*, the narrator reflects:

> If the scriptures had said: "Today, light is born," man's heart would not have leapt. The idea would not have become a legend and would not have conquered the world. They would merely have described a normal physical phenomenon and would not have fired our imagination—I mean our soul. But the light which is born in the dead of winter has become a child and the child has become God, and for twenty centuries our soul has suckled it.[48]

8. Worship is a matter of the heart. On Tuesday, November 13, 2001, the Taliban abandoned Kabul in Afghanistan. Their rule had meant an extremely severe sort of religious repression. Among other things, women were required to wear in public a burqa, a garment covering the entire body. One 32-year-old woman, Nabillah Hasimi, a former school teacher who had continued to teach children secretly in their homes during the rule of the Taliban, said she looked forward to not wearing the burqa, as soon as it would be safe to quit it. She said: "Faith is in the heart, not in the burqa."[49]

The style of worship people are comfortable with is usually a matter of what they have grown up with. And, frankly, our tastes differ. The solemn dignity of a High-Church mass might be perfect for one person's sense of sacrality but dull and tedious for another. The raucous cacophony of Pentecostalism might inspire one person, but drive another to distraction. There is nothing wrong with any of these reactions. What is wrong is the claim that only one form of worship is truly worship. To transpose Nabillah Hasimi's comment about faith and dress: worship is in the heart, not in the style of ritual. One could say that if we cannot "experience" worship in the silence of the Quaker meeting or in the joyful noise of Pentecostalism or in the simplicity of a Reformed congregation, the problem is not with the style of worship, because obviously many people worship in such contexts; the problem is with our hearts. The same holds for worship in the various schools of religions other than Christianity.

So in selecting a faith community, the style of worship might be important for one, but it is good to remember that its importance is a matter of one's up-bringing or taste or personality—and not a matter of which style is the true worship.

Finally there are two additional claims I would make for the spiritual seeker. These are not meant to be helpful in the way the claims above were meant. The eight claims above were meant to facilitate one's participation in religion. These last two claims could be viewed as caveats or warnings about religious faith. They continue to challenge and scare me in my frail, feeble, and clumsy spiritual journey, so I suspect they would frighten others. From time to time, I eye them as a kind of destination, then pull back again, a lot like the unworthy person in Jesus's parable about the person whose hands are on the plow but who keeps looking back.[50] These claims are the spoilers for those who can think of nothing more important than their own self-interests or the interests of their nation, race, family, or even religious sect. If the experience of the Holy Other is the basis for an open-and-critical faith, these are the criteria of judgment for a life of open-and-critical faith.

9. The experience of the Holy gives rise to a sense of incongruity between the Sacred and the world that calls to action. This is to say that religious experience leads to the feeling that something is amiss—not only with one's self but also with the world we inhabit. There is in that encounter with the Holy a deep discrepancy between the "secular" self and world and the "Sacred" Other so that one confesses: *Only you are sacred.*[51] It does not end, however, with the confessor mired in the muck of self-depreciation.

To put it plainly, it engenders in one a drive to go forth with a mission to do something about it. The students of mythology, literature, religious stories, and biography have identified this aspect of the spiritual journey in countless narratives of heroes, saviors, and saints.[52] In the Hebrew Bible we can see it in the Israelites' liberation from Egyptian bondage, the wandering in the wilderness, and the settling of the land where they are then to be "a light to the nations."[53]

As one telling goes, the Buddha finds Nirvana and knows "that the longings of his heart [have] at last come to fulfillment." He looks out over the world with the idea of sharing this new insight. He sees the enormous gap between "the world lost in low views and confused efforts" and "the exceeding subtlety of the Dharma of emancipation." He finds himself tempted to give up the burden of telling others, which they wouldn't understand anyway. But then he remembers his prior commitment "to enlighten all beings." Two heavenly beings, Indra and Brahma, come to him and plead: "Now that you, O Sage, have yourself crossed the ocean of the world of becoming, please rescue also the other living beings who have sunk so deep into suffering!" So Buddha reflects on their words and is "confirmed in his decision to set the world free."[54]

In the gospels, Jesus returns from forty days of temptation in the wilderness and starts "proclaiming the good news of God."[55] According to the Qur'an, Muhammad, frequently retiring to "a cave in the side of Mount Hira," experiences "a dazzling vision of beauty and light," and hears the call to proclaim and to record "the sanctified Book, the Gift of Allah," which he does, then, for twenty-three years "in patience, conflict, hope, and final triumph."[56] There seems to be this recurring pattern in the human experience of the Holy Other: a sense of mission that involves returning to the world of everyday activity with the message of liberation, reconciliation, enlightenment, good news.

Every religion I know of contains a norm for its adherents to live with special care for the world. In other words, to participate in a religion is to share in that religion's mission. I would even go so far as to say that if we do not feel challenged by a religion to live differently, there is something wrong with that religion. I am aware that religion's attempts to fulfill its mission has led too frequently to the kinds of imperialism and brutalities that have damaged religion's image. This is why faith needs to be open and critical. It also highlights the importance of my next and last claim.

10. The experience of the Holy gives rise to a sense of solidarity with all of humanity. The *numinous* experience of the Holy leads to a sense of union, a sense of deep relatedness not only to life and the cosmos but by extension also to humanity. One experiences intensely one's own finitude but also one's participation in the sea of finite human beings.

It should be no surprise, then, that all the world's major religions include— as a central obligation—love and kindness for others. In the Christian New Testament, for example, every book except one includes some statement suggesting that love is to guide one's life, and the one book without it still says, "It is more blessed to give than to receive."[57] It is not difficult to compile teachings from the world's religions that encourage kindness, love, generosity, and service toward others—all others—not just to one's own clan. Here are a few:

Buddhism: "In this world hostilities are *never* appeased by hostility. But by the absence of hostility are they appeased. This is an interminable truth."[58]
Confucianism: "Fan Chi asked about Goodness. The Master replied, 'Care for others.'"[59]
Jainism: "The function of selves is to support each other."[60]

Islam: "But it is righteousness...To spend of your substance, Out of love for Him, For your kin, For orphans, For the needy, For the wayfarer, For those who ask."[61]

The defenders of religion could, and sometimes do, compile long lists of historical examples where the religious have exercised loving care, often quite sacrificially. I would go so far as to say that people the world over expect to feel safe among pious members of Judaism, Christianity, Islam, Hinduism, Buddhism, and so on—and when they do not, they know something is wrong.

The Enlightenment humanists had their blindnesses, parochialisms, and prejudices, but somehow they too were inspired by care for the welfare of humanity. Whether the source of that care was rooted in their own religious backgrounds or in their own sense of human solidarity is probably impossible to ferret out with certainty. It is clear, though, that this concern for human welfare is where they most resonate with the spiritual. This is why they are not the enemies of religion. It might be too much to suggest they are friends of religion, but indeed they are the kind of prophetic antagonists religion needs to keep it honest.

It is precisely because of its consistent and universal call for compassion, care, and kindness toward others that religion is especially vulnerable to damning criticism. Almost certainly, governments have tortured and killed more people than religion has, but this does not discredit government in the same fundamentally troubling way religion is discredited by such actions. After all, governments are not expected to act outside their own interests or the interests of their nations. In the long history of humanity abuse and violence in the family has probably destroyed more people than religion has, but this does not discredit the family quite as deeply as it does religion. We expect families to treat their own well, but we are not surprised when the human struggles for power and control and the trauma of life manifest themselves in unkindness and cruelty even in our intimate relations. Religion is different. We expect more from it because it expects more from itself. Every example of brutality in the name of religion contrasts starkly with its own ideals. The point is, the expectations are lower for any other institution because it is so widely recognized that religion, as the organized response to the Holy Other, calls for love and service. In fact, although this book has not addressed it, except for a couple of early chapters, religion's usual critics come from its own ranks. They are called prophets. And religion needs its prophets—both inside and out.

We are at the end of this particular journey through the history of the criticism of religion. It is fitting, I think, to close with arguably the most famous quotation from one of religion's own prophets. About 150 years before the birth of Buddha, seven hundred years before the birth of Jesus, thirteen hundred years before the birth of Muhammad, the Hebrew prophet Micah looked at the forms of religion practiced in the temple at Jerusalem and elsewhere, and, like other prophets, tried to express what it is that the Lord really expects. He asks, is it genuflection, burnt offerings, large gifts, one's firstborn child? No, he says, The Lord "has told you, O mortal, what is good; and what does the Lord require of you but to do justice, and to love kindness, and to walk humbly with your God."[62]

Notes

1. Patrick Glynn, *God, The Evidence: The Reconciliation of Faith and Reason in a Postsecular World* (Rocklin, CA: Forum, 1999), 147.

2. Albert Camus, *Resistance, Rebellion, and Death*, trans. Justin O'Brien (N.Y.: Vintage Books; Random House, 1960), 93.

3. For the classic sociological discussion of conformity, rebellion, and innovation, see Robert K. Merton, *Social Theory and Social Structure* (N.Y.: The Free Press, 1968).

4. For a discussion of capitalist theory as a solution to the question of chaos or order in society, see Daniel R. Fusfeld, *The Age of the Economist*, 3rd ed. (Glenview, Ill.: Scott, Foresman and Co., 1977), 25-26.

5. See Ayn Rand, *The Ayn Rand Reader*, ed. Gary Hull and Leonard Peikoff (N.Y.: Plume; Penguin, 1999), 79-83.

6. Paul Kurtz, *A Secular Humanist Declaration*, reprinted from *Free Inquiry*, 1, no. 1 (Winter 1980).

7. Camus, *Resistance*, 228.

8. Marx, *Writings*, 240, 227.

9. Exodus 20:19.

10. Armstrong, *A History*, 218.

11. Rudolf Otto, *The Idea of the Holy: An Inquiry Into the Non-rational Factor in the Idea of the Divine and Its Relation to the Rational*, trans. John W. Harvey (London: Oxford University Press, 1923).

12. Otto, *The Idea of the Holy*, 19-22.

13. Otto, *The Idea of the Holy*, 124.

14. For an overview of mystical experience, see F. C. Happold, *Mysticism: A Study of an Anthology* (Middlesex, Eng.: Penguin, 1970).

15. W. T. Stace, "The Teachings of the Mystics," in *To Believe or Not To Believe: Readings in the Philosophy of Religion*, ed. E. D. Klemke, 70-80 (Fort Worth, Tex.: Harcourt Brace Jovanovich, 1992), 72, 76.

16. Sharon Begley, "Religion and the Brain," *Newsweek*, May 7, 2001, 52.

17. Peter J. Wylie, "The Great Globe Itself," in *The New Encyclopaedia Britannica*, 15th ed., *Propaedia* (Chicago: Encyclopaedia Britannica, 1994), 61.

18. Quoted in Sharon Begley, "Searching For the God Within," *Newsweek*, January 29, 2001, 59; see also Begley, "Religion and the Brain."

19. James, *Varieties*, 418-419.

20. Alan Watts, *Behold the Spirit: A Study in the Necessity of Mystical Religion* (N.Y.: Vintage Books, 1971), 127.

21. See Schmidt, *The Origin*; also James, *Comparative*, 286; also Theissen, *Critical Faith*, 34.

22. Quoted in Alan W. Watts, *The Wisdom of Insecurity* (N.Y.: Vintage, 1951), 151.

23. Job 42:3.

24. Lao Tsu, *Tao Te Ching*, no. 1.

25. 1 John 4:8.

26. The Koran, 6:103, p. 435.

27. Romans 11:33, adapted.

28. Walter Houston Clark, *The Psychology of Religion: An Introduction to Religious Experience and Behavior*, (N.Y.: Macmillan, 1958), 22.

29. Keith A. Roberts, *Religion in Sociological Perspective*, 2nd ed. (Belmont, Calif.: Wadsworth, 1990), 21.

30. See the psychologist: Jung, *Psychology*, 4-6; and the sociologist: Joachim Wach, *Sociology of Religion* (Chicago and London: University of Chicago Press, 1944), 13-14.

31. George M. Marsden, *Religion and American Culture* (San Diego: Harcourt Brace Jovanovich, 1990), 4.

32. Paul Tillich, *Dynamics of Faith* (N.Y.: Harper & Row, 1957), 1, 4.

33. Tillich, *Dynamics of Faith*, 12.

34. Exodus 20:2-3; NRSV.

35. See Watts, *Wisdom of Insecurity*.

36. *Buddhist Scriptures*, ed. Edward Conze (London: Penguin, 1959), 186-187.

37. Mark 8:34-35.

38. Durkheim, *Elementary Forms*, 473.

39. For an example, see p. 149 in Voltaire, *Philosophical Dictionary*.

40. Huston Smith, *Why Religion Matters: The Fate of the Human Spirit in an Age of Disbelief* (San Francisco: HarperCollins; HarperSanFrancisco, 2001), 43.

41. Job 38:2.

42. Annie Dillard, *Pilgrim at Tinker Creek* (N.Y.: HarperPerennial, 1974), 28.

43. *Rig Veda* 10:129; *in Rig Veda: An Anthology*, ed. and trans. Wendy Doniger O'Flaherty (London: Penguin Books, 1981), 25-26; Dillard in *Pilgrim* quotes from a different translation.

44. Caputo, *On Religion*, 27.

45. See Leon Festinger, Henry W. Riecken and Stanley Schachter, *When Prophecy Fails: A Social and Psychological Study of a Modern Group that Predicted the Destruction of the World* (N.Y.: Harper & Row, 1956).

46. Lyotard, *Postmodern Condition*, 43.

47. Caputo, *On Religion*, 64.

48. Nikos Kazantzakis, *Zorba the Greek*, trans. Carl Wildman (N.Y.: Scribner Paperback Fiction; Simon and Schuster, 1981 [1952]), 115.

49. Quoted in "Veil of darkness lifts in capital with Taliban retreat," *The Kansas City Star*, 14 November 2001, A2.

50. Luke 9:62.

51. Otto, *The Idea of the Holy*, 50-51.

52. See the classic study by Joseph Campbell, *The Hero With A Thousand Faces* (Princeton, N.J.: Princeton University Press, 1949).

53. Isaiah 42:6.

54. *Buddhist Scriptures*, 51-52.

55. Mark 1:14.

56. Introduction in *The Holy Qur'an*, translated with commentary by 'Abdullah Yusuf 'Ali (Beltsville, MD: Amana Publications, 1422 AH/2001 AC), C. 27, 29, 30,40.

57. Acts 20:35.

58. *The Dhammapada: Verses on the Way*, trans. Glenn Wallis (N.Y.: The Modern Library, 2004), 1:5.

59. Confucius, *Analects: with selections from traditional commentaries*, trans. Edward Slingerland (Indianapolis/Cambridge: Hackett Publishing Co., 2003), 12:22.

60. Sri Acarya Umasvati, *Tattvarthadhigama Sutra*, trans. J. L. Jaini, in *A Source Book in Indian Philosophy*, ed. Sarvepalli Radhakrishnan and Charles A. Moore (Princeton, NJ: Princeton University Press, 1957), 5:21.

61. *The Holy Qur'an*, trans.'Ali, 2:177.

62. Micah 6:8.

Bibliography

Aeschylus. *Prometheus Bound*. Translated by G. M. Cookson. Vol. 5, *Aeschylus, Sophocles, Euripides, Aristophanes*. Great Books of the Western World, edited by Robert Maynard Hutchins et al. Chicago: Encyclopaedia Britannica; William Benton Publisher, 1952 [c. 458 BCE].

Ahmed, Akbar S. *Postmodernism and Islam: Predicament and Promise*. London & N.Y.: Routledge, 1992.

Anderson, Bernhard W. *Understanding the Old Testament*. 2nd ed. Englewood Cliffs, N.J.: Prentice-Hall, 1966.

Anderson, Perry. *The Origins of Postmodernity*. London & New York: Verso, 1998.

Apuleius. *The Golden Ass*. Translated by William Adlington; revised by S. Gaselee. Ware, Hertfordshire, England: Wordsworth, 1996.

Armstrong, Karen. *A History of God: The 4,000-Year Quest of Judaism, Christianity and Islam*. N.Y.: Alfred A. Knopf, 1994.

Ayer, A. J. *Voltaire*. N.Y.: Random House, 1986.

Bainton, Roland H. *Here I Stand: A Life of Martin Luther*. Nashville: Abingdon Press, 1978.

Barbour, Ian G. *Religion and Science: Historical and Contemporary Issues*. San Francisco: HarperSanFrancisco; HarperCollins, 1997.

Barnes, Harry Elmer. "Chapter I: Ancient and Medieval Social Philosophy." In *An Introduction to the History of Sociology*, edited by Harry Elmer Barnes, 3-28. Chicago & London: University of Chicago Press, 1948.

Bauman, Zygmunt. "Postmodernity, or Living with Ambivalence." In *A Postmodern Reader*, edited by Joseph Natoli and Linda Hutcheon, 9-24. Albany, N.Y.: State University of New York Press, 1993 [from *Modernity and Ambivalence*, by Bauman 231-245, Cornell University Press and Blackwell, 1991].

Begley, Sharon. "Searching For the God Within." *Newsweek*, January 29, 2001, 59.

———. "Religion and the Brain." *Newsweek*, May 7, 2001, 50-57.

"Belfast schoolchildren caught in cross fire of religious hate." *The Kansas City Star* (The Associated Press), 4 September 2001, A7.

Bellah, Robert N. "Civil Religion in America." *Daedalus*. 96, no. 1 (winter 1967): 1-21.

ben-Jochannan, Yosef A. A. *African Origins of The Major "Western Religions."* Baltimore: Black Classic Press, 1970.

———. "The African Contribution to Technology and Science." In *New Dimensions in African History*, edited by John Henrik Clarke. Trenton, N.J. and Asmara, Eritrea: Africa World Press, 1991.

Berger, Peter L. *Invitation to Sociology: A Humanistic Perspective*. Garden City, N.Y.: Anchor Books, 1963.

———. *The Sacred Canopy: Elements of a Sociological Theory of Religion*. Garden City, N.Y.: Doubleday & Co., 1967.

Berger, Peter L., Berger, Brigitte, and Kellner, Hansfried. *The Homeless Mind: Modernization and Consciousness*. N.Y.: Vintage, 1973.

Berger, Peter L., and Thomas Luckmann. *The Social Construction of Reality: A Treatise in the Sociology of Knowledge*. Garden City, N.Y.: Anchor Books, 1966.

Besterman, Theodore. Introduction to *Philosophical Dictionary*, by Voltaire. London: Penguin Books, 1972.

———. *Voltaire*. N.Y.: Harcourt, Brace & World, 1969.

Bleicher, Josef. *Contemporary Hermeneutics: Hermeneutics as Method, Philosophy and Critique*. London: Routledge & Kegan Paul, 1980.

Bloch, Ernst. *On Karl Marx*. N.Y.: Herder and Herder, 1971.

Blumenberg, Werner, dargestellter. *Karl Marx: in Selbstzeugnissen und Bilddokumenten*. Reinbeck bei Hamburg: Rowohlt, 1962.

Borg, Marcus J. *Meeting Jesus Again for the First Time: The Historical Jesus & the Heart of Contemporary Faith*. San Francisco: HarperSanFrancisco, 1994.

Boring, M. Eugene. "The Gospel of Matthew: Introduction, Commentary, and Reflections." In *The New Interpreter's Bible*, edited by Leander E. Keck et al. Vol. VIII, 87-506. Nashville: Abingdon Press, 1995.

———. "The 'Third Quest' and the Apostolic Faith." *Interpretation* 50, no. 4 (October 1996): 341-354.

Bridenthal, Renate and Koonz, Claudia, eds. *Becoming Visible: Women in European History*. Boston: Houghton Mifflin Co., 1977.

Bromiley, Geoffrey W. "Zwingli, Huldrych." *The New Encyclopaedia Britannica*. 15th ed. Vol. 12, 946-947. Chicago: Encyclopaedia Britannica, 1994.

Brown, Norman O. *Life Against Death: The Psychoanalytical meaning of History*. Middletown, Conn.: Wesleyan University Press, 1959.

Brueggemann, Walter. *The Prophetic Imagination*. Phila.: Fortress Press, 1978.

———. *Texts Under Negotiation: The Bible and Postmodern Imagination*. Minneapolis: Fortress Press, 1993.

Buber, Martin. *I and Thou*. Translated by Ronald Gregor Smith. 2nd ed. N.Y.: Charles Scribner's Sons, 1958.

Buddhist Scriptures. Edited by Edward Conze. London: Penguin, 1959.

Bulfinch, Thomas. *Bulfinch's Mythology: The Age of Fable, The Age of Chivalry, Legends of Charlemagne*. N.Y.: Avenel Books, 1979.

Bulhof, Ilse and ten Kate, Laurens. "Echoes of an Embarrassment: Philosophical Perspectives on Negative Theology—An Introduction." In *Flight of the Gods: Philosophical Perspectives on Negative Theology*, edited by Bulhof and ten Kate, 1-57. N.Y.: Fordham University Press, 2000.

———, eds. *Flight of the Gods: Philosophical Perspectives on Negative Theology*. N.Y.: Fordham University Press, 2000.

Bultmann, Rudolf, Ernst Lohmeyer, Julius Schniewind, Helmut Thielicke, and Austin Farrer. *Kerygma and Myth*, edited by Hans Werner Bartsch. N.Y. and Evanston: Harper Torchbooks; Harper & Row, 1961.

Butterfield, H. *The Origins of Modern Science 1300-1800*. London: Bell & Hyman, 1957.

Campbell, Joseph. *The Hero with a Thousand Faces*. Princeton, N.J.: Princeton University Press, 1949.

———. *Myths to Live By*. N.Y.: Bantam Books, 1972.

Camus, Albert. *The Rebel: An Essay on Man in Revolt*. Translated by Anthony Bower. N.Y.: Vintage; Random House, 1956.

———. *Resistance, Rebellion, and Death*. Translated by Justin O'Brien. N.Y.: Vintage Books; Random House, 1960.

Capra, Fritjof. *The Tao of Physics: An Exploration of the Parallels Between Modern Physics and Eastern Mysticism*. 2nd ed. Boston: New Science Library, 1985.

Caputo, John. *On Religion*. London and New York: Routledge, 2001.

Carver, Terrell. "Reading Marx: Life and works." In *The Cambridge Companion to Marx*, edited by Terrell Carver, 1-22. N.Y.: Cambridge University Press, 1991.

Clark, Ronald W. *The Life of Bertrand Russell*. N.Y.: Alfred A. Knopf, 1976.

Clark, Stephen R. L. *From Athens to Jerusalem: The Love of Wisdom and the Love of God*. Oxford: Clarendon Press, 1984.

Clark, Walter Houston. *The Psychology of Religion: An Introduction to Religious Experience and Behavior*. N.Y.: Macmillan, 1958.

Confucius. *Analects: with selections from traditional commentaries*. Translated by Edward Slingerland. Indianapolis/Cambridge: Hackett Publishing Co., Inc., 2003.

Copleston, Frederick. *A History of Philosophy*. Vol. 2, *Mediaeval Philosophy*, part 1. Garden City, N.Y.: Doubleday & Co.; Image Books, 1950.

———. *A History of Philosophy*. Vol. 3, *Late Mediaeval and Renaissance Philosophy*, part 1. Garden City, N.Y.: Doubleday & Co.; Image Books, 1953.

Coser, Lewis A. *Masters of Sociological Thought: Ideas in Historical and Social Context*. 2nd ed. N.Y.: Harcourt Brace Jovanovich, 1977.

Crews, Frederick C., ed. *Unauthorized Freud: Doubters Confront a Legend*. N.Y.: Viking, 1998.

Crossan, John Dominic. *Jesus: A Revolutionary Biography*. N.Y.: HarperSanFrancisco, 1994.

Dawkins, Richard. *The God Delusion*. Boston & New York: Houghton Mifflin, 2006.

Day, John. "Baal." In *The Anchor Bible Dictionary*. Vol. 1, edited by David Noel Freedman et al., 545-549. N.Y.: Doubleday, 1992.

Denzin, Norman K. "Postmodern Social Theory." *Sociological Theory* 4 (fall 1986): 194-204.

The Dhammapada: Verses on the Way. Translated Glenn Wallis. N.Y.: The Modern Library, 2004.

Diano, Carlo. "Epicurus." *The New Encyclopaedia Britannica*. 15th ed. Vol. 4, 522-523. Chicago: Encyclopaedia Britannica, 1994.

Dillard, Annie, *Pilgrim at Tinker Creek* (N.Y.: HarperPerennial, 1974).

Donellan, Keith S. "Western Philosophical Schools and Doctrines: Modern Schools: Analytic and Linguistic philosophy." *The New Encyclopaedia Britannica*. 15th ed. Vol. 25, 600-608. Chicago: Encyclopaedia Britannica, 1994.

Drummond, Robert Blackley. "Erasmus: A Biographical Note." In *The Christian Reader: Inspirational and Devotional Classics*, edited by Stanley Irving Stuber. N.Y.: Association Press, 1952 [Drummond's note, 1873].

Dugger, Celia W. "Religious rioting shakes India: Hindu reprisal attacks on Muslims kill 100." *The Kansas City Star*, 1 March 2002, A1, A10.

Durant, Will. *The Story of Civilization: The Life of Greece.* N.Y.: Simon and Schuster, 1966 [1939].

———. *The Story of Civilization: Caesar and Christ—A History of Roman Civilization and of Christianity from their beginnings to A.D. 325.* N.Y.: Simon and Schuster, 1944.

———. *The Story of Civilization: The Age of Faith—A History of Medieval Civilization—Christian, Islamic, and Judaic—from Constantine to Dante: A.D. 325-1300.* N.Y.: Simon and Schuster, 1950.

———. *The Story of Civilization: The Reformation—A History of European Civilization from Wyclif to Calvin: 1300-1564.* N.Y.: Simon and Schuster, 1957.

Durant, Will and Ariel. *The Story of Civilization: The Age of Voltaire—A History of Civilization in Western Europe from 1715 to 1756, with Special Emphasis on the Conflict between Religion and Philosophy.* N.Y.: Simon and Schuster, 1965.

Durkheim, Emile. "The Determination of Moral Facts." In *Sociology and Philosophy.* Translated by D. F. Pocock. N.Y.: The Free Press, 1974 [1906].

———. *The Division of Labor in Society.* Translated by George Simpson. N.Y. and London: The Free Press, 1933 [1893].

———. *The Elementary Forms of the Religious Life.* Translated by Joseph Ward Swain. N.Y. and London: The Free Press, 1915 [1912].

———. *The Rules of Sociological Method.* Translated by W. D. Halls, edited by Steven Lukes. N.Y.: The Free Press, 1982 [1895].

———. *Suicide: A Study in Sociology.* Translated by John A. Spaulding and George Simpson, edited by George Simpson. N.Y.: The Free Press, 1951 [1897].

Edwards, Jonathan. "Sinners in The Hands of an Angry God." In *The Works of Jonathan Edwards.* Vol. II. 1974 ed. Edinburgh, Scotland: The Banner of Truth Trust, 1834.

Edwards, Paul. Introduction to *Why I Am Not a Christian: And Other Essays on Religion and Related Subjects,* by Bertrand Russell. London: Unwin Paperbacks, 1975 [1957].

Ehrlich, Blake and Sousa Rebelo, Luis de. "Lisbon." *The New Encyclopaedia Britannica.* 15th ed. Vol. 23, 72-76. Chicago: Encyclopaedia Britannica, 1994.

Eliade, Mircea. *Patterns in Comparative Religion.* Translated by Rosemary Sheed. N.Y.: New American Library, 1958.

Engels, Frederick. "The Peasant War in Germany." In *Marx & Engels On Religion,* edited by Reinhold Niebuhr, 97-118. N.Y.: Schocken Books, 1964 [1850].

Epicurus. *Letters, Principal Doctrines, and Vatican Sayings.* Translated by Russel M. Geer. N.Y.: Macmillan, 1964.

Erasmus, Desiderius. "Letter to Maarten Van Dorp 1515." In *Praise of Folly* and *Letter to Maarten Van Dorp.* Translated by Betty Radice. London: Penguin, 1993.

———. *Praise of Folly.* In *Praise of Folly* and *Letter to Maarten Van Dorp.* Translated by Betty Radice. London: Penguin, 1993.

Ermarth, Elizabeth Deeds. "Postmodernism." In *Routledge Encyclopedia of Philosophy.* Vol. 7, edited by Edward Craig, 587-590. London & N.Y.: Routledge, 1998.

"Existence of God, The: A Debate Between Bertrand Russell and Father F. C. Copleston, SJ." In *Why I Am Not a Christian: And Other Essays on Religion and Related Subjects,* by Russell, edited by Paul Edwards, 133-153. London: Unwin Paperbacks, 1975 [1948].

Fancher, Raymond E. *Pioneers of Psychology.* N.Y.: W. W. Norton & Co., 1979.

Fellner, Fritz. "Introduction: The Genesis of the Austrian Republic." In *Modern Austria*, edited by Kurt Steiner, Fritz Fellner, and Hubert Feichtlbauer, 1-22. Palo Alto, Calif.: The Society for the Promotion of Science and Scholarship Inc., 1981.

Festinger, Leon, Henry W. Riecken and Stanley Schachter. *When Prophecy Fails: A Social and Psychological Study of a Modern Group that Predicted the Destruction of the World.* N.Y.: Harper & Row, 1956.

Feuer, Lewis S. and McLellan, David T. "Marx and Marxism: Life and works of Marx." *The New Encyclopaedia Britannica.* 15th ed. Vol. 23, 531-535. Chicago: Encyclopaedia Britannica, 1994.

Feuerbach, Ludwig. *The Essence of Christianity.* Edited and abridged by E. Graham Waring and F. W. Strothman. N.Y.: Frederick Ungar, 1957 [1841].

Flew, Antony, ed. *A Dictionary of Philosophy.* 2nd ed. N.Y.: St. Martin's Press, 1979.

Fosdick, Harry Emerson, ed. *Great Voices of the Reformation: An Anthology.* N.Y.: The Modern Library, 1984.

———. *The Man from Nazareth: As His Contemporaries Saw Him.* N.Y.: Harper & Row, 1949.

Freke, Timothy. *The Illustrated Book of Sacred Scriptures.* Wheaton, Ill.: Quest Books; Theosophical Publishing House, 1998.

Freud, Sigmund. *Civilization and Its Discontents.* Translated by Joan Riviere. Vol. 54, *The Major Works of Sigmund Freud.* Great Books of the Western World, edited by Robert Maynard Hutchins et al. Chicago: Encyclopaedia Britannica; William Benton Publisher, 1952 [1929].

———. *Leonardo Da Vinci: A Memory of His Childhood.* London: Ark Paperbacks; Routledge & Kegan Paul, 1957 [1910].

———. *Massenpsychologie und Ich-Analyse & Die Zukunft einer Illusion.* Frankfurt am Main: Fischer Taschenbuch Verlag, 1993 [1921, 1927].

———. *Moses and Monotheism.* Translated by Katherine Jones. N.Y.: Vintage Books; Random House, 1967 [1939].

———. *An Outline of Psychoanalysis.* Translated by James Strachey. N.Y.: W. W. Norton, 1949 [1940].

———. *Three Case Histories.* N.Y.: Collier Books; Macmillan, 1963.

———. *Totem and Taboo: Some Points of Agreement between the Mental Lives of Savages and Neurotics.* Translated and edited by James Strachey. N.Y. & London: W. W. Norton & Co., 1950 [1913].

———. "Zwangshandlungen und Religionsübungen." In *Der Mann Moses und Die Monotheistische Religion: Schriften über die Religion.* Frankfurt am Main: Fischer Tachenbuch Verlag, 1975 [1907].

Fromm, Erich. *Escape from Freedom.* N.Y.: Avon, 1941.

———. *Psychoanalysis and Religion.* New Haven: Yale University Press, 1950.

Fukuyama, Francis. *The End of History and the Last Man.* N.Y.: Avon, 1992.

Funk, Robert W., Roy W. Hoover and The Jesus Seminar. *The Five Gospels: The Search for the Authentic Words of Jesus.* N.Y.: Macmillan, 1993.

Fusfeld, Daniel R. *The Age of the Economist.* 3rd ed. Glenview, Ill.: Scott, Foresman and Co., 1977.

Gay, Peter. *Freud: A Life for Our Time.* N.Y. & London: W. W. Norton & Co., 1988.

———. "Sigmund Freud." *Time*, March 29, 1999, 66-69.

Geer, Russel M. Introduction to *Letters, Principal Doctrines, and Vatican Sayings*, by Epicurus. N.Y.: Macmillan, 1964.

Gellner, Ernest. *Nations and Nationalism.* Oxford, England: Basil Blackwell, 1983.

———. *Postmodernism, Reason and Religion*. London and New York: Routledge, 1992.

Giddens, Anthony. *Émile Durkheim*. N.Y.: Penguin Books, 1978.

Glasner, Peter. "Mass." In *Fifty Key Words: Sociology*, edited by David Martin, 44-45. Richmond, VA: John Knox Press, 1970.

Glynn, Patrick. *God, the Evidence: The Reconciliation of Faith and Reason in a Postsecular World*. Rocklin, Calif.: Forum, 1999.

Gough, Alfred, and Miles Millar, writers. "Premiere." *Smallville*. Produced by Gough, Millar, Mike Tolin, Brian Robbins, and Joe Davola. Directed by David Nutter. Warner Bros. Television. KSMO, Kansas City. October 16, 2001.

Graham, Billy. "Young people practicing Satan worship are playing with fire." *The Kansas City Star*, July 2, 1994, E11.

Gray, John. *Voltaire*. N.Y.: Routledge, 1999.

Green, Vivian. *A New History of Christianity*. N.Y.: Continuum, 1996.

Griffin, David Ray, William A. Beardslee, and Joe Holland, eds. *Varieties of Postmodern Theology*. Albany, N.Y.: State University of New York Press, 1989.

Gritsch, Eric W. *Martin—God's Court Jester: Luther in Retrospect*. Phila.: Fortress Press, 1983.

Guérard, Albert. *France: A Modern History*. Ann Arbor: The University of Michigan Press, 1959.

Habermas, Juergen. *Knowledge and Human Interests*. Translated by Jeremy J. Shapiro. Boston: Beacon Press, 1971.

———. *The Theory of Communicative Action*. 2 vols. Translated by Thomas McCarthy. Boston: Beacon Press, 1981.

Hall, Calvin S. *A Primer of Freudian Psychology*. N.Y.: Mentor; New American Library, 1954.

Hammarskjöld, Dag. *Markings*. Translated by Leif Sjöberg & W. H.Auden. N.Y.: Alfred A. Knopf, 1964.

Happold, F. C. *Mysticism: A Study of an Anthology*. Middlesex, Eng.: Penguin, 1970.

Harris, Sam. *The End of Faith: Religion, Terror, and the Future of Reason*. N.Y. & London: W. W. Norton, & Co., 2005.

Harvey, David. *The Condition of Postmodernity: An Enquiry into the Origins of Cultural Change*. Oxford, Eng.: Basil Blackwell, 1989.

Hayman, Ronald. *Nietzsche*. N.Y.: Routledge, 1999.

Held, David. *Introduction to Critical Theory: Horkheimer to Habermas*. Berkeley & Los Angeles: University of California Press, 1980.

Herberg, Will. *Protestant—Catholic—Jew: An Essay in American Religious Sociology*. Revised. Garden City, N.Y.: Doubleday, 1960.

Hitchens, Christopher. *God is not Great: How Religion Poisons Everything*. N.Y. & Boston: Twelve, 2007.

Hobsbawm, E. J. *The Age of Revolution, 1789-1848*. N.Y. and Toronto: Mentor; New American Library, 1962.

Horkheimer, Max and Adorno, Theodor W. *Dialectic of Enlightenment*. Translated by John Cumming. N.Y.: The Seabury Press, 1972.

Houlgate, Stephen. *Freedom, Truth and History: An Introduction to Hegel's Philosophy*. London and N.Y.: Routledge, 1991.

Hovind, Ken. *Are You Being Brainwashed? Propaganda in Science Textbooks*. Pensacola, FL: Creation Science Evangelism, n.d.

Hume, David. *An Enquiry Concerning Human Understanding*. Vol. 35. *Locke, Berkeley, Hume*. Great Books of the Western World, edited by Robert Maynard Hutchins et al. (Chicago: Encyclopaedia Britannica; William Benton Publisher, 1952 [1758]).

Hunter, James Davison. *Culture Wars: The Struggle to Define America*. N.Y.: BasicBooks, 1991.

Isaacson, Walter. "Thinkers vs. Tinkerers, and Other Debates." *Time*, March 29, 1999, 6.

James, E. O. *Comparative Religion*. N.Y.: Barnes & Noble, 1961.

James, William. *The Varieties of Religious Experience: A Study in Human Nature*. N.Y.: The Modern Library, 1902.

Janik, Allan and Stephen Toulmin. *Wittgenstein's Vienna*. N.Y.: Touchstone; Simon and Schuster, 1973.

Jaspers, Karl. *Nietzsche: An Introduction to the Understanding of His Philosophical Activity*. Translated by Charles F. Wallraff and Frederick J. Schmitz. South Bend, IN: Regnery/Gateway, 1965.

John Paul II. *Crossing the Threshold of Hope*, edited by Vittorio Messori. N.Y.: Alfred A. Knopf, 1994.

Jones, Robert Alun. *Emile Durkheim: An Introduction to Four Major Works*. Masters of Social Theory. Vol. 2. Newbury Park, Calif.: Sage Publications, 1986.

Jung, Carl Gustav. *Psychology and Religion*. New Haven and London: Yale University Press, 1938.

Kant, Immanuel. *The Critique of Pure Reason*. Translated by J. M. D. Meiklejohn. Vol. 42, *Kant*. Great Books of the Western World, edited by Robert Maynard Hutchins et al. Chicago: William Benton, Publisher; Encyclopaedia Britannica, 1952 [1781]).

———. "What is Enlightenment?" In *Foundations of the Metaphysics of Morals* and *What is Enlightenment?* Translated by Lewis White Beck. Indianapolis: Bobbs-Merrill, 1959 [1784].

Kaufmann, Walter. *Nietzsche: Philosopher, Psychologist, Antichrist*. 4th ed. Princeton, N.J.: Princeton University Press, 1974.

———. Introduction to *The Case of Wagner*, by Friedrich Nietzsche. N.Y.: Vintage Books; Random House, 1967.

———. Introduction to *On The Genealogy of Morals*, by Friedrich Nietzsche. N.Y.: Vintage Books; Random House, 1967.

———. Introduction to *The Portable Nietzsche*, by Friedrich Nietzsche. Middlesex, Eng.: Penguin Books, 1968.

Kazantzakis, Nikos. *Zorba the Greek*. Translated by Carl Wildman. N.Y.: Scribner Paperback Fiction; Simon and Schuster, 1981 [1952].

Kephart, William M. and Zellner, William W. *Extraordinary Groups: An Examination of Unconventional Life-Styles*. 5th ed. N.Y.: St. Martin's Press, 1994.

Kierkegaard, Søren. "Against Proofs of God." In *To Believe or Not to Believe: Readings in the Philosophy of Religion*, edited by E. D. Klemke, 127-130. Fort Worth, Tex.: Harcourt Brace Jovanovich, 1992. [From Kierkegaard, *Philosophical Fragments*. 1936, Princeton University Press, 1962 renewed; 31-36.]

Klemke, E. D., ed. *To Believe Or Not to Believe: Readings in the Philosophy of Religion*. Fort Worth, TX: Harcourt Brace Jovanovich, 1992.

Kopp, Sheldon. *An End to Innocence: Facing Life Without Illusions*. Toronto: Bantam, 1978.

Koran, The. Translated by N.J. Dawood. Middlesex, England: Penguin, 1974.

Küng, Hans. *Freud and the Problem of God*. Enlarged ed. Translated by Edward Quinn. New Haven and London: Yale University Press, 1990.

Kuhn, Thomas S. *The Copernican Revolution: Planetary Astronomy in the Development of Western Thought.* Cambridge, Maine, & London, England: Harvard University Press, 1957.

———. *The Structure of Scientific Revolutions.* 2nd ed. Chicago: University of Chicago Press, 1962, 1970.

Kurtz, Paul. *A Secular Humanist Declaration.* Reprint from *Free Inquiry* 1, no. 1 (Winter 1980).

Kushner, Harold S. *When Bad Things Happen to Good People.* N.Y.: Avon, 1981.

Lao Tsu. *Tao Te Ching.* Translated by Gia-Fu Feng and Jane English. N.Y.: Vintage Books, 1972.

Lao Tzu. *Tao Te Ching.* Translated by D. C. Lau. London: Penguin Books, 1963.

Lash, Scott. *Sociology of Postmodernism.* London and N.Y.: Routledge, 1990.

Leith, John H., ed. *Creeds of the Churches: A Reader in Christian Doctrine from the Bible to the Present.* Revised. Richmond, VA: John Knox Press, 1973.

Lenski, Gerhard. *The Religious Factor: A Sociological Study of Religion's Impact on Politics, Economics, and Family Life.* Garden City, N.Y.: Doubleday & Co., 1961.

Lester, Toby. "Oh, Gods!" *Atlantic,* February 2002, 37-45.

Levi, A. H. T. Introduction to *Praise of Folly* and *Letter to Maarten Van Dorp 1515,* by Erasmus. London: Penguin, 1993.

Lichtheim, George. "Historical and Dialectical Materialism." In *Dictionary of the History of Ideas: Studies of Selected Pivotal Ideas,* Vol. IV, edited by Philip P. Wiener, 450-456. N.Y.: Charles Scribner's Sons, 1973.

Littell, Franklin Hamlin. *The Origins of Sectarian Protestantism: A Study of the Anabaptist View of the Church.* N.Y.: Macmillan, 1964.

Lucretius. *On The Nature of Things.* Translated by H. A. J. Munro. Vol. 12, *Lucretius, Epictetus, Marcus Aurelius.* Great Books of the Western World, edited by Robert Maynard Hutchins et al. Chicago: Encyclopaedia Britannica; William Benton Publisher, 1952.

Lukes, Steven. *Individualism.* N.Y.: Harper & Row, 1973.

Lyotard, Jean-François. *The Postmodern Condition: A Report on Knowledge.* Translated by Geoff Bennington and Brian Massumi. Theory and History of Literature, vol. 10. Minneapolis: University of Minnesota Press, 1984 [1979].

Magnus, Bernd. "Nietzsche." In *The New Encyclopaedia Britannica.* 15th ed. Vol. 24, 936-938. Chicago: Encyclopaedia Britannica, 1994.

Mandel, Ernest and George Novack. *The Marxist Theory of Alienation.* N.Y.: Pathfinder Press, 1970.

Mannheim, Karl. *Ideology and Utopia: An Introduction to the Sociology of Knowledge.* Translated by Louis Wirth and Edward Shils. N.Y.: Harcourt, Brace & World, 1936.

Marcuse, Herbert. *Eros and Civilization: A Philosophical Inquiry Into Freud.* Boston: Beacon Press, 1966.

Marsden, George M. *Religion and American Culture.* San Diego: Harcourt Brace Jovanovich, 1990.

Marx, Karl. *Karl Marx: Selected Writings,* edited by David McLellan. Oxford: Oxford University Press, 1977.

———. *Writings of the Young Marx on Philosophy and Society.* Translated and edited by Loyd D. Easton and Kurt H. Guddat. Garden City, N.Y.: Anchor Books, 1967.

———. *Economic and Philosophic Manuscripts of 1844.* Translated by Martin Milligan, edited by Dirk J. Struik. N.Y.: International Publishers, 1964 [1844].

————. *The Communist Manifesto*. In the Norton Critical Edition with annotations, sources, and background, edited by Frederic L. Bender, 41-86. N.Y. & London: W. W. Norton, 1988 [1848].

————. *Capital*. Translated by Samuel Moore and Edward Aveling, edited by Friedrich Engels. Revised with additional translation by Marie Sachey and Herbert Lamm. Vol. 50, *Marx, Engels*. Great Books of the Western World, edited by Robert Maynard Hutchins et al. Chicago: Encyclopaedia Britannica; William Benton Publisher, 1952 [1867-1890].

Marx, Karl and Frederick Engels. *The German Ideology: Part One*. With selections from Parts Two and Three together with Marx's "Introduction to a Critique of Political Economy." Edited by C. J. Arthur. N.Y.: International Publishers, 1947 [1845-46].

Mayer, Arno J. *The Persistence of the Old Regime: Europe to the Great War*. N.Y.: Pantheon Books, 1981.

McKay, John P., Bennett D. Hill, and John Buckler. *A History of Western Society*. 2 vols. *From Antiquity to the Enlightenment*. 4th ed. Boston: Houghton Mifflin, 1991.

Meaning of the Holy Qur'an, The. Translated by 'Abdullah Yusuf 'Ali. Beltsville, MD: Amana Publications, 1422 AH/2001 AC.

Merton, Robert K. *Social Theory and Social Structure*. N.Y.: The Free Press, 1968.

Miller, Denning. *Popular Mathematics: The Understanding and Enjoyment of Mathematics*. N.Y.: Coward-McCann, 1942.

Miller, Jonathan. *The Body In Question*. N.Y.: Random House, 1978.

Miller, Madeleine S. and J. Lane Miller. *Harper's Bible Dictionary*. N.Y.: Harper & Row, 1961.

Miller, Perry. *Jonathan Edwards*. n.p.: William Sloane Associates, 1949.

Mills, C. Wright. *The Sociological Imagination*. N.Y.: Oxford University Press, 1959.

Monk, Ray. *Bertrand Russell: The Spirit of Solitude, 1872-1921*. N.Y.: The Free Press, 1996.

————. *Bertrand Russell: The Ghost of Madness, 1921-1970*. N.Y.: The Free Press, 2000.

Montagu, Ashley and Matson, Floyd. *The Dehumanization of Man*. N.Y.: McGraw-Hill, 1983.

Nagel, Ernest. "The Enlightenment: The Scientific Revolution." In *The Columbia History of the World*, edited by John A. Garraty and Peter Gay, 681-692. N.Y.: Harper & Row, 1972.

Natoli, Joseph and Linda Hutcheon, eds. *A Postmodern Reader*. Albany, N.Y.: State University of New York Press, 1993.

New Oxford Annotated Bible, The. With the Apocryphal/Deuterocanonical Books, edited by Bruce M. Metzger and Roland E. Murphy. (N.Y.: Oxford University Press, 1991).

Newell, William Lloyd. *The Secular Magi: Marx, Freud, and Nietzsche on Religion*. N.Y.: The Pilgrim Press, 1986.

Niebuhr, H. Richard. *Christ and Culture*. N.Y.: Harper, 1951.

————. *The Social Sources of Denominationalism*. N.Y.: New American Library, 1957.

Niebuhr, Reinhold. *The Children of Light and the Children of Darkness: A Vindication of Democracy and a Critique of Its Traditional Defense*. N.Y.: Charles Scribner's Sons, 1972 [1944].

Nietzsche, Friedrich. *Also Sprach Zarathustra: Ein Buch für Alle und Keinen*. In *Friedrich Nietzsche: Werke in Zwei Bänden*. Band I. München: Carl Hanser Verlag, 1967 [1883-85].

————. *The Antichrist.* In *The Portable Nietzsche.* Translated and edited by Walter Kaufmann. Middlesex, Eng.: Penguin, 1968 [1888].

————. *Beyond Good and Evil: Prelude to a Philosophy of the Future.* Translated by Walter Kaufmann. N.Y.: Vintage; Random House, 1966 [1886].

————. *The Birth of Tragedy.* Translated by Walter Kaufmann. N.Y.: Vintage; Random House, 1967 [1872, 1886].

————. *The Case of Wagner.* Translated by Walter Kaufmann. N.Y.: Vintage; Random House, 1967 [1888].

————. *Ecce Homo.* Translated by Walter Kaufmann. N.Y.: Vintage; Random House, 1967 [1888].

————. *The Gay Science: with a prelude in rhymes and an appendix of songs.* Translated by Walter Kaufmann. N.Y.: Vintage, 1974 [1882, 1887].

————. *Nietzsche Contra Wagner.* In *The Portable Nietzsche,* edited by Walter Kaufmann. N.Y.: Penguin, 1968 [1888].

————. *On the Genealogy of Morals.* Translated by Walter Kaufmann R. J. Hollingdale. N.Y.: Vintage; Random House, 1967 [1887].

————. *The Portable Nietzsche,* edited by Walter Kaufmann. N.Y.: Penguin, 1968.

————. *Thus Spoke Zarathustra: A Book for All and None.* In *The Portable Nietzsche,* edited by Walter Kaufmann. N.Y.: Penguin, 1968 [1883-85].

————. *Twilight of the Idols.* In *The Portable Nietzsche,* edited by Walter Kaufmann. N.Y.: Penguin, 1968 [1889].

————. *The Will To Power.* Translated by Walter Kaufmann and R. J. Hollingdale, edited by Walter Kaufmann. N.Y.: Vintage; Random House, 1967 [1901].

Noss, John B., *Man's Religions.* 4th ed. London: Macmillan, 1969.

Ogden, Schubert M. *The Reality of God and Other Essays.* N.Y.: Harper & Row, 1966.

O'Neill, J. C. "Biblical Criticism: History of Biblical Criticism." In *The Anchor Bible Dictionary,* edited by David Noel Freedman et al. Vol. 1, 726-730. N.Y.: Doubleday, 1992.

Otto, Rudolf. *The Idea of the Holy: An Inquiry Into the Non-rational Factor in the Idea of the Divine and Its Relation to the Rational.* Translated by John W. Harvey. London: Oxford University Press, 1923.

Pappe, Hellmut O. "Enlightenment." In *Dictionary of the History of Ideas: Studies of Selected Pivotal Ideas,* edited by Philip P. Wiener. Vol. IV, 89-100. N.Y.: Charles Scribner's Sons, 1973.

Pascal, Blaise. *Pensees.* Translated by W. F. Trotter. Vol. 33, *Pascal.* Great Books of the Western World, edited by Robert Maynard Hutchins et al. Chicago: Encyclopaedia Britannica; William Benton Publisher, 1952.

Perkins, Pheme, "The Gospel of Mark: Introduction, Commentary, and Reflections." In *The New Interpreter's Bible.* Vol. VIII, edited by Leander E. Keck et al., 507-733. Nashville: Abingdon Press, 1995.

Peters, H. F. *Red Jenny: A Life With Karl Marx.* London: Allen & Unwin, 1986.

Peters, John Durham. *Speaking into the Air: A History of the Idea of Communication.* Chicago and London: University of Chicago Press, 1999.

Peyre, Henri. "Durkheim: The Man, His Time, and His Intellectual Background." In *Essays on Sociology and Philosophy,* edited by Kurt H. Wolff, 3-31. N.Y.: Harper Torchbooks; Harper & Row, 1960.

————. Foreword to *Montesquieu and Rousseau: Forerunners of Sociology,* by Emile Durkheim. Ann Arbor: University of Michigan Press, 1975.

Pfister, Oskar. "The Illusion of a Future: A Friendly Discussion with Prof. Dr. Sigmund Freud." Appendix A in *Affirming the Soul: Remarkable Conversations Between Mental Health Professionals and an Ordained Minister*, by Jeffrey H. Boyd. Translated by Ted Crump and Jeffrey H. Boyd, 177-215. Cheshire, Conn.: Soul Research Institute, 1994 [1928].

Pippin, Robert B. "Hegel, Georg Wilhelm Friedrich." *The Cambridge Dictionary of Philosophy*, edited by Robert Audi, 311-317. Cambridge: Cambridge University Press, 1995.

Plato. *Apology*. Translated by Benjamin Jowett. Vol. 7, *The Dialogues of Plato*. Great Books of the Western World, edited by Robert Maynard Hutchins et al. Chicago: Encyclopaedia Britannica; William Benton Publisher, 1952.

———. *Crito*. Translated by Benjamin Jowett. Vol. 7, *The Dialogues of Plato*. Great Books of the Western World, edited by Robert Maynard Hutchins et al. Chicago: Encyclopaedia Britannica; William Benton Publisher, 1952.

———. *Phaedo*. Translated by Benjamin Jowett. Vol. 7, *The Dialogues of Plato*. Great Books of the Western World, edited by Robert Maynard Hutchins et al. Chicago: Encyclopaedia Britannica; William Benton Publisher, 1952.

———. *The Republic*. Translated by Benjamin Jowett. Vol. 7, *The Dialogues of Plato*. Great Books of the Western World, edited by Robert Maynard Hutchins et al. Chicago: Encyclopaedia Britannica; William Benton Publisher, 1952.

Plumb, J. H. *The Italian Renaissance: A Concise Survey of Its History and Culture*. N.Y. and Evanston: Harper & Row; Harper Torchbooks, 1961.

Pope, Alexander. *An Essay On Man*, edited by Frank Brady. Indianapolis: Bobbs-Merrill; The Library of Liberal Arts, 1965 [1733-34].

Pope, Liston. *Millhands & Preachers: A Study of Gastonia*. New Haven and London: Yale University Press, 1942.

Powell, Jim. *Postmodernism for Beginners*. Illustrated by Joe Lee. N.Y.: Writers and Readers Publishing, 1998.

Rand, Ayn. *The Ayn Rand Reader*, edited by Gary Hull and Leonard Peikoff. N.Y.: Plume; Penguin, 1999.

"Religious violence flares in Nigeria." *The Kansas City Star* (The Associated Press), 9 September 2001, A20.

Remarque, Erich Maria. *Der schwarze Obelisk: Geschichte einer verspäteten Jugend*. Frankfurt/M: Ullstein, 1956.

Restivo, Sal. "Critical Sociology of Science." In *Science Off the Pedestal: Social Perspectives on Science and Technology*, edited by Daryl E. Chubin and Ellen W. Chu, 57-70. Belmont, Calif.: Wadsworth, 1989.

Rich, Norman. *The Age of Nationalism and Reform: 1850-1890*. 2nd ed. N.Y. & London: W. W. Norton, 1977.

Rickett, Richard. *A Brief Survey of Austrian History*. Wien: George Prachner Verlag, 1966.

Ricoeur, Paul. *Freud and Philosophy: An Essay on Interpretation*. Translated by Denis Savage. New Haven and London: Yale University Press, 1970.

Rig Veda: An Anthology. Edited, translated, and annotated by Wendy Doniger O'Flaherty. London: Penguin Books, 1981.

Ringgren, Helmer. *Israelite Religion*. Translated by David E. Green. Phila.: Fortress Press, 1966.

Rizzo, Tony. "Event on homosexuality draws protests: Demonstrators represent wide range of views." *The Kansas City Star*, 23 June 2002, B4.

Roberts, Keith A. *Religion in Sociological Perspective.* 2nd ed. Belmont, Calif.: Wadsworth, 1990.

Rubin, Lillian Breslow. *Worlds of Pain: Life in the Working-Class Family.* N.Y.: Basic Books, 1976.

Russell, Bertrand. *The Autobiography of Bertrand Russell—1872-1914.* Boston and Toronto: Little, Brown and Co., 1967.

———. *Autobiography.* London and New York: Routledge, 1996 [1967-69].

———. *A History of Western Philosophy.* N.Y.: Simon and Schuster, 1972 [1945].

———. *Human Knowledge: Its Scope and Limits.* London: Routledge, 1948.

———. *An Inquiry Into Meaning and Truth.* London: George Allen and Unwin, 1940.

———. *Marriage and Morals.* N.Y.: Liveright, 1929, 1957.

———. *An Outline of Philosophy.* Cleveland and New York: Meridian Books; World Publishing Co., 1960 [1927].

———. "Philosophy and Politics." Appendix to *Authority and the Individual,* by Russell, 81-101. Boston: Beacon Press, 1949 [1946].

———. *The Philosophy of Logical Atomism.* La Salle, Ill.: Open Court, 1985 [1918, 1924].

———. *The Practice and Theory of Bolshevism.* N.Y.: Simon and Schuster, 1964 [1920, 1948].

———. *Religion and Science.* N.Y. and Oxford: Oxford University Press, 1997 [1935].

———. *Why I Am Not a Christian: And Other Essays on Religion and Related Subjects,* edited by Paul Edwards. London: Unwin Paperbacks, 1975 [1957].

Samuelson, Kurt. *Religion and Economic Action: A Critique of Max Weber.* Translated by E. Geoffrey French, edited by D. C. Coleman. N.Y. and Evanston: Harper & Row, 1961.

Santayana, George. *Three Philosophical Poets: Lucretius—Dante—Goethe.* Garden City, N.Y.: Doubleday Anchor, 1954.

Sartre, Jean-Paul. *The Philosophy of Jean-Paul Sartre,* edited by Robert Denoon Cumming. N.Y.: Random House, Vintage Books, 1965.

Sawyer, John F. A. "Isaiah, The Book of." In *The Oxford Companion to the Bible,* edited by Bruce M. Metzger and Michael D. Coogan, 325-329. N.Y. & Oxford: Oxford University Press, 1993.

Singer, Peter. "dialectic." *The Oxford Companion to Philosophy,* edited by Ted Honderich, 198. Oxford & N.Y.: Oxford University Press, 1995.

"*The Schleitheim Confession of Faith,* From." Translated by John C. Wenger. In *Great Voices of the Reformation: An Anthology,* edited by Harry Emerson Fosdick, 286-295. N.Y.: The Modern Library, 1952. First published in *The Mennonite Quarterly Review,* Oct. 1945.

Schmidt, W. *The Origin and Growth of Religion: Facts and Theories.* Translated by H. J. Rose. N.Y.: Cooper Square Publisher's, 1972 [1931].

Schorske, Carl E. *Fin-De-Siècle Vienna: Politics and Culture.* N.Y.: Vintage Books; Random House, 1979.

Schroyer, Trent. *The Critique of Domination: The Origins and Development of Critical Theory.* Boston: Beacon Press, 1973.

Seidman, Steven. *Contested Knowledge: Social Theory in the Postmodern Era.* Oxford, UK & Cambridge, USA: Blackwell, 1994.

Seitz, Christopher R. "Isaiah, Book Of (First Isaiah)." In *The Anchor Bible Dictionary.* Vol. 3, edited by David Noel Freedman et al., 472-488. N.Y.: Doubleday, 1992.

Shestov, Lev. *Athens and Jerusalem.* Translated by Bernard Martin. N.Y.: Simon and Schuster, 1966 [1937].

Simons, Menno. "From *The Writings of Menno Simons.*" In *Great Voices of the Reformation: An Anthology,* edited by Harry Emerson Fosdick, 316-327. N.Y.: The Modern Library, 1952. [From *Menno Simons' Life and Writings,* edited by Harold S. Bender. Scottdale, PA: Mennonite Publishing House, 1936].

Singer, Peter. "dialectic." *The Oxford Companion to Philosophy,* edited by Ted Honderich, 198. Oxford & N.Y.: Oxford University Press, 1995.

———. *Hegel.* Oxford and N.Y.: Oxford University Press, 1982.

Smith, Adam. *An Inquiry Into the Nature and Causes of the Wealth of Nations.* Vol. 39, *Adam Smith.* Great Books of the Western World, edited by Robert Maynard Hutchins et al. Chicago: Encyclopaedia Britannica; William Benton Publisher, 1952 [1776].

Smith, Huston. *Why Religion Matters: The Fate of the Human Spirit in an Age of Disbelief.* San Francisco: HarperCollins; HarperSanFrancisco, 2001.

Stacey, John. "Wycliffe, John." *The New Encyclopaedia Britannica.* 15th ed. Vol. 12, 786-787. Chicago: Encyclopaedia Britannica, 1994.

Rodney Stark and William Sims Bainbridge. *The Future of Religion: Secularization, revival, and cult formation.* Berkeley: University of California Press, 1985.

Stace, W. T. "The Teachings of the Mystics." In *To Believe or Not To Believe: Readings in the Philosophy of Religion,* edited by E. D. Klemke, 70-80. Fort Worth, Tex.: Harcourt Brace Jovanovich, 1992.

Stearns, Peter N. *1848: The Revolutionary Tide in Europe.* N.Y. & London: W. W. Norton & Co., 1974.

Stern, Fritz. "The Great World War: 1914-1945." In *The Columbia History of the World,* edited by John A. Garraty and Peter Gay, 981-993. N.Y.: Harper & Row, 1972.

Strathern, Paul. *Descartes in 90 Minutes.* Chicago: Ivan R. Dee, 1996.

———. *Hegel in 90 Minutes.* Chicago: Ivan R. Dee, 1997.

———. *Sartre in 90 Minutes.* Chicago: Ivan R. Dee, 1998.

Swatos, William H. and Christiano, Kevin J. "Secularization Theory: The Course of a Concept." *Sociology of Religion* 60, no. 3 (1999): 209-228.

Szasz, Thomas. *The Myth of Psychotherapy: Mental Healing as Religion, Rhetoric, and Repression.* Syracuse, N.Y.: Syracuse University Press, 1988.

Tallentyre, S. G. (pseud. for Evelyn Beatrice Hall). *The Life of Voltaire.* N.Y.: Loring & Mussey, n.d.

Tarnas, Richard. *The Passion of the Western Mind: Understanding the Ideas That Have Shaped Our World View.* N.Y.: Ballantine Books, 1991.

Taylor, A. J. P. *From Sarajevo to Potsdam.* London: Harcourt, Brace & World, 1965.

Theissen, Gerd. *A Critical Faith: A Case for Religion.* Phila.: Fortress Press, 1979.

Thiel, Winfried, "Ahab," in *The Anchor Bible Dictionary.* Vol. 1, edited by David Noel Freedman et al., 101-104. N.Y.: Doubleday, 1992.

Thompson, Henry O., "Yahweh," in *The Anchor Bible Dictionary.* Vol. 6, edited by David Noel Freedman et al., 1011-1012. N.Y.: Doubleday, 1992.

Thompson, William Irwin. *Coming Into Being: Artifacts and Texts in the Evolution of Consciousness.* N.Y.: St. Martin's Press, 1996.

Tillich, Paul. *Dynamics of Faith.* N.Y.: Harper & Row, 1957.

Tocqueville, Alexis de. *Democracy In America,* edited by J. P. Mayer, translated by George Lawrence. Garden City, N.Y.: Anchor Books, 1969 [1835].

Tracy, James D. "Erasmus." *The New Encyclopaedia Britannica*. 15th ed. Vol. 18, 489-491. Chicago: Encyclopaedia Britannica, 1994.

Tracy, Patricia J. *Jonathan Edwards, Pastor: Religion and Society in Eighteenth-Century Northampton*. N.Y.: Hill and Wang, 1980.

Turner, Bryan S., ed. *Theories of Modernity and Postmodernity*. London: Sage, 1990.

Turner, Denys. "Religion: Illusions and liberation." In *The Cambridge Companion to Marx*, edited by Terrell Carver, 320-338. N.Y.: Cambridge University Press, 1991.

Umasvati, Sri Acarya. *Tattvarthadhigama Sutra*. Translated by J. L. Jaini. In *A Source Book in Indian Philosophy*, edited by Sarvepalli Radhakrishnan and Charles A. Moore. Princeton, N.J.: Princeton University Press, 1957.

Urban, Linwood. *A Short History of Christian Thought*. Revised and expanded. N.Y. & Oxford: Oxford University Press, 1995.

"Veil of darkness lifts in capital with Taliban retreat." *The Kansas City Star*, November 14, 2001, A1-A2.

Voltaire. *Candide*. Translated by Lowell Blair. N.Y.: Bantam Books, 1959 [1759].

———. "History of Scarmentado's Travels." In *Candide, Zadig and Selected Stories*. Translated by Donald M. Frame. N.Y.: New American Library, 1961 [1756].

———. "The Lisbon Earthquake." In *The Portable Voltaire*. Translated by Tobias Smollett et al., edited by Ben Ray Redman. N.Y.: The Viking Press, 1963 [1755].

———. *Philosophical Dictionary*, edited and translated by Theodore Besterman. London: Penguin Books, 1972 [1764].

———. *Philosophical Letters*. Translated by Ernest Dilworth. Indianapolis, IN: Bobbs-Merrill, 1961 [1733/34].

———. *Treatise on Tolerance*. Translated by Brian Masters, edited by Simon Harvey. Cambridge: Cambridge University Press, 2000 [1763].

Von Rad, Gerhard. *Old Testament Theology*. Vol. I, *The Theology of Israel's Historical Traditions*. Translated by D. M. G. Stalker. N.Y. and Evanston: Harper & Row, 1962.

Wach, Joachim. *Sociology of Religion*. Chicago and London: University of Chicago Press, 1944.

Walker, Williston. *A History of the Christian Church*. 3rd ed. Revised by Robert T. Handy, Cyril C. Richardson, and Wilhelm Pauck. N.Y.: Charles Scribner's Sons, 1970.

Walsh, Jerome T. "Elijah," in *The Anchor Bible Dictionary*. Vol. 2, edited by David Noel Freedman et al., 463-466. N.Y.: Doubleday, 1992.

Walzer, Michael. *The Company of Critics: Social Criticism and Political Commitment in the Twentieth Century*. N.Y.: Basic Books, 1988.

Ward, Graham. "Introduction, or, A Guide to Theological Thinking in Cyberspace" to *The Postmodern God: A Theological Reader*, edited by Ward. Malden, Mass.: Blackwell Publishers, 1997.

———, ed. *The Postmodern God: A Theological Reader*. Malden, Mass.: Blackwell Publishers, 1997.

Watterson, Bill. *The Essential Calvin and Hobbes: A Calvin and Hobbes Treasure*. Kansas City, MO, and N.Y.: Andrews, McMeel, & Parker, 1988.

Watts, Alan. *Behold the Spirit: A Study in the Necessity of Mystical Religion*. N.Y.: Vintage Books, 1971.

———. *The Two Hands of God: The Myths of Polarity*. Toronto: Collier Books, 1963.

———. *The Wisdom of Insecurity*. N.Y.: Vintage, 1951.

Weaver, C. Douglas, ed. *A Cloud of Witnesses: Sermon Illustrations and Devotionals from the Christian Heritage*. Macon, GA: Smyth & Helwys, 1993.

Weber, Max. *Economy and Society: An Outline of Interpretive Sociology*. Vol. 1, edited by Guenther Roth and Claus Wittich. Berkeley: University of California Press, 1978.

———. *Economy and Society: An Outline of Interpretive Sociology*. Vol. 2, edited by Guenther Roth and Claus Wittich. Berkeley: University of California Press, 1978.

———. *The Protestant Ethic and The Spirit of Capitalism*. Translated by Talcott Parsons. N.Y.: Charles Scribner's Sons, 1958 [1904-05].

Weil, Simone. *Waiting for God*. Translated by Emma Craufurd. N.Y.: Harper & Row, 1951.

Weir, Peter, dir. *Witness*. Paramount Pictures, 1985.

"Weird News." *The Kansas City Star*. September 25, E1.

Wells, Alan. "Mass Society." In *Encyclopedia of Sociology*, 172. Guilford, Conn.: The Dushkin Publishing Group, 1974.

Westphal, Merold. *Overcoming Onto-Theology: Toward a Postmodern Christian Faith*. N.Y.: Fordham University Press, 2001.

Wheen, Francis. *Karl Marx: A Life*. N.Y. and London: W. W. Norton, 1999.

White, E. B. *Charlotte's Web*. Pictures by Garth Williams. N.Y.: Dell, 1952.

Wiedmann, Franz. *George Wilhelm Friedrich Hegel: in Selbstzeugnissen und Bilddokumenten*. Reinbek bei Hamburg: Rowohlt, 1965.

Wilde, Lawrence. "Logic: Dialectic and contradiction." In *The Cambridge Companion to Marx*, edited by Terrell Carver, 275-295. N.Y.: Cambridge University Press, 1991.

Winokur, Jon, ed. *The Portable Curmudgeon*. N.Y.: New American Library, 1987.

Witherington, Ben, III. *The Jesus Quest: The Third Search for the Jew of Nazareth*. 2nd ed. Downers Grove, Ill.: InterVarsity Press, 1997.

Wolfe, Alan. "The Opening of the Evangelical Mind." *Atlantic*, October 2000, 55-76.

Wollheim, Richard. *Freud*. Glasgow: Fontana Paperbacks, 1971.

Wood, Allen. "Karl Marx." In *The Philosophers: Introducing Great Western Thinkers*, edited by Ted Honderich, 167-172. N.Y.: Oxford University Press, 1999.

———. "Dialectical Materialism." *Routledge Encyclopedia of Philosophy*, edited by Edward Craig. Vol. 3, *Descartes to Gender and Science*, 53-58. London & N.Y.: Routledge, 1998.

Wycliffe, John. "from *The Trialogus*." In *Great Voices of the Reformation: An Anthology*, edited by Harry Emerson Fosdick, 23-29. N.Y.: The Modern Library, 1952.

Wylie, Peter J. "The Great Globe Itself." In *The New Encyclopaedia Britannica*, 15th ed, *Propaedia*, 61-63. Chicago: Encyclopaedia Britannica, 1994.

Wyntjes, Sherrin Marshall. "Women in the Reformation Era." In *Becoming Visible: Women in European History*, edited by Renate Bridenthal and Claudia Koonz, 165-191. Boston: Houghton Mifflin Co., 1977.

Zimmer, Heinrich. "The Meeting of East and West." In *Readings In Eastern Religious Thought*. Vol. 1, *Hinduism*, edited by Allie M. Frazier, 17-49. Phila.: The Westminster Press, 1969.

Index

207

About the Author

Anton K. Jacobs teaches philosophy and religion at the Kansas City Art Institute, and sociology at Park University. He received his B.A. from the University of Missouri–St. Louis, his M.Div. from Eden Theological Seminary, his M.A. from the University of Louisville, and his Ph.D. from the University of Notre Dame. He is also a UCC clergyman, having pastored churches in Kentucky, Indiana, Missouri, and Kansas. He is a co-editor and translator, with Anthony Blasi and Mathew Kanjirathinkal, of Georg Simmel's *Sociology: Inquiries Into the Construction of Social Forms* (2009). He has published articles in social theory, sociology of religion, the political imagination in literature, and urban history; and written a local newspaper column for several years on the interface between religion and culture. He lives with his wife in Kansas City, Missouri.